destination
Papua New Guinea

The publication Destination Papua New Guinea

Project Manager:
Gudmundur Vidar Fridriksson

Contributing Editors:
Dr. Suzanne Campbell-Jones
Meg Sheffield
Michael Smee
Dr. Martin Regal
Abby Yadi

Text Editor:
Simon Campbell-Jones

Photography Researcher:
Susan Turner

Principal photographers:
Susan Turner, Robert Burroughs, Bragi Thor Josepsson, Rocky Roe

Other contributing photographers:
Ron and Georgie McKie, Frederick Roll, Hugh Davies

Art Director:
John Kipong

Layout:
Kjartan Jonsson

Designers:
Jon Armann Steinsson, Dennis Livinai, Arthur Levi, Kelly Lomon

Other contributors:
Anthony Smee, Lei Lokoloko, Dr. Moale Kariko, Vavine Iamu, Maxine Aihi, Irene Dallas, Catherine Killiu, Louisa Westley, Fiti Asigau, Baea Motu, Birgir Vidar Halldorsson, Thomas Undi and Gudmundur Orn Johannson.
National Archives, The National Library, Air Niugini, PNG Tourism Promotion Authority and Westpac Bank - PNG - Ltd.

Printing:
Sanon Printing Corporation SDN BHD

Published by Destination Papua New Guinea, Pty Ltd.
Port Moresby, Papua New Guinea.

© 1995 Destination Papua New Guinea, Pty Ltd.

ISBN-9980-85-118-X

The publishers whish to give special thanks to Sir Wiwa Korowi, Sir Julius Chan, Mr. Chris Haiveta, Mr. Arnold Marsipal, Mr. Seri Hegame, Mr. John Painap, Mr. Renagi Lohia, Mr. Franz Albert Joku Mr. Mark Basausau and Mr. Romanus Pakure for their initiative and foresight which helped make this book a reality.

destination
Papua New Guinea

Foreword by His Excellency
The Governor General
of Papua New Guinea

It gives me great pleasure to write the introduction for Destination Papua New Guinea. I am confident this book will swing our country's doors wide open and finally reveal its many riches to the outside world.

With our 20th year of Independence it is the ideal time to promote Papua New Guinea. Not only its unique people and culture but its increasingly dynamic political, social and economic developments.

In my lifetime alone, Papua New Guinea has been transformed from a civilisation stuck in a timewarp to an efficient and modernised country. Papua New Guineans have always been proud of their past but only recently have they started to embrace their future. Papua New Guinea now wants to step out of the shadows and grab its share of the limelight.

From the misty mountains of the Highlands to the white beaches of Milne Bay this country is a natural paradise. It is a place which has successfully blended the ancient with the modern. It has spear-wielding tribesmen and sharp-suited businessmen living in harmony under the same sky. Providing a home for this vibrant mishmash of humanity is a delicate balancing act. The fact Papua New Guinea has managed it so effectively is a huge feather in its cap.

Papua New Guinea has a distinguished track record. Its administrative structure was originally masterminded by the Australians and loyalty to Australia was nowhere more evident than during the two world wars when the Papua New Guineans fought side by side with the Allies against the Japanese and Germans. But since September 16, 1975, when the country won its Independence, it has proved it is eminently capable of standing on its own feet.

This book focuses on many features, not only the people and the culture of our unique land but its politics, economics and, especially, its natural resources

We, as individuals, have a country which calls for everyone, whether families, tribal groups or political parties, to make sacrifices that will ensure Papua New Guinea becomes an even more impressive place than it is now. We must pass onto our children the valuable traditions we have learnt from the generations before. They, in turn, must carry on the bond of trust and the spirit of advancement through to the next generations.

With this current mood of optimism I am confident Papua New Guinea's future will be a bright one.

Sir Wiwa Korowi, GCMG, KStJ

The Governor General

Papua New Guinea

WELCOMING ADDRESS

by The Prime Minister

I am an exceedingly proud Papua New Guinean, when I look back on the 20 years that we have just been through, and likewise, without an inkling of hesitation, I can say with strong personal conviction that we can only look to the future with determined hope and confidence. That, in a nutshell, is perhaps the simplest way to sum up my feelings about Papua New Guinea's achievements and the prospect of taking on the challenges that await us ahead.

The past two decades certainly represents a period of great change and achievement for us as a modern-day nation-state of Papua New Guinea. For myself, having devoted the past 27 years to an uninterrupted parliamentary career in this country, the past 20 years have been exciting and fulfilling. I wish I were 20 years younger, so that I could contribute another 20 equally vigorous years of service to a potentially great country. We have had our ups and downs, and will continue to do so into the future. That is the inevitable fact of life. No person or nation can experience change without some pain, and achievements can not occur unless there is some honest sweat. And by any measure at all, Papua New Guinea has indeed experienced pain and expended honest sweat. More pain and more sweat will be needed if we are to meet the challenges on hand and fulfil the aspirations of our people. The task is even more challenging, given the geographic nature and the multiplicity of the language and ethno-cultural groups we have in this country.

The Bougainville secessionists movement and the pain and the many hardships that it has inflicted on Papua New Guinea is perhaps the biggest test ever for our national unity, resilience and sensibility. I am confident, however, that with renewed commitment, tact and sense of purpose, we will be able to achieve total peace and normalcy in the province soon.

Our domestic problems aside, Papua New Guinea is also firmly committed to the principles of creating a more peaceful, harmonious and prosperous region in the South Pacific. We, therefore, in defence of our future will continue to vehemently deplore and oppose in any way possible, any form of military, political and economic oppression and exploitation of our peoples and our environment. We are by no means in dire danger, but it would be grossly foolish to say that all is well with our society, our economy, and particularly our attitudes. It is the latter area where, I think, we possibly face the greatest danger.

We tell ourselves we are a country rich in natural resources, but we fool each other, if we think that those resources represent tangible wealth when they stand still on the land or lie idle in the ground. Of course we are a potentially rich nation, but we will never realise that potential, unless we exploit what nature has given us and harvest it in a sustainable manner.

We have an equally rich cultural heritage. We tell ourselves that we have many fine traditions and customs, forming an unique and proud Papua New Guinean culture. But we would be naive, if we continue to retain certain negative aspects of our traditions and sit by comfortably and idly, wishing and hoping that we can be part of a modern and increasingly international world economy. Culture is a living creature, but if it is allowed to stagnate, then we may as well drop out of the rest of the world and be content to deteriorate into a Third World backwater.

Having said that , I am confident that Papua New Guinea is back on the right track again. We must, however, be ready to accept some more pain and should not expect miracles to happen overnight. Above all else we must agree that there is more room for change and adjustment. To achieve this, complacency and greed must be thrown out the window.

There was a tremendous sense of achievement when we proclaimed our independence back in September 1975. We have come a long way since. Although it has sometimes been a case of three steps forward and two steps backwards or sideways, we are nevertheless ahead. And only when we are able to overcome the major problems facing the country at present, will we be able to stand tall under the sun once again and claim our rightful place among the nations of the world. But it must be through our own efforts that we must get there. And I know that, together, we can take the country through the path of success to the year 2000 and beyond!

Destination Papua New Guinea is, therefore, our way of informing all potential overseas investors and extending our hand of friendship to warmly welcome them when they choose to make our country a haven for their investments. You are most welcome!

The Rt. Hon. Sir Julius Chan GCMG KBE MP
Prime Minister and Minister for Foreign Affairs and Trade

CONTENTS

Introduction
Foreword by The Governor General 4
Welcoming Address by The Prime Minister . 6
The Scope and purpose of ths book 9

Political and Legal structure
Government 12
The Prime Ministers 14
Department of Prime Minister and NEC . . . 16
Minister of State Assisting The Prime Minister 18
Minister for State Affairs & Admin. Services 20
The Ombudsman Commission 21
Department of Public Service 22
Political Parties overview 25
Parliament and the Speaker 26
Foreign Affairs overview 30
Foreign Trade overview 31
Department of Foreign Affairs and Trade . . . 32
Defence overview 34
PNG Defence Force 36
Legal System overview 38
Judiciary overview 41
Department of Justice and Attorney General 42
PNG Law Society 44
Royal PNG Constabulary 46
Correctional Institutional Services 48
Securimax Security Group 51
Guard Dog Securities 52

Environment and resources
Geography overview 56
Department Lands and Physical Planning . . 58
Geology overview 60
Department of Mining and Petroleum 62
Mineral Resources Development Company . 65
Chevron Niugini 70
PNG Electricity Commission 72
Wildlife and Environment overview 74
Department of Environm. and Conservation 78
Forests and Forestry overview 83
Ministry of Forests 84
Forest Industries Association 86
Vanimo Forest Products 90
Agriculture and Livestock overview 93
Department of Agriculture and Livestock . . 94
Coffee Industry Corporation 96
Angco Coffee 99
Ilimo Poultry Producers 100
Mainland Holdings 102
Ramu Sugar Limited 104
Higaturu Oil Palms 107
Fish and Fishing overview 108
Dept. of Fisheries and Marine Resources . . . 110
Gulf Papua Fisheries 113
Trans Melanesian Marine 114
New Guinea Marine Products 116
The Net Shop 117

Business Potential
The Economy overview 120

Finance and Planning overview 123
Department of Finance and Planning 124
National Computer Centre 128
Central Bank of PNG 130
Investment Corporation of PNG 132
National Provident Fund Board of Trustees . 133
Westpac Bank PNG Ltd 134
PNG Banking Corporation 135
McIntosh Securities 136
Price Waterhouse 138
Helandis Management Services 140
Commerce and Industry overview 142
Department of Commerce and Industry 144
PNG Investment Promotion Authority 148
Industrial Centres Development Corporation 150
PNG Chamber of Commerce 152
PNG Chamber of Manufacturers 153
Hornibrook NGI 154
Howard Porter (Lae) 155
Mobil Oil 156
BOC Gas 157
Boroko Motors 158
Ela Motors 159
Computers and Communications 160
Remington Pitney Bowes 161
Daltron Electronics 162
BNG Trading Company 163
Collins and Leahy 164
Treid Pacific 166
Woo Textiles 167
Lae Biscuits and Coastal Shipping 168
Wills 170
Fairdeal Liquors 173
Labour and Employment overview 174
Department of Industrial Relations 176
Employers Federation of PNG 178
Trade Union Congress 179
Transport and Communication overview . . . 180
Ministry of Transport 182
PNG Harbours Board 184
Steamships Shipping and Transport 186
Tourism overview 189
Department of Tourism and Civil Aviation . 190
Air Niugini 194
Aiways Hotel and Apartments 198
Avis Rent A Car 200
Colin Ritchie 201
Coral Sea Hotels 202
Loloata Island Resort 204
Islands Nationair 205
Niugini Adventures 206
MBA Airlines 208
Trans Niugini Tours 210
PNG Tourism Promotion Authority 212

People and culture
Language overview 219
The People – Demographics overview 220
Department of Works and Supply 222
Ministry of Housing 224

Ministry of Health 226
City Pharmacy 229
Ministry of Home Affairs and Youth 230
Rugby League 234
Religion overview 236
Bible Society 237
Education overview 238
Department of Education 240
Higher Education 242
International Education Agency of PNG . . . 245
Arts and Culture overview 246
The Media overview 249
Information and Communication 250
Telikom 252
National Broadcasting Commission 254

Regional perspectives
Regions overview 258
Dept of Village Services and Prov. Affairs . . 260
Provinces overview 262
Western Province 264
Gulf Province 266
Central Province 268
NCD Port Moresby 270
Milne Bay Province 274
Oro Province 280
Southern Highlands Province 282
Enga Province 286
Western Highlands Province 288
Simbu Province 290
Eastern Highlands Province 292
Morobe Province 294
Lae City Authority 298
Madang Province 300
East Sepik Province 306
Sandaun Province 310
Manus Province 312
New Ireland Province 316
East New Britain Province 320
West New Britain Province 322
North Solomons Province 324

Historical Perspectives
Early history overview 328
The Europeans overview 330
Colonization overview 332
The Twentieth Century overview 334
Post War order overview 336
Independence 337
The 1995 Anniversary Celebrations 338

Information
Cabinet Ministers 352
Government Departments 354
Subscribers 356
Churches and Missions 359
Acknowledgements and Credits 360

THE SCOPE AND PURPOSE
OF THIS BOOK

On September 16th 1995 Papua New Guinea celebrated the twentieth anniversary of its Independence. This book is an extension of that celebration, paying tribute to the country, its people and to their spirit of independence. It shows you something of the country's past and its traditions, but also much about its opportunities and its goals. The profiles of government ministries and agencies provide a unique and up-to-date view of the nation's administration and its plans for the future. The profiles of the world of commerce, which represent a substantial cross-section of the country's economic activity, from the multinational companies to small independent retailers, are a testament to their commitment to PNG's prosperity. This book may be considered to be opinionated, contradictory and notably frank as it reflects the views of the many different people who were interviewed and their different interpretations of the situation of PNG at this time. We hope you will appreciate their interesting and original insights.

However, while Destination Papua New Guinea provides overviews and practical information for foreign investors, it simultaneously offers a guide to those visitors who want to explore Papua New Guinea in a more leisurely fashion. The country, its people, its flora and fauna cannot be condensed into a few hundred pages. In offering a glimpse of the multifaceted cultures and spectacular landscapes for which Papua New Guinea is renowned, this book goes some way towards presenting the splendour and the beauty that draws so many people to this special part of the world.

Papua New Guinea is at the geographical hub of the new grouping of South East Asian and Australasian economies. Since Independence, it has found that it has not only the resources to compete successfully with its close neighbours, but also the energy and the incentive to make its presence felt as an international commercial force. Like many 'new' nation states, Papua New Guinea has been subject to a range of European influences. After it was 'discovered' in the early sixteenth century, it became part of a trade route that encompassed the whole South Pacific. It was eventually divided up and annexed by the British and the Germans in 1884. Twenty years after Independence it still has strong European links. But Papua New Guinean culture goes back beyond its European links for fifty millennia with a plethora of traditions, rites and customs. It has a diversity of peoples and languages unparalleled anywhere else in the world.

The ancient societies of Papua New Guinea contrast sharply with the modern technological age, but beware of the clichés. The tribesman standing beside a jet plane may make an arresting image, but it does inadequate justice to the real Papua New Guinea at the turn of the twenty-first century. The truth is that while PNG does retain many of the structures and customs of the past among its predominantly rural population, it is simultaneously one of the fastest developing countries in the world. It has enormous untapped wealth and an increasingly qualified workforce. Its government has proved itself capable of tackling its national and international problems. It is a modern parliamentary democracy. Papua New Guinea now invites you, without sacrificing its unique past, to discover its exciting future.

Tau Asigau Fridriksson

politics and le

Papua New Guinea (or PNG as it is more familiarly known) became an independent parliamentary democracy on September 16th 1975. The day marked not only the end of colonial rule but a new dawn in the history of the people.

Almost five hundred years had passed since the first Europeans arrived and it was nearly a century since the country last had full authority over its affairs. With the coming of independence, PNG looked forward to a future in which it could shape its own

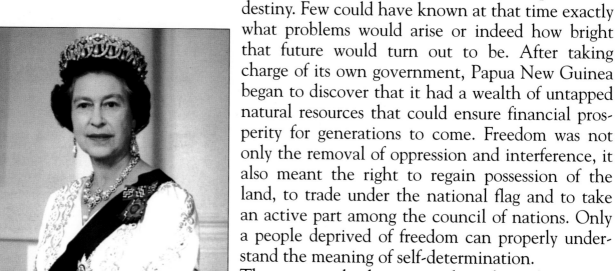

destiny. Few could have known at that time exactly what problems would arise or indeed how bright that future would turn out to be. After taking charge of its own government, Papua New Guinea began to discover that it had a wealth of untapped natural resources that could ensure financial prosperity for generations to come. Freedom was not only the removal of oppression and interference, it also meant the right to regain possession of the land, to trade under the national flag and to take an active part among the council of nations. Only a people deprived of freedom can properly understand the meaning of self-determination.

The process leading towards independence had been slow. Papua New Guineans first gained the right to some representation in the parliament of their own country in 1951. However, at that time they had only three elected members. Today, there are 109 Members of Parliament, elected by universal suffrage to represent the nineteen provinces of Papua New Guinea. Government exists at three levels: national, provincial and local. This three-tiered system has remained the model for the last twenty years.

The National Parliament is styled on both the Australian and British systems and is elected to a five-year term of office. Its formal head of state is Queen Elizabeth II, while its ceremonial head is the Governor-General, who is elected by parliament and subsequently approved by the British monarch. In 1977, just over a year after independence, the decentralised Provincial Assembly was inaugurated, comprising the nineteen

provinces and the district of the national capital, Port Moresby. Like the central government, each of these provincial governments had a premier and a constitution. Each also had the right to impose and collect certain taxes and to control areas such as education, health care and the local economy. All were ultimately answerable to the National Parliament. Recent reforms (July 1995) have changed the status of provincial governments, replacing premiers with centrally-appointed governors. At a third level of government are the local councils, funded either by their particular provincial government or by their district MP.

One of the most significant and distinctive characteristics of PNG politics is the concept of consensus. Unlike many other democracies, there seems to be little ideological disparity between the various political parties and the electorate usually votes according to clan or personal allegiance. Moreover, there is a first-past-the-post system, which means that the successful candidate may carry only a small percentage of the vote. Political debate is therefore always susceptible to partisanship, but a consensus of opinion must be reached on all matters and discussions will generally continue until all parties are satisfied that their interests have been protected and their views represented.

Where self-interest on the part of provincial governments has threatened to upset the country's interests as a whole, central government has had the power to veto and suspend them and, in a very recent case, to amend the constitution. But whatever changes are effected and whatever disagreements may arise, and however many times individual parties split and regroup, the parliamentary democracy of PNG remains stable, providing continuity for both domestic and economic planning. Despite the fact that a changing patchwork of alliances has sometimes meant that certain parliamentary members have retained ministerial positions while the government itself has been replaced, all such changes have been democratic, peaceful and orderly.

The Prime Minister is the political head of PNG. He is elected by Parliament. Since Independence only four men have been Prime Minister. The first was the man who saw the country through to Independence, Sir Michael Somare "The Chief" from East Sepik.

"I came with a vision. I wanted to see Papua New Guinea as an independent sovereign nation which could stand with the rest of the people in the Pacific and Asia region", said Sir Michael. "A lot of people said it wouldn't be possible to make a country out of 700 different dialects, different languages, but I was able to prove to them that it can be done. People are beginning to see themselves as Papua New Guineans." Sir Michael formed PANGU (Papua andNew Guinea Unite, known just as Pangu Pati) in 1967. He worked assiduously for Independence. He became Chief Minister in 1972 and in 1975 (at Independence) Prime Minister. But while his party has so far achieved the largest number of seats at each election, it has never commanded an overall majority.

When Sir Michael became Prime Minister he relied on a coalition to keep him there. The first coalition was with Sir Julius Chan's Peoples Progressive Party. In 1978 that coalition came apart largely because Somare wanted to tighten up on the leadership code which would have restricted the business interests of politicians. Chan's party is essentially a businessman's party. Somare struck a deal with the opposition and continued in power until 1980 when Somare lost a no confidence vote and Sir Julius Chan, from New Ireland, became the second Prime Minister of PNG.

For two years Sir Julius Chan successfully fought to keep his government intact and built up his numbers to 70 as members switched allegiance and crossed the floor. 1982 was election year. However, it turned out to be a triumph for Somare. PANGU achieved 34% of the vote and won almost half the Parliamentary seats. Somare was Prime Minister for the next three years by which time his party was splitting apart. Sir Julius Chan tabled the motion of no confidence nominating Paias Wingti, the MP for Mt. Hagen in the Western Highlands, as alternative Prime Minister. Somare survived one vote and then fell. Paias Wingti became Prime Minister.

Sir Michael Somare

Mr. Rabbie Namaliu

Paias Wingti had been a member of PANGU party and had taken office in successiveSomare governments, but in 1985 had split and formed his own party, the PDM, the People's Democratic Movement. He was thirty four when he took the Office of Prime Minister. "There will be a different style of leadership", he promised. "There will be discipline and control of expenditure." Wingti had eighteen months to the next election. It was close run. In a desperate attempt to save his party Somare stepped down and Rabbie Namaliu from East New Britain took over as PANGU leader. He was to be the fourth man to become Prime Minister.

The next four years were swings and roundabouts as first Namaliu and then Wingti tried to keep their coalition governments together. By 1992 it became clear that the vote of no confidence mechanism might turn consensus into instability and the constitution was modified to allow successive governments a period of grace. In 1993, Paias Wingti, resigned, called a snap election, and was subsequently re-installed. The opposition objected and one year later the Supreme Court ruled that it was unconstitutional for a prime minister to resume office after having tendered his resignation. Sir Julius Chan then led a coalition government of the People's Progress Party and the Pangu Party.

Sir Julius once described PNG politics as "regionalistic and tribally based. Each member has a strong commitment to directly benefit his immediate electorate. In a way that is a good thing." It puts pressure on members to service the needs of their electorate. It makes a logic out of a system that frequently seems illogical to an outsider. Sir Julius is an astute politician. He began as an officer in the Australian Administration. He has led his party since 1970. In the 1970's he was a Governor of the International Monetary Fund, the World Bank and the Asian Development Bank. He has always shown great interest in matters of finance, trade and industry. In 1980 he was awarded a KBE and became Sir Julius Chan. In 1994 his service to Papua New Guinea was recognised by the highly prestigious award Knight Grand Cross of the Order of St.Michael and St.George (GCMG). Sir Julius remains head of government today and is also Minister for Foreign Affairs.

Mr. Paias Wingti

Sir Julius Chan

In August 1994 Sir Julius Chan once again became Prime Minister. He took time to reflect, not just on the past 10 or 20 years, but on the past 60 years.

Under the Department of the Prime Minister and National Executive Council fall several functions of government including the PNG Fire Services, National Security Organisation, National Intelligence Organisation, National Planning Office, the Office of the Legislative Council and the Office of Information and Communication. The Prime Minister is assisted in this by department Secretary, John Painap.

One of the biggest issues facing the government today, is the question of land — in particular land compensation. If this is not resolved then PNG could fall back on the old solution--tribal conflicts.

There are still occasional outbreaks. In a country where 85% of the land is rural and the land represents the only wealth people have, it assumes enormous importance. A villager owns the land beneath his feet and, while customary laws might vary from district to district, there has been a need for some normalisation which will recognise reasonable rates of compensation for legitimate owners. Steps have been taken to prevent any possibilities of dispute.

In addition to accepting a Structural Adjustment Programme which applies stringent free market principles to the economy, PNG is committed to trade liberalisation. All export and import licensing

requirements, import bans and quotas and other quantitative restrictions, particularly for cement, rice, sugar, fresh fruits and vegetables, meat and fish, will be phased out as soon as legal circumstances permit.

The restoration of government authority and services on Bougainville has cost Papua New Guinea considerable time, energy and money. But that is a price the government had to pay to ensure national unity, resilience and sensibility. Prime Minister Sir Julius Chan, since taking office in mid 1994, undertook to resolve the Bougainville dispute and bring back peace and normalcy on the island, which once was a major contributor to the national income through the Panguna copper mine and the province's cocoa and coconut produce.

In undertaking the settlement of the Bougainville dispute, Sir Julius not only committed himself and his cabinet, but also his department - the Department of Prime Minister and the National Executive Council. The department has the huge task of providing administrative services to the restoration exercise as well as advising the Prime Minister and other government leaders on the very difficult task of dealing with leaders on Bougainville, a task that has proven to require sensitive handling. So far there have been achievements, with over 80 per cent of Bougainville now under government control. Now, the only detriments to lasting peace are the hard-core rebels and their leaders. Again from the Bougainville restoration, the department of Prime Minster has other major tasks which it performs to ensure smooth running of the government as well as other functions. After the July, 1995 cabinet reshuffle - the first by Sir Julius since taking over the reins the previous year - the functions of the department were upgraded, and in some cases expanded. Twenty five areas of responsibilities for the department have been gazetted after the change.

"PNG looks to a bright future", says Sir Julius Chan. "We are looking to a rapid improvement in our overall investment picture with the Lihir gold project, the largest in the world outside South Africa, approved and ready to go. Development work on this project, along with work

already underway, or about to start, on a number of other major infrastructure and development projects, will give our economy the injection that it needs".

17

"Our office is in charge of the administration of the Prime Minister's Department" explained Minister of State Assisting the Prime Minister, Arnold Marsipal. He was being modest. His office is often in the front line dealing swiftly with problems, implementing decisions and negotiating political settlements.

The Minister is responsible for four constitutional offices, that of Auditor General, Electoral Commission, Boundaries Commission and Ombudsman. He is member of three committees, Infrastructure, Law and Order and Administration. By virtue of recently being appointed Justice Minister he is also a member of the National Security Council.

The Prime Minister delegates responsibility to his Minister of State requiring him to deal with protocol and Foreign Affairs. This has brought Arnold Marsipal into heavy involvement with the South Pacific Forum and with APEC (Asian Pacific Economic Community). On the home front he is looking after the rehabilitation of Bougainville.

The Minister deals with grievances against the government from Papua New Guinea citizens. It may mean dealing with irate leaders of a student demonstration surging outside the building. It may mean calming landowners, angry and frustrated by delays in what they see as rightful compensation. It involves being able to talk in common terms with many different people. It requires tact and high level public relations, especially when dealing with other government departments or ministries. The Minister is ably assisted by a staff of eight including First Secretary, Seri Hegame, who has been a principal political advisor since Independence.

Arnold Marsipal is also Deputy Parliamentary leader of Pangu Party, Member of Parliament representing the Islands and a member of the Manus Lapan Assembly. He does not find conflict in these roles. "At Independence we had one goal, to be united. Pangu stands for Papua and New Guinea Unite. It is there to serve the people. So am I. I am not interested in a struggle for power. When I discuss matters with the Prime Minister, I address him as a brother, as a citizen, and discuss issues openly and honestly."

One of Arnold Marsipal's most trying jobs has been Chair of the Implementation Committee. It looks at all the projects over the last twenty years and asks why they have not been completed. "You can imagine it requires skills and professional officers to sort things out. It really needs a separate division. It gets so complicated. But it does leave the Prime Minister free to deal with policy and with forward planning."

The Minister for State and Administrative Services has a rich and varied portfolio which includes volcanic eruptions and floods as well as looking after the nearly 400 public servants who work for the present Prime Minister. He also looks after three former Prime Ministers, the Speaker, each of the 27 Government Ministers and seven Parliamentary Party leaders. He also keeps the accounts for the money spent by all Members of Parliament on projects in their own areas.

The present Minister is the Honourable Paul Tohian, QPM, MP, Regional Member for New Ireland.

The first set of duties derives from fact that the National Disaster and Emergency Services come under his control. When Tavurvur and Vulcan erupted in Rabaul in September 1994 and Karkar volcano blew up in Madang the same year, when the Sepik or any other river floods causing deaths and damage, and when there are major landslips in the mountainous areas, it is this Ministry, and the Minister himself, who is responsible for making sure that the Emergency Services do their duty.

Natural disasters often involve fires and the Ministry controls the Fire Service, which operates fourteen permanently established Fire Stations throughout the country, employing nearly 400 people. Active consideration is being given to the use of volunteers to extend the work of this force which, according to its own reports, has become overstretched.

The National Liquor Licensing Commission, a statutory organisation, also comes under the Ministry for State Affairs. This is a small but crucial organisation, whose workload and income-generating capacity will increase dramatically if powers presently held by provincial governments are abolished as part of the reform of local government. At present decisions about the sale and consumption of liquor are made by each province.

But perhaps the most well known part of the job of the Ministry for State Affairs is to do with the regulation of a fund called 'The Electoral Development Fund'. An amount of K300,000 is provided annually to each Member of Parliament to support projects in his or her constituency.

In a democracy, power resides with the people. But how do democracies ensure that their elected representatives and public officials do their job properly? How can they make sure that power is not abused, that ill-gotten gains do not accrue in the bank accounts of unprincipled leaders?

One of Papua New Guinea's answers to this question is through the office of an Ombudsman. Twenty years ago, as part of its Independence Constitution, PNG set up its own Ombudsman Commission with the highest powers to act as public watch-dog. Ombudsmen elsewhere have the main function of taking up the cases of individuals with complaints against the system, and, if the case is upheld, of

seeking redress without delay. But PNG required more than this of its Ombudsman, adding a whole new, and possibly unique, function: that of monitoring the actions of its most senior representatives and officials according to a "Leadership Code". The Code itself, and the list of post-holders to whom it was to apply, was also specified.

At present approximately 3,500 persons are subject to the requirements of the code and therefore have to be monitored, while about 2,000 cases a year might be brought to the Ombudsman under the complaints procedure with cases ranging from unfair dismissal to theft.

Papua New Guinea has enjoyed an enviable reputation for many years as being relatively free of the kind of corruption that is routine in many other nations, some of whom are neighbours. In fact PNG, after 20 years' experience, is now ready to assist other Pacific territories in setting up Ombudsmen on similar lines. But it is a continual battle to keep standards high.

The complicated financial opportunities made possible by electronic bank transfer of funds, together with the global reach of many industries, has meant that public life in PNG is harder to penetrate. But while that might make the day-to-day work of the Ombudsman more difficult, the moral position remains as clear as it was on the day that it was formed, that is: to safeguard society from abuse by those elected or appointed to serve it.

The public sector is a major part of PNG's economy. It is the single biggest employer in the country, accounting for roughly one quarter of formal employment.

But public service performance in delivering services has been questioned by various leaders, particularly elected leaders at the national and provincial levels over the past ten years.

"This Department is at the heart of the Administration of Papua New Guinea", said outgoing Public Service Minister Bart Philemon. "I have made a public statement on my concern that after Independence we have gone backwards and that it is a reflection of our capacity to administer. If you look at the indicators, in terms of gross national product and per capita income we are a middle level country. But most of our social indicators, infant mortality, maternal mortality, literacy and so forth are much below those of

other countries within the region, in fact they are in line with low income earning countries. To me that's a reflection of the failure of government machinery to manage the system properly."

There is a general concern that services are not reaching rural areas. Certain parts of the country lack essential health, education and infrastructure services, or people need to travel long distances to be able to access these services. Yet administration is

costing the country 80% of total government expenditure. Coming from the private sector where administration costs would never exceed 30%, Bart Philemon thinks that costs must be reduced, fast. The National Executive Council agrees with him. They have asked for a 7.5% reduction within the year, reducing the salary bill by K45 million. It will mean putting four and a half thousand people out of a job. But it must be done if the country is to free up money for development.

How is it that before Independence the public service was small yet services reached people at the grassroot level? Bart Philemon says that there is no "capacity to manage". There are no recruitment criteria. There is no available training in Business and Public Administration at a post-graduate level in PNG. He has put a policy document before Government which will build capacity at every level from entry to Department Heads. "We want to appoint people to positions based on their qualifications or merits rather than on political patronage. It is going to be hard selling that idea to the rest of the Ministers who want to appoint their own wantoks", Philemon admits ruefully. ("Wantok" is pidgin for a friend or relative or someone who speaks the same language - "one talk".)

The Public Service Management Act provides the legal basis and parameters for personnel management matters. It initiates training programmes at Cadetship and Senior Executive levels and it suggests ways of developing administrative skills. "There is a need for

public servants to have a sense of purpose, by following a clearly defined career path which creates a professional working atmosphere where personnel are so skilled that they can survive in any working environment be it public or private," declares a recent discussion paper. "The public service personnel should compete for excellence." At present there are no performance standards or even agreed mechanisms for measuring performance. It is almost impossible to assess the productivity of the workforce. The proposed training programme will, it is hoped, ensure that all staff are appropriately skilled, motivated and productive.

All public service jobs will be classified along the broad lines of International Labour Organisation classifications, that is: Professional and Executive,

Skilled Manpower (including professionals), Semiskilled Workers and Unskilled Workers. Minimum entry qualifications will be set. Sponsorship will be available to assist personnel in attaining qualifications. Bilateral agreements have been established with Australian universities until a graduate business school can be established in PNG.

It remains to be seen whether Public Service will be able to deliver the goods. "It's not the system, it is the capacity to manage the system that has been at fault" says Bart Philemon. "First we will deal with capacity and then with decentralisation." Building a skilled bureaucracy responsive to Parliament, accountable to the people, is perceived as the most important task for the future administration of Papua New Guinea.

After one particularly volatile Parliamentary session, Prime Minister Sir Julius Chan was heard to comment, "I have often read foreign commentators refer to our politics as 'crazy and without ideology'. But our politics are not illogical, unstable or even unpredictable."

Papua New Guinea has maintained the democratic process in its own inimitable style. One feature of this is a plethora of parties which appear to have little fixed ideology. Parties have so little commitment to a manifesto that members are able to step in and out of them as they do their clothes. In traditional village politics, debates and allegiances would form over single issues and no one was expected to commit themselves to long term loyalties.

Of all the parties in PNG the People's Progress Party, Pangu Party and People's Democratic Movement have been the most successful. The Melanesian Alliance, led by Bougainville MP Father John Momis has always been seen as the 'conscience' party and is the closest to a leftist party on the PNG political scene. There are at least five other smaller parties including one with just a single member.

One of the mechanisms that keeps coalitions and ministers in power is the 'lock-up' or 'camp'. In the days immediately after an election, the Parliament and Port Moresby will be denuded of politicians. They will have been lured away to an island resort or remote 'camp' where they cannot be 'got at' by the opposition. Here the political groupings are cemened, at least temporarily. It is a version of a traditional big man's feast.

In the 1987 elections, independents won 41% of the vote. Gaining their allegiance was essential if a party leader was to make any headway in the Parliamentary chamber. Much the same thing happens prior to a major or tricky piece of legislation It is a different but perfectly practical and logical way of doing parliamentary business.

"Parliament has helped develop and strengthen our own brand of parliamentary democracy", says Speaker Rabbie Namaliu. "Despite all the predictions prior to independence that it wouldn't survive, it is thriving and flourishing and I think it always will for the future." There are none who would disagree. Though quite how government can be conducted through the shifting allegiances of the house frequently baffles outsiders.

Speaker Namaliu points to the parliamentary building itself to provide the answer. "The strength of this country, the resilience of our people, is partly due to the diverse nature of it, its ethnic and tribal makeup. No one region or tribal grouping is sufficiently large to dominate the rest." The building combines two traditions, the diversity of Papua New Guinea and the Westminster model of parliamentary democracy.

The design is monumental. See it from the air and it looks like a great bird settled on the gentle slopes of Waigani, just outside Port Moresby. Rising above the main entrance to the Chamber is a peaked roof modelled on the haus tambaran, the men's spirit house of the Sepik region. The roof sweeps down over a central office building to end in a round house whose form comes directly from the Highlands.

The interior and decorative elements are equally eclectic. Door handles are shaped like kundu drums. The ceiling above the main hall is decorated with tapa designs, like the court houses of the Sepik. The speakers chair is surrounded by intricate carvings originating from the ceremonial canoes of the Trobriand and Milne Bay areas. The Chair itself is Westminster, but the whole effect is more reminiscent of the orator's stool which features in village ceremonies along the Sepik river. And carved into the base is a garamut, a long cylindrical drum from Manus island used to call people together.

Each of the 109 MPs has a large desk and earphones

on which he can hear proceedings translated into Tok Pisin, Motu, or English. The debates can be watched by 600 spectators. The floor of the chamber is arranged as a sweeping semi-circle around the Speaker. "I find it a very convenient arrangement", says Speaker Namaliu. "It's much easier to control. You can see everyone and as they all have fixed positions it makes identification easy." Individuals may have fixed seats but they take a more cavalier attitude to party allegiance. There are parties in PNG but discipline is loose and members are prone to act independently. Successive government have been dependent on shaky, unreliable coalitions. Parties are distinguished more by the personality of their leaders and their regional bases than by ideology.

"In our tradition," one MP declared, "leaders are leaders because they are wealthy men. By wealth I mean pigs, material goods and sometimes many wives. Sometimes they are leaders because they have magical powers and can use these powers to catch fish, win negotiations, make rain." Speaker Rabbie Namaliu would like to see an end to such extravagant claims and the development of a proper party system. Enduring stability will depend on the development and maturing of political parties who can be identified by philosophy, by shared values and a legal

organisation. There is a proposed bill before the house which will set down minimum standards and requirements to comply with party status. "That should stabilise them", says the Speaker. "It will commit them to certain principles so that they can be recognised on the floor of the house."

The original constitution provided for a six month grace period after a government was sworn into office

either after an election or after a vote of no confidence. Just about everyone was agreed that this was very destabilising. "Even during the first six months people were jockeying for position", said Speaker Ramaliu. "So we tried for thirty months grace period which would translate into half-way through the normal term of five years. Some people in the opposition objected and we compromised on eighteen months."

Rabbie Namaliu was one of the first intake into the University of Papua New Guinea in 1966. He took a Master's degree in history and political science from Victoria University, Canada, and entered politics as Sir Michael Somare's principal private secretary in the year of Independence. He won the seat of Kokopo in the 1982 national elections and Somare appointed him Minister for Foreign Affairs. Six years later, in July 1988, Namaliu was Prime Minister. A journalist decribed the scene when he went home to his Raluana village in East New Britain. "A watermelon shatters at his feet. The old Tolai women from his father's side of the family wail as they splinter sticks of sugarcane for him to walk over, and cast white, powdery lime on his legs. His father presents him with a spear, places a band around his head and bids his own, leaf-bedecked, sacred Tubuan spirit figure to dance around his son."

"Tolai traditional society is very strong," Namaliu confides. "If you come from it and don't accept it as being part of your backbone, you won't be accepted as a leader, as a true leader."

But Namaliu was to suffer under the old no-confidence procedures. "It can be very destabilising because it takes your mind off everything else, including governing, and concentrates your mind entirely on the vote."

Namaliu would be the first to acknowledge the changes that have come to Parliament since independence. He is proud of them. "Parliament is the one supreme law-making body and as such it has grown enormously in its responsibilities and is going to build up its own traditions, its own practice, its own reputation and standing in the community. It hasn't been easy but its something for which we can hold our heads high. It is an enormous achievement."

With Independence came responsibility in the international arena. The fledgling sovereign nation had to make up its mind about foreign affairs. When to be friendly. When to be cool. These decisions could have a profound influence at home. Very sensibly the first Foreign Minister Sir Albert Maori Kiki announced that "Papua New Guinea wishes to establish friendly relations with as many countries as possible and to be hostile to none." This stance was called 'universalism'. It gave PNG a breathing space.

The first white paper on Foreign Affairs was seen through parliament in 1981 by then Foreign Minister Noel Levi. He summed up the new approach as "active and selective engagement." This orientation, for it is hardly a policy, enabled PNG to continue with universalism while pursuing specific interests. Over the years it had tended to keep the Soviets at arms length while welcoming the Chinese. The West was favoured over the East. Indonesia was treated with caution. As for the old colonial power Australia, PNG was anxious to be seen not as a stooge but as a natural friend.

It is significant that Papua New Guinea did not have to win Independence from Australia. Relations with Australia were amicable, often based on personal ties. Certain elements of Australian popular culture, beer, pies and rugby had been welcomed by PNG. Australian political institutions and administrative structures were left in place. Unlike other colonial powers Australia was a close neighbour. PNG and Australia were affected by the same strategic and regional issues.

In the mid to late 80's a series of formal agreements were made which remain today: a treaty with Indonesia, membership of ASEAN (Association of South East Asian Nations), a joint declaration with Australia and a pan-Melanesian pact. Together with membership of the United Nations, the Commonwealth, the South Pacific Forum and the South Pacific Commission these are the main planks of PNG Foreign Affairs. PNG has close international relations with over sixty countries. Twenty seven nations have a diplomatic mission in PNG, over half of them European.

For PNG as with most other sovereign nations, it is trading relations which take up most of the Foreign Affairs effort. Trade with Australia, Japan and Germany accounts for two thirds of all trade. But by far the most important trading relationship is with Australia.

Before Independence, Australia gave aid and took advantage of the market. Australian companies dominated the formal economy. Burns Philp, Steamships and Carpenters were everywhere as were Australian banking and financial services and the effects of the massive Bougainville copper mine.

After Independence, Australia stepped up the aid and took further advantage of the opening market. Until 1986, up to 40% of PNG's budget came directly from Australian aid. Then in 1986 Australia unilateraly reduced the grant by 10 million Australian dollars. The time had come for a reappraisal of the 'special relationship'.

1987 and 1989 saw the formalisation of the relationship into one of self reliance and mutual defence (Australia still helps PNG maintain a viable well-trained defence capacity). Australia's development assistance to PNG shifted from budget support (direct financial transfers to government revenue) to programmed assistance (investment tied to particular sectors and projects). Both govern ments are committed to completing this shift by the year 2000. AusAID is now directed at health, education, law enforcement, infrastructure and the rehabilitation of Bougainville.

What is remarkable is that Australian programme aid has actually increased, by almost 40% over the last year. And this rapid growth will continue. In 1995-96 Australian aid will increase to A$118.6 million (approximately K110 million). Programme aid will be more than 50% higher than in 1994-95. Australia provides more programme aid to PNG than it provides to any other country, although Indonesia runs a close second. Australia clearly has an interest in seeing PNG through its current economic problems.

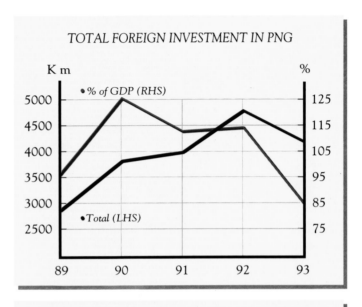

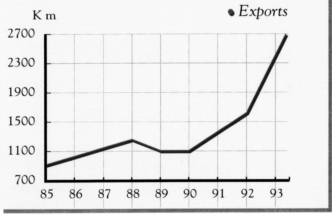

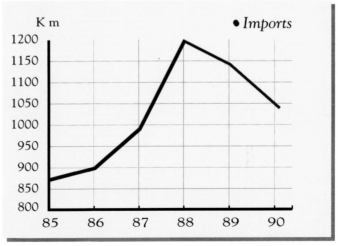

Courtesy of McIntosh Baring, Papua New Guinea Resources Review, March 1995

"The Ministry of Foreign Affairs is twenty years old, just like the country. In that time we have built a fully localised national Foreign Service," said Gabriel Dusava, Secretary to the Department of Foreign Affairs and Trade. "Only Papua New Guineans are responsible to the government for policy advice on international relations in trade, on investments, on a whole series of challenges that PNG faces as a member of the international community preparing to face up to the year 2000 and beyond." Gabriel Dusava was reassured by this achievement. For how can a nation be truly independent without being wholly in charge of its relations with other countries, near neighbours and far?

In the beginning we had the policy of universalism", Gabriel Dusava continued. "PNG had to be a friend to everybody and an enemy to none. This is not the same as neutrality. If you are neutral then you take sides with those who are in the middle. We wanted to be friendly to everyone so that they would know us and we could know them."

After five years, in 1981, Sir Julius Chan became Foreign Minister. He introduced a White Paper with a new policy. "We moved from an initial foreign policy stance of Universalism to one of Selective Engagement, a policy which we pursue to this day, with regular refinements as the needs, interests and issues of our nation dictate," explained Sir Julius, who once again holds the position of Minister for Foreign Affairs in addition to the Prime Ministership. He identified PNG's role in the Vanuatu uprising in 1981 as a crucial point. "It was a moment when Papua New Guinea committed itself to looking past its own borders, in a manner more decisive than ever before, and to taking on the responsibility of behaving as a member of the South Pacific group of nations. It was a pivotal event in developing a view of ourselves as a member of a wider community."

PNG was now more mature, able to distinguish between governments and to identify those that had made a more positive impression. As Gabriel Dusava said, "We could now choose our friends. We opened up diplomatic

missions in strategic places in addition to those already established with traditional friends such as Australia, New Zealand, Indonesia, the United Kingdom, the United States and Japan."

At that time, in the early eighties, PNG started looking at relations with China, Malaysia and Fiji. It joined the South Pacific Forum. It opened up consulates in twenty strategic places like the west coast of the United States, Canada, Germany, Israel, Hong Kong, Vanuatu and, in the last few years, in Seoul, Singapore and Paris. PNG is working world-wide to create awareness of its potential. Opening up a consular office is the first step to facilitating foreign investment and tourism.

In 1995 the most important trading partners were Australia (with billions in investments) and the Asian countries, Japan, Malaysia, Korea, Taiwan and Hong Kong. The most important neighbours were Indonesia and the Solomon Islands. The relationship with both could be described as 'close friends'.

PNG has one land border, that with Indonesia. It is 750 km long. There are a scant 11 border posts, no roads, few people, steep mountains covered in jungle and swamp. Kiaps used to regard it as a punishment posting. Yet this border is one of the most sensitive items in PNG's foreign policy. In 1975 Indonesia invaded East Timor and a shudder went through the fledgling state of PNG. But it held its nerve. Under the policy of universalism it wanted to remain friendly. In 1979 and 1980 border treaties recognised Indonesia's claim to Irian Jaya. But it was this border which caused the biggest headache. Guerrilla war surged this way and that across the border leaving in its wake thousands of refugees. By 1984 the refugee situation was critical and UNHCR was called in. Somehow the two countries maintained a dialogue and by 1987 a new agreement was reached. For PNG it signalled a further move from Australia towards the Asian countries.

The other factor which has affected PNG Foreign Affairs, in particular in its relations with it's close neighbours the Solomon Islands, is the trouble on Bougainville. It erupted in 1989 with sabotage and violence. By 1990 many businesses and banks had stopped trading. Plantations had repatriated migrant workers. Air Niugini ceased all commercial flights. Lloyds of London withdrew insurance cover. It was as bad as having a war zone within your borders. By the time the police and army withdrew, in March 1990, more than seventy people had lost their lives. PNG's neighbours were sympathetic but distanced. This was an internal problem. When it was solved, and in 1995 it does seem that a solution has at last been reached, they would come in and help. Australia, in particular has pledged a lot of programme aid to the rehabilitation of Bougainville.

If there is a direction to Foreign Policy it is towards recognition of PNG as a Pacific Island country. One of Sir Julius Chan's first actions as Prime Minister was to tour all the Pacific Island countries. It made a statement. PNG is Melanesian first and foremost. In 1986 the Melanesian Spearhead Group was formed by Papua New Guinea, Solomon Islands and Vanuatu. After a short while in the doldrums it is now back on track and its members have just signed a trade agreement by which tea, tuna and beef will be traded duty-free. The Kanak Socialist National Liberation Front of New Caledonia has joined the group which engages in cultural exchanges and law enforcement initiatives as well as trade agreements.

Papua New Guinea is also a mainstay of the South Pacific Forum. It is the premier political organisation for leaders throughout the region to meet and formulate policies on a whole range of activities including development programmes, trade, environment, fisheries, forestry and the general health and well-being of the membership. It is of course, firmly opposed to nuclear armaments, the testing of nuclear weapons and the dumping of nuclear waste in the South Pacific. In 1995 PNG are hosting the forum in Madang, bringing 150 leaders and their staff to PNG just before the Independence celebrations.

Sir Julius Chan concludes, "While it would be the height of folly for a small nation to feel that it can call the shots internationally, we do not have to sit by as passive observers. We have our roles to play, ideas to generate. We have a contribution to make to the community of nations. Let us begin on our own doorstep, in our own region."

Twenty years ago there were those who questioned whether Papua New Guinea needed a defence force. Wasn't it just a status symbol like a national airline? There were fears that a standing army would be a temptation to a power-hungry general and that PNG would be dragged into the scenario of military coups and counter coups that dogged so many other small countries. These fears have been confounded. As one commentator wrote, "The low profile of the military in PNG is one of the country's many political surprises."

Before Independence the Australian administration maintained two infantry battalions, the 1st and 2nd Battalions of the Royal Pacific Islands Regiment which had a proud and tough record stretching back to World War 2. At hand-over there was a force of 3,500 Papua New Guineans and 465 Australians. Overall control was vested in the NEC (National Executive Council) with the proviso that the Minister of Defence could not be a serving member of the armed forces.

At Independence the Defence Force was a confident elite. The soldiers had high educational level and material possessions. Their public image was good. It remained good until after the successful expedition to Vanuatu

when the troops where welcomed home like heroes. But a slow rot had set in. Government after government reduced spending, which not only reduced administrative efficiency but also pay and conditions. In 1989 the soldiers rioted. It came soon after Bougainville - an unhappy experience for the Defence Force in which they were in conflict with local people. They felt humiliated.

The question remains: does PNG need a Defence Force? The answer from most Papua New Guinea politicians is 'yes' but only with considerable foreign defence assistance and with a devolved responsibility which allows for civil activities. This has, in a sense, been a success story both for the Australians and for the PNGDF. In the Southern Highlands there is a 23-man unit of engineers, based in Mendi, who virtually run the provincial works department. In 1989 a second unit was based in Sandaun which also helps with civil works. It has a double benefit. Trained troops undertake extremely useful activities like road and bridge building, and other capital projects. This could be the best justification for maintaining an army in peacetime.

The Papua New Guinea Defence Force is currently under review pending a Defence White Paper, but it is safe to say that its goals and objectives are enshrined in the Constitution and are unlikely to change. Defence protects PNG's sovereignty against external threats. It assists PNG in fulfilling international obligations. It comes to the aid of civil authorities in civil emergencies and contributes to nation-building and to promoting national unity. So the Defence Force has both an external and an internal rationale.

There are, in 1995, about 5,200 in the Defence Force. It is one force consisting of Land, Maritime and Air Elements. There are two infantry battalions (of approximately 1,000 men each), one Engineering Battalion, a Preventive Medical Platoon and a Signal Squadron. The maritime element consists of a Patrol Boat Squadron, a Landing Craft Squadron, an Explosive Ordinance Disposal Unit and a small Riverine Operations Unit. The Air element includes Fixed Wing and Rotary Wing Flights and a Training Flight. In addition there are a number of support elements: Supply, Transport, Movements, Health Centres, Field Medical Section, Provost, Regional Engineer Units and Defence training institutions.

There is no doubt that the Defence Force is small in relation to the country but there is no immediate external threat at present. PNG is geographically located in one of the least troubled regions of the world. PNG is living in harmony with immediate neighbours on all three borders. But uncertainty still prevails. There is a need to be ready for anything. Perhaps PNGDF's most successful incident in the international arena occurred in 1980 when PNG went to the aid of the legitimate government of Vanuatu in a peacekeeping operation.

"The training was such that they could hit rats and bandicoots at night if they moved", boasted the Brigadier General in charge. The force, led by the then Colonel Tony Huai was formidable. Ninety-five combat-ready troops were dropped

onto Santo airfield. "Led by Huai clutching an Israeli sub-machine gun, the men leapt out prepared for trouble. They were in full battle dress, armed with automatic rifles and heavier weapons. They had the dark visors of their battle helmets pulled down over their faces and fearsome-looking, long-bladed bush knives strapped to their waists. They secured the airport... With the arrival of the Papua New Guineans the British and French soldiers packed up and left, having picked up no honours but excellent suntans." This deployment of soldiers from one Pacific island to another for the first time ever was significant. It marked the beginning of a new sense of cohesiveness among Melanesian countries.

The internal situation presents more of a problem for the Defence Force. The operation in Bougainville is uncomfortable. A small band of guerrillas has been able to tie up a large section of PNGDF. The Army's activities have brought them into disrepute, with charges of human rights violations. The Defence force is recruited on a quota system so that all regions are represented. They do not like getting involved in partisan or regionalist arguments, but they have a duty to maintain law and order. They also have to help in times of national disaster such as volcanic eruptions.

The present Minister, Mathias Ijape, sees the future development of the Force in maintaining a highly mobile core force which is structured and strategically located throughout the country to meet low-level conflicts which may arise at short notice. "Despite the commonly recognised conventional roles of the Defence Forces, PNGDF must play a leading role in nation building" the Minister says. "Almost 80% of our people live in the mountains and rural areas with little or no access to developed infrastructures. I see PNG Defence Force with assistance from our neighbouring armed forces carrying out civic action tasks in future. Instead of keeping the soldiers in barracks, let's send them out to the villages to build roads, set up water supplies, aid posts and schools. It would not diminish their military capability and it would be immensely helpful to the nation."

As the day of Independence approached twenty years ago there was much concern in certain circles about what to do about the existing law. For most people it was an alien system, brought by colonialists to serve their own ends. The Australian patrol officers, the Kiaps, who first brought order and attempted to subdue tribal fighting, papered over a complex traditional system. They were largely successful in resolving disputes peacefully albeit on a biannual round of mobile patrols to remote villages.

In the 1950's the Australian administration attempted to codify the laws and make them apply to the whole population. They established a system of visiting foreign magistrates. From 1962 there was to be a single system of courts administering a single body of law. All work on village courts came to a stop and was not resumed until after Independence.

The first Papua New Guinean Minister of Justice, John Kaputin wrote: "Law only has legiti-macy when it comes from the people and responds to their requirements. This truth by itself is enough to question the legitimacy of the Criminal Code. As Minister of Justice I am obliged to ensure that our country's present laws are altered, and our future laws are framed, to fit our people and our society."

The Constitutional Planning Committee agreed with him and brought custom into the legal system. Unfortunately the combination of customary and western law has often led to contradictions which has sometimes resulted in an apparent disregard for law and order and a bad reputation abroad. It is important to recognise that PNG is not a lawless society and that this reputation is undeserved by any measure.

In a country as huge and diverse as PNG there can be no common body of customary law. Traditional society was held together in a pattern of shifting allegiances, mechanisms and understanding of mores which varied from place to place. The only point in common was that it aimed to restore balance and order in the community. It was speedy. It often involved compensation. The accused had few rights. The difficulty now of maintaining law has to do with the speed with which the 700-odd separate independent 'states', each with its own customs and practices, have been welded together into a single modern 'State'.

When it comes to maintaining the law, Papua New Guinea has a combination of traditional and introduced court systems. It is a three-tier system. The Supreme Court and the National Court have many formal rules and hold jurisdiction over both civil and criminal matters.

The Supreme Court of Justice is the highest court of the land; having its inherent powers and enabling jurisdiction established under the Papua New Guinea Constitution. It is the ultimate and final court of appeal which hears appeals from the National Court of Justice. The judiciary is headed by a Chief Justice and is augmented by several judges and numerous magistrates.

The National Court of Justice also has inherent powers and original jurisdiction. It hears or tries criminal cases and indictable offences. It deals with civil litigation cases involving K11,000 damages or compensation and above. This court of record reviews various administrative or executive decisions of government departments or statutory authorities and body. It is a Court of Appeal that hears appeals from the District Court.

District Courts are run by Magistrates and handle the bulk of cases brought by the police. Local village courts are more informal and deal with customary law. Their aim is to encourage local people to settle their own disputes in their own way.

There are some other specialised courts like the Children's Court for those under 16, or the Coroner's Court which deals with unexpected deaths, or the Court of Disputed Returns which deals with complaints by losers in political elections. A Warden's Court deals with disputes relating to mining and there are other courts with responsibility for determining ownership of land and for assessing the right of customary landowners to compensation.

The Clifford report in the mid 1980's was critical of the National court system in the first ten years since independence.

Conviction rates had fallen from 80% to 50% and court delays had escalated so that the average number of days from committal to verdict was 344. Police inefficiency, poor quality of prosecution work, lack of resources, including a short supply of court reporters and interpreters hampered the course of justice. In contrast the District courts were found to be working well and even getting better.

The village courts are not traditional Melanesian institutions but they try to take Melanesian norms, values and modes of organisation into account. In general it is felt that they have contributed to the maintenance of law and order though there are criticisms such as "wantokism" by court personnel, arbitrary punishments and ignorance of proper procedure. From the first days of Independence custom was seen as an essential ingredient of nation-building. Customary law was no exception, though its integration into the legal system has been slower than was hoped. What the Justice system is looking for now are the skills, training, experience and appropriate technology to take it past the year 2000.

When he took over as Minister for Justice in September 1994, Robert Nagle was given a list of his legislative duties. There were nearly a hundred statutory responsibilities in his brief. They covered everything from Organic Law on Provincial and low-level governments, the Power of Mercy, Companies Acts, land disputes, trusts and trustees, matrimonial causes and parole to sorcery, village courts and vagrancy.

Robert Nagle is not a lawyer. He is an accountant by profession. He has an Attorney General to administer the legal side. He also has 19 offices and branches within his Ministry. There are 409 trained staff.

The work of the Ministry has increased since Independence with the establishment of the Parole Board, for example, and the Village Courts Secretariat. There are about 950 village court officials in the country each of whom receives an allowance from the State for carrying out his duties. The idea is that they should come under Provincial government. The spread of justice throughout the country is also the concern of the National Narcotics Control Board which was established in 1992. The bureau is concerned with a new Controlled Substances Act, with a pilot project to raise awareness in schools, village courts and other target groups as well as with international linkages.

The Ministry also works with various constitution-

al offices which are free from political control. The Public Prosecutor's office controls the performance of prosecutions in the National and Supreme Courts. It is entitled to bring proceedings under the Leadership Code for misconduct in office. The Public Solicitor provides legal advice and assistance to persons in need. The Law Reform Commission is an independent body which reviews the law with a view to its development, including modernisation, simplification and the elimination of defects.

One of the first things the Minister for Justice did was to look at costs. "The previous government went outside the Department drawing on certain lawyers from the private sector and this cost a lot of money," points out the accountant-turned-Minister with feeling. "We intend to restructure the department to get the best legal advise and the best terms.

"Then the next thing is to ensure that all lawyers practising in PNG are Papua New Guinean nationals or at the very least 60% in any one practice. In special technical fields we will let the outsiders in, but it should be on a reciprocal basis with that country. We have agreements only with the United States, the United Kingdom and Australia at present."

The law of Papua New Guinea is a complex interweaving of 'customary and constitutional or 'Western' law. It takes the very best advice to sort it out. Minister of Justice Robert Nagle is very aware that foreign investors want to be confident they will not run into conflict over ownership of land or rights. However, while he has no power over the National Lands Commission which hears disputes and settlements over national land, he may act to transfer customary land to registered title and he may also be able to agree to compensation. Though currently he does none of these things without expert advice from the department. The department is currently setting up a compensation tribunal which will cover all compensation claims for damage to property arising from a renewable or non-renewable resource development project. However, it is considered that this is a notoriously difficult area in which to legislate. It could well be that a Steering Committee will have to be set up to advise on the form of the tribunal, its terms and legal functions or role.

In the last few years there has been some concern about corruption in high places. Minister Robert Nagle is determined to deal with it. He hopes to set up a Federal Investigation Branch, run on the lines of the FIB in Australia or the FBI in the United States. "There are crooked deals involving two and three million kina. A lot of bribery. The culprit walks free. Or it takes two to three years to prosecute. Why should it be different for him and others in high places than for every other person on the street who gets locked up for a lousy two kina", says the Minister for Justice with passion. "What is required is a high level investigation which will make an example of the culprit. That should wipe out corruption at a stroke."

One of this Ministry's most important plans concerns Human Rights. For too long, especially in regard to Bougainville, Papua New Guinea has come under the United Nations spotlight for apparently transgressing human rights. Now there will be a Human Rights Commission which will, to quote the Minister, "protect the grassroots people who are ignorant of their rights." Even the preparations for the establishment of the Commission have improved Papua New Guinea's international image. They may well result in the withdrawal of complaints from the UN agenda. And they serve to present PNG as a civilised and democratic nation to the rest of the world.

43

Establishing a proper regard for the law and creating a proper professional body to protect both lawyers and clients was one of the many tasks of the newly independent state of PNG. It was not until 1986 that the Lawyers Act established a statutory body, the Papua New Guinea Law Society.

The Act sets out the functions and objectives of the Society. Not only was it to protect the public and the lawyers, it was to encourage proper conduct by lawyers. That meant establishing codes of practice, suppressing illegal, dishonourable and improper conduct, and preserving and maintaining the integrity and status of lawyers. Being admitted to the bar automatically conferred membership of the society - although, in a nice legal twist, it could not be compulsory because that would infringe the freedom of association under the Constitution. There has never yet been a refusal of membership.

Members have to pay a fee on joining and to pay for a certificate to practice, which has to be renewed annually. A certificate may be restricted or unrestricted. A restricted certificate entitles the lawyer to practice as an employee lawyer only. There are currently 287 lawyers working with restricted certificates. To work on their own a lawyer has to have held a restricted certificate for at least two years. They can then be issued an unrestricted certificate and can take the further responsibility of holding clients money on trust. There are 152 unrestricted certificates mostly held by senior partners.

Since the Law Society was created in April 1987 there have been 758 members. Currently there are 46 female lawyers practising and the numbers have been steadily increasing. The total numbers fluctuate because some no longer practise within PNG jurisdiction, or they become judges or magistrates, or they leave the law.

The Society has certain regulatory functions in addition to the issue of certificates to practice. These include the scrutiny of trust account audit reports and the setting of standards of professional conduct. It can charge its own members for it is able to appeal to a disciplinary body, the Lawyers Statutory Committee, with complaints of improper conduct by lawyers. By these means the Society is able to ensure that the public is protected and that standards are set.

To ensure high standards the Society intends to promote continual legal training by organising conferences and workshops. It also supports the publication of local legal materials by providing financial support and it is attempting to publish the proceedings of conferences held to date. Future plans include the publication of materials designed to increase awareness of the law amongst the general public.

A major initiative, begun four years ago, has been the introduction of a legal aid scheme. First point of call for legal aid is the Public Solicitor's Office. If it is not able to help, then the claimant will be referred to the Society. At the Society the first person people meet is the Secretary who helps with administrative details. In most cases legal aid will be considered and a private lawyer from the 'pool' will be assigned to the case.

The scheme is funded from interest accrued on trust accounts maintained by lawyers. It is mandatory for banks to forward the interest each quarter. Certain legal problems are not covered, such as adultery and enticement cases, land disputes, taxation claims, conveyancing, wills and testaments, defamation actions, election petitions and traffic offences. It may seem a long list but there are still plenty of cases which get legal aid, the most common of which are matrimonial or family matters, breaches of contract, motor vehicle injury claims and dependency claims. Once the panel has accepted the case all costs and fees are met. It is only rarely, in very big compensation cases, that any of those costs are recouped by the Society.

The Law in PNG, at twenty, feels young but maturing fast. "It is," said one member of the Society's council, " growing more mature in outlook and more professional." The Society is now making proposals for Law Reform. Members of the council are represented on important government Committees. They have been expanding their activities to attend Pacific Island Law Officers meetings and regular gatherings of Australian Law Societies. All these activities have strengthened Papua New Guinea's profile in regional and international legal forums.

In modern Papua New Guinea, the policeman is expected to be a leader and set the example for the community to follow. During its 107 years of service the 'Constabulary' as it is affectionately known, has seen many changes.

Currently, in 1995, the Royal Papua New Guinea Constabulary has a manpower strength of 5000 men and women in the Regular Constabulary Branch, 900 in the Reserve and 1200 in the Community Auxiliary Police Branch. They serve the entire population of PNG - four million people scattered in town and country across the length and breadth of the nation.

PNG's first police service was established in British Papua in 1884 to protect settlers and to introduce law and order. The success of the Papuan model was noted by the Imperial administration in German New Guinea and soon there emerged an armed 'Expedition Troop' to protect their small outposts that they were establishing in coastal areas and inland waterways. Both forces were paramilitary in nature, constables were armed with rifles and training was generally conducted along military lines by European officers and NCO's.

In 1939 King George the Sixth honoured the Papuan force with the title 'Royal' for the outstanding work done during the early years of pacification of the country. During World War Two members of the police served with distinction and after that a single force for the whole country was established.

Throughout the 1950s and early 1960s, armed police accompanied and protected administration patrols into the most remote and wildest parts of PNG. It was during this time, in towns and urban areas, that the more usual police role began to emerge with new aids and responsibilities including motor traffic patrols, communications, dog patrols and CID investigations.

In 1971 the Bomana Police Training College stepped up the training of commissioned officers, NCO's and recruits. In the run up to Independence massive inputs in police numbers and police capability were made. New police stations, barracks and police houses were built. The Constabulary led the way for other government departments in fulfilling the national goal of 'localising' positions filled by expatriate contract officers. By Independence national officers were holding the top command

positions of the Constabulary including that of Police Commissioner.

The 20 years since Independence have not been easy for the Constabulary or for the men and women who serve in its ranks. The Clifford report in the mid-80's was damning in its conclusions. It said that a lack of training, improper supervision and inadequate resources "deny police a fighting chance against most crimes". Further, it said that police in towns had become isolated in their barracks and had lost the confidence of the community. They began to be seen as an alien force which sallied out on punitive raids.

In recent years, the Constabulary has adopted the concept of "community policing" where a greater emphasis is placed on dialogue and consensus with communities rather than the harsh ways of olden times. It is finding different ways in which it can work in partnership, discussing specific community law and order problems and listening to the community's ideas and input of how the police and the people can work together to find a solution to local crime problems.

In these modern times the police emphasis worldwide is shifting from 'who-dun-it' to crime prevention. The Constabulary is abreast of the latest developments in this field and is a regional leader in some aspects of community policing.

The Royal Papua New Guinea Constabulary put out this statement: "As we stand together to celebrate this observance of 20 years of Indepen-dence, the Royal Papua New Guinea Constabulary is ready to serve the government and the people of Papua New Guinea to help us gain our national goals of law and order, when we can truly be 'One community, One Nation, One People'".

The price of progress is sometimes high. Ever since independence parts of Papua New Guinea have experienced higher than average crime rates. Some public areas have acquired the unenviable reputation of being quite unsafe. The "raskol" problem is fundamentally one of alienated, jobless youths, many of whom have drifted to the cities from their villages, only to discover that neither work nor other occupation can be found there. They resort to violent crime to live and the result may be that they end up in prison.

The prisons of Papua New Guinea contain 3,500 inmates, about half of whom are prisoners on remand, that is, awaiting their trials. Both convicted prisoners and prisoners on remand provide a challenge to the Ministry of Correctional Institutional Services. "Prisons cannot be just dumping grounds," says Minister Sylvanius Siembo, echoing educated opinion worldwide. "A prison sentence is not only punishment. It is an opportunity to effect behavioural change in the prisoner and to equip him with the skills which he can use to lead a crime-free life on his release."

The fundamental cause for the criminalization of sections of Papua New Guinean society seems to lie in the loss of significant roles for young men brought about by the shift from tribal to globalized modern society. In the very recent past many young men in Papua New Guinea spend long periods being initiated into the duties expected of them in their tribal society. These often involve the maintenance of the very rules by which that society lived, the tabus, rituals and behaviours which governed not only daily life but which also held the key to the understanding of both this world and the spirit world. Suddenly, with western contact and especially with missionization, this vocation was demolished and nothing has replaced it. So while young women can find their traditional roles

both confirmed and expanded by the process of modernization, this is not quite so easy for young men. They are susceptible to the power of macho images and concepts such as "pay-back", which at its worst is merely a form of revenge.

The problem remains of what to do for these young men, as does the problem they constitute for the rest of society. Many have not been apprehended because of problems experienced by the police in carrying out their duties. In fact there is a fear that some of the gangs have become institutionalized and are already involved in rackets and crimes involving politicians and village leaders who protect them. Those raskols who have been apprehended eventually find themselves in one of the correctional service's institutions.

The correctional institutions have suffered from poor conditions, with overcrowded premises, no new buildings and low staff morale. The recent elevation in status of the former Department to a Ministry, putting it on the same footing as the Ministry of Police and the Ministry of Defence, is expected to have a beneficial effect. There has already been an improvement in staff morale. Australia has provided an aid package worth K50 million for the correctional institutions. Conditions in gaols are planned to improve. "The law and order issue is the most significant issue for Government," says Minister Siembo.

Securimax Security Group has rapidly established itself as the premier security company in Papua New Guinea. Founded in 1987 by David Pringuer, MBE, it prides itself on offering all aspects of security work, including: armoured car services, payroll packing and delivery, guard dogs and handlers, computerised alarm systems, emergency radio network, process serving, fraud enquiries, quick response teams, and security at mining sites, exploration areas and remote bushcamps.

Founded in 1987 by David Pringuer, MBE, Securimax Security Group prides itself on offering all aspects of security work, including: armoured car services, payroll packing and delivery, guard dogs and handlers, computerised alarm systems, emergency radio network, process serving, fraud enquiries, quick response teams, and security at mining sites, exploration areas and remote bushcamps.

David Pringuer has brought all his experience as a Major in the British Army and as a Superintendent in the Royal Papua New Guinea Constabulary to form and manage the Group. It now consists of two companies with over 800 men.

Securimax Security Pty Ltd. has its head office in Mt.Hagen in the Western Highlands Province. It is especially proud of its record with mining and petroleum companies. In early 1991 it provided security at the Moro bushcamp in Southern Highlands Province for what was to become the Chevron oil fields. It won the tender with a Joint Venture agreement with Fasu landowners in the area. Over the next three years training was given to all levels of staff including a General Manager. The entire company was then sold back in December 1994 to the Fasu people who now run it as an independent security company.

Training is of paramount importance to Securimax. It opened the first residential training centre in PNG in Mt. Hagen in 1991 and now has two other centres in Port Moresby and Rabaul.

Securimax - Islands Security Pty Ltd. was formed in November 1993 expressly to provide security to the Lihir Island gold project. It took over a small ailing security company and retrained the staff. They showed their worth in the aftermath of the Rabaul volcano. Men stayed at their posts as the town was wrecked by the eruption, and the compa-

ny threw its weight, free of charge, behind the Provincial Government and the National Disaster Committee in shepherding refugees from the area, and providing anti-looting patrols.

There are few prospects more terrifying for a criminal than being confronted by a snarling Rottweiler. Guard Dog Security Services not only provides Rottweilers but a selection of over 70 other highly trained dogs - including German Shepherds and Dobermans - in its quest to keep Port Moresby a safer place.

"Our dogs are used primarily to protect our guards and to provide a deterrent," explained Dale Smith, who runs the Port Moresby business. "But when the need arises these dogs can be lethal weapons."

Dale knows his dogs only too well. He has seen first-hand the gruesome injuries they are capable of inflicting. For this reason training is paramount and all his guards are sent on rigorous dog handling courses at the National Security Training Academy in Lae.

Guard Dog Security Services was masterminded in Lae by Dale's Papua New Guinean friend, Dennis Bux. This was back in 1986 and the Lae branch now boasts over 350 guards and 80 dogs. The Moresby branch opened five years ago but it is already almost similar in size and has just opened its own dog handling facility.

Training is conducted in groups of 60 with the recruits selected through the Labour department. Young men aged 18 to 21, single, no commitments,

are given a three week induction course. If they pass they are given employment in the company. Quite a few fail to make the grade. Some find that, faced with a highly trained attack dog, they just can't get rid of their fear.

Both Dale and Dennis work in close contact with the police in a concerted effort to crack-down on crime. Every one of the business's guards has a radio so they can call for help or backup if necessary.

But guards with dogs are by no means the only security the company deals with. It sells everything from sophisticated alarm systems to personal radio monitoring.

"Personal radios are excellent because they provide 24-hour contact," said Dale. "If somebody's car breaks down in the middle of the night, they can call for assistance and help will immediately be on its way. If someone suspects their house is being broken into they can also call. It is a very effective service."

Guard Dog Security Services likes to move with the times. As the criminals get more advanced, security also has to keep pace. Hi-tech electronic fences are now becoming more commonplace in Papua New Guinea. They are another service supplied by the company.

They are now pushing into electronic surveillance. Dale is just completing the designs for a Grade 1 Monitor room which will enable them to track any area anywhere in the country. Using a series of radio repeater links they'll be able monitor what's going on inside or outside any building in PNG.

"I would like to see the whole of the country's security systems regulated." said Dale. "I think all security firms should be licensed and that all individuals should be made to hold ID cards. This would help pinpoint criminals.

I have been in Papua New Guinea for 33 years and genuinely love the place. It has so much going for it but law and order is a problem. We will continue to do everything we can to remedy this."

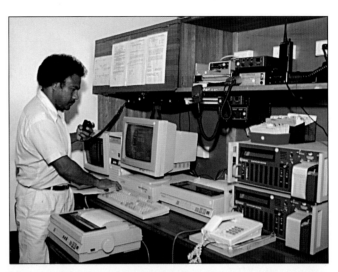

environ

and resc

Papua New Guinea lies just below the equator in the eastern South Pacific. It shares its main island with Indonesia. Its other nearest neighbours are the Solomon Islands, Australia and Vanuatu to the south, Micronesia to the east and Malaysia, Singapore and the Philippines to the north. It comprises more than 600 islands, covers a total area of over 474,000 square kilometres and has a population of 3.7 million.

One of the most striking features of PNG is the immense variety of landscape. Highlands, plateaux, valleys, savanna, rain forest, mangrove swamps, gardens, plantations, island archipelagoes and coral atolls provide a spectrum hardly matched anywhere else in the world. Almost a quarter of the country is over 1,000 metres above sea-level and many of its mountains are over four times that height.

There are at least one hundred volcanoes, some of them still active, and a large number of geothermal springs. South of the central cordillera on the main island stretch luxuriant lowlands, interlaced with one of the largest river systems in the world. The longest of these rivers is the Fly, some 1200 km in all, which empties into the Gulf of Papua where it deposits about 100 million tonnes of sediment a year. Some of PNG's rivers have hydroelectric development, some are major transport routes

and others provide additional irrigation for the plenteous crops of coffee, cocoa and copra and sugar cane.

Situated in the wet and humid equatorial tropics, PNG has little seasonal temperature variation. Regional variation, on the other hand, is quite substantial. Coastal temperatures range from 23° to 30° Celsius, while the highland areas are considerably cooler, very occasionally falling to zero degrees. Most of the country has more than 2,000 millimetres of rain a year and some parts are subject to an annual deluge five times greater. The wettest seasons are January to April and September to December, the first period bringing the northwesterly monsoons and the latter carrying heavy rain on the south east trades. The national capital, Port Moresby, has less rain than the rest of the country – about 1000 millimetres a year.

This rainfall gives rise to and nourishes the vast rainforests that cover 70% of the country. A further 10% is covered with other woodland. It is not just the extent of the forest but the variety of species it contains that makes it such a fascinating natural phenomenon. Besides the hundreds of different kinds of trees, there are over 10,000 other species of flora. The main reason for the great wealth and variety of vegetation in PNG is the corresponding diversity of habitat, the most common of which is lowland forest. With a canopy towering 30–40 metres high, the lowland forests are made up of palms and vines, and strewn with ferns and orchids. Where drainage is poor, the predominant vegetation is sago palm and pandanus. At a higher altitude, mountain forests comprise of oaks, laurels and conifers and ultimately give way to low dense scrub.

57

A nodding acquaintance with the history and geography of Papua New Guinea might lead you to suspect that the portfolio of Lands and Physical Planning was not going to be one of the easiest for a government minister. You would be right.

The present Minister, Sir Albert Kipalan, who has held four other ministerial positions, including Justice and Health, says he has never come across so much paperwork in his life as in the Lands Department.

The reason for this is the way that the land is owned in PNG, where it is rightly perceived to be not only the source of all wealth and security but also the repository of ancestral remains and the home of spirits.

There are only two kinds of landowners in PNG: the customary land owners and the State. By 'land' is meant what grows on the land and what lies underneath it as well as the surface itself.

97% of the land is owned by customary land owners and most of this is owned collectively, that is, by all of the people who live there. They manage the land according to time-honoured custom which varies from area to area. Rights to use land for houses and gardens are handed down from generation to generation, without written record. It is usually by inheritance from father to sons but in a minority of areas, such as in parts of East New Britain and Milne Bay, where matrilineal inheritance is the custom, land can be inherited by daughters and managed by the mother's brother in her absence. It is not possible for an individual to bequeath land to whomsoever they wish, if that goes against the traditional practice. Nor is it possible for land to be sold to foreigners or even other PNG citizens unless they acquire the status of customary land owner by consent of the group. The only body which can buy the freehold of customary land is the State. The State then grants leaseholds to interested parties.

The 3% of the land of PNG which is owned by the State has usually been acquired by purchase. This 3% is actually a declining figure, because, ever since Independence, and even before, various customary land-

owners have successfully challenged state ownership in the courts, usually on the grounds that the original purchase, which may have been many years ago, was unfair for one reason or another. Since 1972 the State has handed back more that 180 parcels of land. The land that has reverted to customary ownership in this way has exceeded that purchased by the State in the meantime.

When the Government wants land, for example to build a road, school or aid-post, or for other public purpose, it must negotiate with all the customary land-owners, first for their permission and then to agree a price. This is the famous 'compensation' of land transactions in PNG. Such is the power of customary law that despite its powers of compulsory purchase, enshrined in the 1963 Land Act, government has never yet felt that making a compulsory purchase was worth the trouble. All its transactions have been with landowners who have voluntarily agreed to the purchase.

Once the government has acquired land it can lease it to organisations and individuals, including foreign companies and missions, or use it for its own purposes, such as state-owned businesses or roads. The government can also acquire rights in customary land, such the rights to extract timber, or mining rights, and lease these to rights to others.

Disputes about land ownership, land use rights, leasehold, access and inheritance are referred to land courts which sit in each province. There are many such disputes.

The suggestion that land ownership should be registered once and for all is one that divides the nation. Some landowners and economic advisers see an advantage in it, because land that is registered would be invaluable as collateral for loans. The World Bank would dearly like to see the land registered. However, much of the population see land registration as the first step towards alienation and have risen up against the idea. The Department of Lands and Physical Planning claims to have no point of view about it at all, but it would obviously make their work easier and perhaps reduce Sir Albert Kipalan's paperwork if land were registered.

The remaining functions of the Department, such as town planning, cartography, valuation, surveying and the management of the new computer system that will allow records to be consulted from the regions, do not compare in terms of excitement with land ownership and the disputes that arise from it. However, all are engrossing and fundamentally important areas of work, without which debates about ownership would be even more difficult to resolve than they are at present.

Take a look at a map of the eastern hemisphere of the world. A great sweep of land and islands flows from India through Malaysia and Indonesia, round the top of PNG and down via Vanuatu to New Zealand. This is the leading edge of the Indo-Australian plate. Using PNG as a hammer head, Australia seems to be thrusting it's way into the Pacific, leaving strings of islands draped over PNG like a fold in the fabric of the Earth's crust.

This in effect is just what has been happening over the last couple of hundred million years. Two of the major tectonic plates have been in conflict. The Pacific plate is being invaded and crushed at the edges by the Australian plate. As each massive slab of crust tries to slide over or under the other, the earth cracks and moves. Earthquakes regularly shake the islands and the north western parts of PNG.

As the floor of the Pacific ocean slips under the part of the Australian plate on which PNG rests, deep ocean trenches are formed offshore. The New Guinea Trench is to the north of Irian Jaya and the Mariania Trench, a long way north, is the deepest part of the ocean in the world - over seven miles deep. The Pacific plate sinks into the earth's mantle of molten rock and, 40 to 200 miles below the surface, begins itself to melt. Being of a different consistency parts of it try to float and come upwards through the crust under PNG. The result is the scattering of active volcanoes throughout the north western parts of PNG.

In September 1994, as if to anticipate the first 20 years of Independence, the volcanoes Vulcan and Tavurvur, on the tip of East New Britain, exploded and blew clouds of volcanic material almost into the stratosphere. Much of Rabaul and surrounding districts were buried. The natural harbour of Rabaul is itself an old circular volcanic caldera with the sea flowing in on one side. The newer active volcanoes are around the edge. New land is slowly being built up.

Where two crustal plates meet like this, an arc of islands is usually formed. These eventually build up to form more continuous land. You can see examples of the process in the Caribbean, off Alaska, in Java and Japan. It can get very complicated. Bits of crust breaking off and themselves form ocean trenches, volcanoes and island arcs at the margins of these microplates. PNG has at least two, Bismarck and Solomon In PNG the effect of the movement of the main plates and these microplates can be clearly seen in the shapes of New Britain and New Ireland and the continuation of the line that follows through to Manus. Further offshore, the latest new islands can be seen beginning to emerge. One of them is Lihir. These represent the leading edge of the progression of PNG into the Pacific - geologically speaking.

Step many millions of years back in time and you can see that the main island of PNG was once that leading edge, a string of islands that built up and amalgamated to form a flowing sweep from the Highlands to the Owen Stanley range.

The result of all the melting far beneath the ground is that minerals, especially heavy elements of similar atomic weights, tend to gather together. The heaviest, gold and silver, concentrate the most, copper slightly less so. The copper deposits of PNG - Bougainville, OK Tedi and others - are usually accompanied by the other two metals. The Frieda deposit, now being investigated on the borders of East Sepik and Sandaun has a cap of gold sitting on top of the more diffuse copper.

A secondary result of the crustal movement is that many sediments on the floor of shallow seas and lakes are buried. They ferment into oil and seep upward through the layers until some of it gathers in a dome of impermeable rock. The rest seeps to the surface and dissipates.

The mineral wealth of PNG exists because of millions of years of geology, millions of years of the Australian plate pushing its way into the Pacific.

Papua New Guinea has mineral and petroleum deposits today because of geological events which took place millions of years ago. Petroleum is the result of the compression, over millions of years, of the remains of marine life which accumulated on the sea floor. Covered by deposits of sand and material from volcanic eruptions, it was then trapped under layers of solid rock. It did not become available to humans in any quantity until the advent of drilling technology.

Although some of the minerals, for example gold, eventually came up to the surface of the land and could be collected from the gravel of river beds, the use of metal was not a tradition among the indigenous people in PNG. However, there was traditional quarrying of rock and minerals for implements, weapons and dyes.

The first prospectors were foreigners who arrived only last century. The first gold was found (on Sudest Island) in 1880. Prospecting and exploring continued from then on. In the 1930's an alluvial gold mine was started at Wau, and gold was dredged there until 1965.

As the exploration of the country continued, the sophisticated methods of mid-20th century geologists enabled them to find valuable minerals in the hard rocks that exist both as outcrops throughout the land and deep within the earth. Gold was still the metal that attracted most interest, but copper and silver in large quantities are as valuable as smaller quantities of gold. Often the three are found together.

The first large modern mine started producing income at Panguna, on Bougainville island, in 1972, eleven years after the first report of possible deposits there and eight years after the beginning of initial exploration. Gold, copper and silver were mined from Panguna until 1989, when agitations by the local people caused its closure. Until that time it was a very profitable mine, accounting for 10% of the gross domestic product and 36% of the total export earnings of the country, and its closure was a major loss.

However, since then a number of other large mining projects have become established in PNG and an oil industry has begun. The receipts from mining, together with those from petroleum, still constitute the bulk of PNG's export earnings (over 70%) and make up over 20% of GDP. Over the past twenty years the government's income from this sector has derived from direct profits from its share holdings, together with the licence fees charged and the taxes payable by companies, employees and land-owners who have received compensation payments.

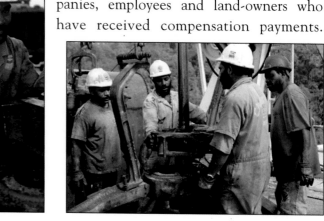

The country also receives benefits in kind, in the form of road-building and other infra-structures, for example, health services and schools in the local area.

Apart from Bougainville, there are four main mining sites in PNG. Ok Tedi, in Western Province, started as a gold mine in 1984 and began extracting copper in 1987. It is now a major world producer of premium copper concentrate. Misima, on Misima Island in Milne Bay Province, had a history of alluvial gold mining that went back to the early years of the century and had underground mines before the war. The modern mine, however, came into production in 1989. It produces both gold and silver. Porgera, in Enga Province, one of the world's largest gold mines, started production from an underground shaft in 1990 and continues with both underground and open pit mines, processing 10,000 tonnes of ore per day. The latest gold mine, Lihir, on Lihir Island, in New Ireland Province, expects to begin operations in the near future.

The Department of Mining and Petroleum has been centrally involved in all developments in this major wealth-creating sector of the economy since Independence in 1975. It is the Minister who, acting in Cabinet, determines the policy framework, embodies it in legislation and is responsible for administering it. Advised by the Department, the Minister makes the decisions on which the continuing development of the industry depend.

The Department is also responsible for managing the latest extractive industry: petroleum. Unlike gold, the presence of oil had been known by some local residents prior to its discovery by twentieth-century oil explorers and, in areas where it occasionally occurred on the ground surface, it had been used by them as an emollient. In 1987 Chevron Niugini discovered oil near Lake Kutubu in Southern Highlands Province, deep in the heart of the country, and since then a major development has taken place. The first production of oil was in 1992. In 1995 the 100 millionth barrel of crude oil had been pumped from

Kutubu Oilfield and sent down a pipe-line which passes the whole length of Gulf Province to the terminal 40 kms out to sea in the Gulf of Papua. More exploration has been taking place in the same general area of Kutubu and along the pipe-line and more discoveries have been made, in particular of natural gas deposits at Hides. Development of PNG´s next petroleum project is well underway at Gobe to the southeast of the Kutubu Oilfield, and construction should take place during 1996.

Apart from the obvious financial benefits to PNG in generating foreign income. PNG´s mining and petroleum projects play a major role in promoting education, training, services, infrastructure, employment and business opportunities to communities who live in remote locations that previously had little or no government services or economic activity.

MINERAL RESOURCES DEVELOPMENT COMPANY

Nearly thirty years ago amendments to the mining laws of PNG made a momentous and now famous distinction.

The new laws differentiated between the owners of land (and thus those who control access to it), and the owners of the mineral resources under the surface. The law now says that the State owns the minerals but must pay "access fees", or compensation, to the surface owners when it issues a mining licence. In doing so the state must exercise control over the mining process, that is regulate it, and it must at the same time extract revenue from it and distribute this to the people.

But there is a problem with this. The concept of 'customary law', widely accepted and even written into the Constitution, conflicts with these 'new' laws. The land, and the minerals beneath it, cannot so easily be bought and sold - by the state or by anyone else. This conflict has already been the source of major difficulties.

Nonetheless these pre-Independence laws were the reason why, twenty years ago, just before Independence, the government set up a 100% state-owned company called the Mineral Resources Development Company as custodian of its interests in mining and petroleum resource projects. Nobody knew then just how huge these would be.

Between 1992 and 1994 the MRDC paid corporate taxes to the State amounting to K33 million. MRDC intends to continue paying dividends and taxes to the National Government, while ensuring that the operations of the projects in which the company has an interest are maintained on the maximum possible profit basis.

MRDC has (or will shortly have) considerable equity interests in:

• Porgera, the largest gold mine in the world outside

South Africa,

- the Kutubu oil project, producing 40 million barrels of light sweet crude oil per year,
- the Misima gold and silver mine,
- the Ok Tedi and Bougainville gold and copper mines and,
- the most recently finalised prospect, the Lihir gold mine.

The mining and petroleum industries (and the list above is by no means complete) are the most significant contributors to the PNG economy and the largest single contributor to Gross Domestic Product, accounting for more than 70% of total export values

"I would say we run the most valuable milking cow in the country", says MRDC Managing Director, Mr Charles Lepani, "but we have to contend with the strong current of international opinion on public policy, which runs against State ownership and participation in the production process. Currently we're seeking some form of privatisation which will keep the milk without selling the cow for beef."   The MRDC is concerned not only with government interests in the purchase, control and management of PNG's mineral and petroleum resources, but also with those of the local land-owners. As an ex-UNDP consultant to the Prime Minister's Department, Mr Lepani has voiced the view that in the past the State has not always pursued a coherent approach to resource projects. This prevented it from representing effectively the interests of landowners in the initial stages of negotiations with investors. Hence perhaps the tragic events in Bouganville which led to the 1989 closure of the immensely productive copper mine at Panguna, with disastrous consequences, in the short term, for the Mineral Resources Stabilisation Fund into which all government revenues from minerals and oil are paid.

However, there is a strong belief that the evolution of democratic and administrative processes, which allow the landowners to challenge unilateral decisions about their land, have created a positive atmosphere in the mining and petroleum industry. It is thought

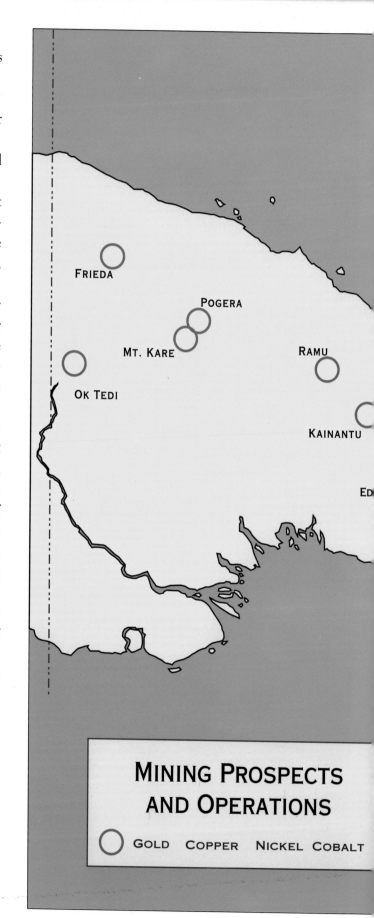

FRIEDA

POGERA

MT. KARE

RAMU

OK TEDI

KAINANTU

ED

MINING PROSPECTS AND OPERATIONS

GOLD COPPER NICKEL COBALT

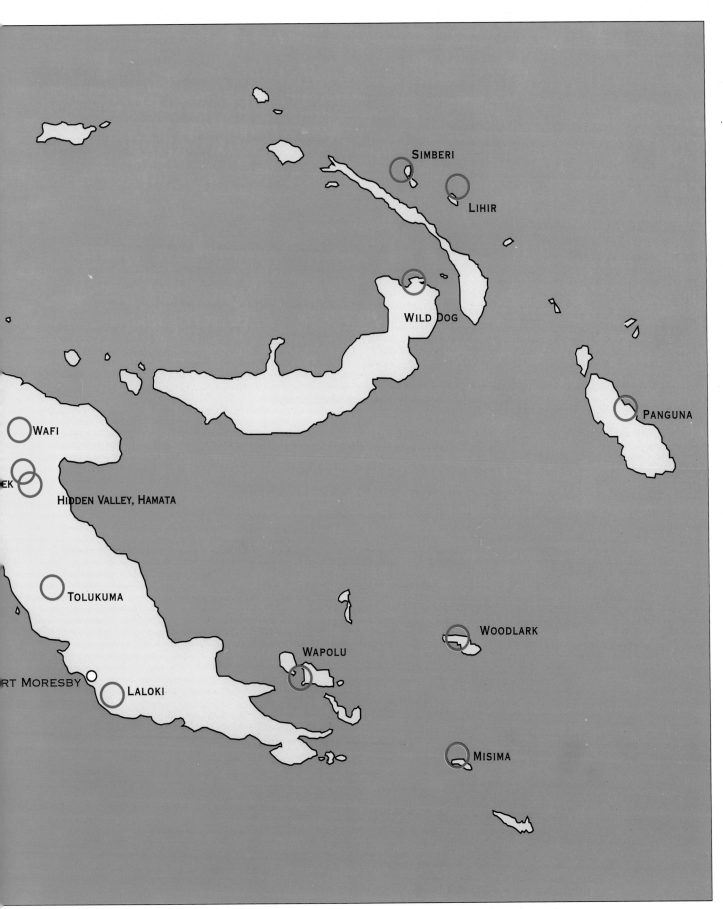

SIMBERI

LIHIR

WILD DOG

PANGUNA

WAFI

EK

HIDDEN VALLEY, HAMATA

TOLUKUMA

WOODLARK

WAPOLU

RT MORESBY

LALOKI

MISIMA

67

that the institutional framework, if properly managed and adequately resourced, should provide sufficient means for building consensus and resolving conflict .

Although MRDC holds stakes in some very large mines, the company has a long term focus on small to medium scale mining and petroleum projects, where MRDC can participate in the equity for the benefit of landowners. This is a strategic decision because it is this scale of project that PNG can effectively own and operate over the medium to long term. The company maintains that it is only through such management that Papua New Guineans will benefit directly and indirectly. Small-scale projects are spread over the whole country, so wealth is distributed more effectively and fairly over the whole economy - hence the company's investment in the medium sized Tolukuma Gold Mine, where the recoverable ore is measured in

hundreds of thousands of tons, as against the millions of tons that are estimated for Porgera.

Of course MRDC holds a 10% stake in the Porgera gold mine too, through its subsidiary, Mineral Resources Porgera Pty. Ltd. of which MRDC has 51% and the remaining 49% is shared between the Provincial Government and the local Porgera landowner groups.

MRDC's other investments include 20% in the Misima gold mine. It also has 30% of the Lihir gold mine through it's subsidiary, Mineral Resources Lihir Pty. Of this 50% is held by MRDC and 50% by the landowner groups. It is part of MRDC's role as the people's trustees to ensure that the optimised return is to all the stakeholders, not just to the national government and that it is in proportion to the equity held.

Another subsidiary is Petroleum Resources Kutubu Pty. Ltd. - known as PRK - which holds a 22% equity in

the Kutubu oil project. To date, MRDC has relied on borrowings and cash flow from its subsidiaries to finance its participation in the resource projects.

A recent study of its finances has shown that the ratio of its debts to the equity it holds, in the jargon its 'gearing', is higher than many mining houses would sustain, but it has the capacity to reduce this as cash flow from investments, measured in tens of millions of kina, approaches its peak in less than 10 years time.

All mines have a finite lifespan - an estimated 8 years for Porgera's underground mine, 19 years for its open pit. As Mr Lepani says, "Without vision and increased management skills, the mining industry will leave this country with huge holes in the ground and little or no benefits to the landowners and the nation." Nevertheless, Papua New Guinea is still a prospector's dream, and MRDC feel certain that landowners do not have too much to fear, with MRDC protecting their interests."

Miners and oil men look to the long term. It has taken thirteen years, since the geologists first struck gold at Lihir, to get the new gold mine to the point of construction. Whatever style the government chooses for MRDC to 'go public', it looks as if Mr Lepani's milking cow will live to a ripe old age.

The discovery of industrially-viable deposits of oil in Papua New Guinea followed later than the discovery of precious mineral ores but in many respects the chain of events was similar and oil is now potentially as valuable an export commodity as gold, silver and copper.

Chevron Niugini is the operator of the Kutubu Joint Venture that was set up to drill for oil in PNG's first discovered oilfield near Lake Kutubu in Southern Highlands Province. Starting in 1987 with an oil exploration licence, its geologists discovered what it believed to be an oil reserve of approximately 250 million barrels. But the geographical maps showed that it was in a place that had not only no road access but where it would be too difficult to build a road anyway. It was also a long way from the coast and any port that could serve as a terminal.

One by one solutions to these problems were proposed. It was decided that the main site could be built and serviced by helicopters and that a pipeline could be built from Kutubu to an oil terminal 267 kilometres away in the Papuan Gulf. Then came the long process of working with the local people to ask for their permission and their co-operation to have access to the land, to put up the necessary buildings, to sink the bores and to cross the land with the pipeline. Compensation had to be paid to many people to achieve these agreements.

But Chevron Niugini also knew from the beginning that, whether compensation was large or very large, only a project that also paid serious attention to the cultural, social and environmental disruption that such first-time development would cause would have any chance of success in the Papua New Guinean situation. The tragic example of Bougainville, where the mine was closed by disaffected citizens and there was considerable loss of life of both Bougainvilleans and PNG Government forces, is all too recent a memory in this part of the world for any new enterprise to take these matters lightly. Besides, Chevron Niugini had a positive belief in the benefits they would be bringing to the local people. They planned what roads they could, they built schools, installed health services, took on and trained local staff and employed a 40-strong community relations unit to bridge the gap between cultures. One of the innovations of this unit was to create a set of written genealogical records for the people of the area.

On the environmental side, Chevron's engineers and scientists designed and built the facilities to a

standard that equalled or exceeded their existing global policy of causing minimal environmental impact. The first thing they took care about was to design systems which would keep the oil contained at all times, so that there was very little chance of accidental spillage in the area of the oilfield, along the pipeline, or into the waters of the Gulf. In fact it is quite hard to see oil at Kutubu – it is all in pipes. They also tried to minimize the damage caused to the environment during the construction stage, when helicopters were flying in and out every hour and there were hundreds of workers moving around with bulldozers and earth-movers and trucks of spoil. They pre-

served whatever vegetation they could – important in a society where single trees are claimed in ownership - and insisted that the track used to lay the pipeline was particularly narrow, so that regeneration would cover it as soon as possible.

It all paid off. Although it has not been easy - the intrusion of one culture into another can never be thought of as being "easy" - Chevron Niugini has not experienced the major setbacks that might have been expected. Oil has been pumped out of the reserves, carried along the pipeline and sold in the international market for a profit. Taxes and fees have been paid to the government and the land-owners. People have been employed, have been trained and have gained experience. Businesses have been founded and will probably remain. All without disaster – and all because of oil.

For Chevron Niugini, of course, it has not been a one-off success. Kutubu will be exhausted in the next three or four years. Chevron Niugini is already looking to their next oil-field – and their next set of solutions.

In its first year of operation, when it took over from the state system some thirty two years ago, Elcom produced 56 Gigawatts of power for only eight thousand consumers. Today fifty five thousand consumers are regularly using more than 620 gigawatts. For the people of Papua New Guinea power means progress and the nineties have been record-breaking years in the generation of electricity. Approximately 75% of this power is generated from hydro sources and 25% from diesel or gas thermal power stations.

Mountainous countries typically produce cheap power from water sources but in PNG, mountainous though it certainly is, hydro power is never an easy option. The rugged terrain and harsh conditions, which include both drought and flood, and the long distances between the best sources and the populations they might supply, have meant that Elcom's constant search for new dam sites and plant locations has only too often been frustrated by financial considerations.

"The hydro potential is immense", says Chief Development Engineer and Deputy Director, Sev Maso. "The dam project on the Purai river west of Port Moresby, for example, would produce about 2300 mega watts, compared with the daily consumption in the capital of only 65 megawatts. But the development costs and the costs of high voltage cable transmission to get the power to the city mean that it won't be viable for some years to come. But the potential is certainly there!"

Elcom was set up by government statute but it is required to act as a commercial body - in fact it has to show a minimum 10% return on capital. It has been hard hit by recent circumstances. Heavy electrical generating equpment has to be imported and paid for in foreign currency. Servicing the consequent debt with last year's devalued kina hit the profit and loss account

hard. Then just to compound matters the eruption of Vulcan which partly destroyed the city of Rabaul, simultaneously took away one of Elcom's major profit centres.

At the same time it scarcely needs saying that Elcom supports the government's policy of bringing power to the majority of people who live in the rural areas. That very often this means an unprofitable investment which must, of necessity, be covered by the profits generated in the heavily populated centres where economies of scale are possible.

When villages are first connected to the supply, Elcom's Minimum Service Supply Kit, which simplifies domestic connections, comes into play. So popular is it that demand regularly outstrips the manpower that can be allocated. In villages which are built over the sea the kit is sometimes installed using low-voltage bundled aerial cable.

The major hydro schemes have certainly contributed to Elcom's capacity to fulfil its obligations to the rural people. The K100 million Yonki Dam Project for example, completed in 1992, not only contributed a significant increase of generating power from the coast at Lae and Madang right up into the Highlands of Mt Hagen and Wabag, it also produced spin-offs like sixteen kilometres of local roads and the creation of the Arona Valley Development Authority.

Established with assistance from Elcom, the authority has helped to transform the kunai grass-lands into profit-able coffee estates. It takes a leading role in the develop-ment of an effective village communication system and the provision of extension services in health and hygiene through-out the valley. Village produce now travels across the reservoir created by the dam, using a boat service set up by AVDA.

Overhead power lines are a common sight in the valley and of course in all the areas where electricity is available, but 4000 kilometres of such cables make life unusually difficult for Elcom's maintenance engineers. Tree growth 3 degrees south of the Equator is rapid and frequently threatens the company's lines and pylons. The problem is exacerbated by the reluctance of tree owners to allow trees to be cut. In a dangerous partnership with the trees, lightning, rain and wind take their toll too.

Indeed nature is always likely to be the enemy of the power providers in PNG. In 1993 a tropical cyclone passing over the north east of the country brought enough heavy rain with it to flood the Warangui River near Rabaul and put the hydro power station there out of action from January until March. Thousands of tons of silt and rocks were deposited into the water intake. At the other extreme a severe and prolonged drought in the Port Moresby area threatened the Rouna hydro-power supply for the capital throughout much of 1992 and 1993.

It may surprise people to learn that PNG's top class hotels, especially in the capital, are some of Elcom's largest customers. Air conditioned rooms, conference centres, bars and restaurants all use massive amounts of power. The swimming pool, tennis courts and gym, pile on even more. Indeed, without electricity, these top hotels would find it hard to meet the comfort and convenience standards which their customers demand.

And the price is not unduly high. Elcom's prices have fallen in real terms over the last few years and there's an outstanding commitment that any electricity price increases will be less than inflation.

While there is still much to do before all this country's people can enjoy the benefits of electricity, expansion must of necessity be carried out carefully. It's unlikely that we will see projects like the big Yonki Dam in the near future. What we will see is concentration on improvement to service, a more reliable supply, greater efficiency and a large emphasis on working in partnership with customers for the good of the country. Whether it's electricity for homes, to allow people to enjoy a better lifestyle, or electricity to power the growth of business and industry, Elcom plans to work with the people.

73

OVERVIEW

The separation between the North and South Pacific land masses is known as the Wallace Line, after the naturalist who first noticed the essential differentiation between marsupial and non-marsupial mammals in the region.

The birds and reptiles of Papua New Guinea are also mostly from this side of the Wallace line. The flora, conversely, is predominantly South East Asian. However, both flora and fauna have evolved long enough in this part of the world to become distinct species with unique features. There are more than 700 species of birds and over 150 species of mammals.

Many Papua New Guinea birds are restricted to the lowland forest areas, where a typical square kilome-

tre may support no less than 150 species. An unusually large proportion of them are fruit- or nectar -eaters, nearly twice as many as in comparable lowland forest areas of the South American continent. Perhaps the best known of all Papua New Guinea's birds is its national emblem, the splendid Raggiana Bird of Paradise (<u>Raggiana Paradisaea</u>). All in all, there are thirty eight species of birds of paradise here, their plumage ranging from pure black to red, orange and irridescent green. Hardly less striking in appearance are the over three hundred species of parrot, lory and cockatoo. New Guinea parrots range in size from the pygmy-parrots to the huge Palm Cockatoo, nearly ten times larger. PNG also boasts eleven species of the renowned bowerbird, nine of which can be found in the wooded highland areas and the other two on lowland grassland and savanna. In most of these species, it is the male who builds a sophisticated nest or 'bower' and decorates it with flowers and berries. The large flightless cassowary, standing at anywhere from 1.3 - 1.7 metres tall and weighing up to 60 kg, is particularly valued in PNG, both for its meat and its feathers. Various species of kookaburra and kingfisher abound, though most of the latter rarely go near water or feed on fish like their counterparts elsewhere in the world. Although many of the birds in PNG are sedentary, a number migrate from nearby Australia and some from

much further afield. The largest group of migrants are the waders and seabirds, but the variety is enormous. PNG is truly a birdwatchers paradise.

In addition to its large number of birds, PNG has nearly two hundred indigenous species of mammals, only about one third less than the whole of the Australian continent. Most of these are marsupial, the largest being a type of tree kangaroo known as the tenkile, a full-grown male weighing up 20 kg. One of the best-known species of mammal, the cuscus, can be found in the remote lowland forest areas. There are over fifty species of bat, several species of wallaby and Raffray bandicoot, one of the largest in the world. There two species of crocodile, freshwater and saltwater.

Among the ninety species of snake, forty three of which are poisonous but only seven that are regarded as deadly, are the death adder, a variety of Papuan Taipans (with one of the most potent toxins of any snake in the world) and a host of smaller species. The non-poisonous snakes include the pythons and boas, the largest measuring eight metres. Nearly two hundred types of lizard inhabit the mainland and the islands and fall mainly into four groups: monitors, dragons, geckos and skinks. The Salvadori Dragon, at nearly four metres, is the longer even than the Komodo Dragon of Indonesia which makes it the longest lizard in the world and one of the Bougainville skinks has a prehensile tail and grows to a length of nearly one metre. Among the several hundred species of spider, only two are dangerous to humans, the huge Bird-Eating Spider, and the smaller Redback Spider. similar in appearance to the South American Tarantula, but quite harmless to human beings. There are hundreds of indigenous species of moths and butterflies. The reddish-brown male Hercules Moth with its long, distinctive tail-like hind wings is the largest known moth and the famous Queen Alexandra are even larger with a wingspan of up to twenty seven centimetres. Exquisitely coloured, they are a marvel to the eye.

Riches beyond compare: Papua New Guinea is one of the most bio-diverse nations on earth, harbouring 5% of the world's species in only 1% of the world's land area - from insects to crocodiles, orchids to hardwood, sea-snakes and corals to fish, the Department of Environment and Conservation has the responsibility of conserving and sustaining eco-systems which are consistently under threat.

Minister for Environment and Conservation, Parry M. Zeipi is one of the world's longest serving environment ministers. "I love nature. It beautifies the world. I am just the right mind in the right place", he says modestly. His efforts over the last ten years have placed Papua New Guinea in the enviable position of having much protective legislation in place. "My idea was to develop a policy for sustainable development. Following on from the Rio conference, we are the first country to develop legislation and to create a permanent sustainable development commission".

Papua New Guinea was also the first country to introduce legislation against the movement of hazardous waste. "We have no intention of being used as a dumping ground by some super-power," said Mr. Zeipi. "A US company wanted to dump radio-active waste in Oro province. We sponsored a regional treaty to ban trans-boundary movements."

But what of the temptation to make fast bucks? The Department has a division devoted to explaining environmental matters to the people. They go out into the villages to explain what the effects of, say, logging might be so that villagers can make informed judgements.

In Papua New Guinea 97% of the land is owned by local communities who have traditionally held a strong spiritual attachment to the nature on which they depend for subsistence and survival. Ownership or the right to exploit carries social, cultural and moral responsibilities. Where the needs of families, clans or regions conflict with national or international objectives then the government takes responsibility for guardianship. A key mechanism to this end has been the establishment of partnerships, starting at the grassroots level, between adjacent clans, expanding outward to South Pacific neighbours, ultimately to the United Nations system.

It is not enough for International bodies to insist on conservation. They must provide practical support.

For example, how best to sustain the different forest types in Papua New Guinea. Three quarters of the land area is forest which ranges from high alpine to mangrove swamp. But the lowland rain forest constitutes the greatest wealth and is under the greatest threat. It is probably the most valuable long term natural asset the country possesses. "Uncontrolled logging is just like wild fire which catches grassland and spreads all over the place", says Mr. Zeipi. Proper management can renew and improve forests both quantitatively and qualitatively.

All too often the forest becomes a bale of logs, a source of cellulose or wood-chips instead of a multifaceted resource used by most of the community. In a West New Britain timber area, Department of Environment and Conservation research established that hunting animals for food for the protein they provided and harvesting wild plants and the eggs of megapodes (a kind of turkey) brought immeasurably more value to the local community than selling off logging rights. As a result forest corridors were redrawn to leave precious megapode egg grounds intact.

Humans have been living in Papua New Guinea for 50,000 years. The traditional knowledge base is an asset all too often neglected by western-educated scientists. Now recognition of the efficacy of 'fever' cures has led to the development of a new source of anti-malarial drugs. Soil maps have been constructed using local knowledge and chemically analysed samples. Fishermen are consulted for local knowledge of the sea Where traditional knowledge and western science are combined the potential is realised and the resource is available for generations to come.

The Department of Environment and Conser-vation is responsible for protected wildlife such as the famous Birds of Paradise. Of the world's 43 species of birds of paradise, Papua New Guinea has 33. Twelve of those, including the national emblem, the Raggiana bird, live

only in PNG. They come under the CITES convention to which PNG is a signatory. They may only be hunted with traditional weapons and even then they may not be sold to foreigners or taken out of the country.

The species management branch of the Department looks after, amongst other things, crocodiles and butterflies. Officers have been monitoring the wild crocodile population and declared it stable at the moment. But the biggest butterfly in the world, the Queen Alexandria Butterfly, is under threat from the extension of a nearby oil palm project. The Department is working closely with the Oro Butterfly project in Popondetta in Oro province to resolve the conflict of interests.

Finally the Department maintains an interest in PNG's independent research institutes and privately run breeding programmes including the Wau Institute, the Christensen Research Institute and the National Botanical Gardens.

The Botanical Gardens in Port Moresby have a plan to create and restore as many PNG orchid species as possible. Director, Justin Tkatchenko claims that Papua New Guinea is a world leader in orchids. "We have over 3,000 species that are found nowhere else in the world plus there could be thousands out there yet to be discovered. Most of the other countries, like Singapore and Thailand, developed their cut-flower industries using PNG orchids as a basis in their breeding programmes. In the early days there were no regulations. Orchids were stripped out of this country and the population of at least seven species were totally devastated."

The legislation is in place which bans the export of rare orchids but conservationists are still concerned about the number of species that are being lost through logging. The Botanical Gardens is a scientific institution for research, teaching, conservation and the protection of orchids in PNG. In a joint project with the Japanese government they maintain a glass house in Goroka to propagate Highland species. Justin Tkatchenko has an eye for display. He takes his collection abroad accompanied by arts and crafts items. At the Australian orchid conference, the Botanical Gardens won the award for the best display. Now an ambitious plan for a show house, to be opened in 1997, is under construction. It is a huge tent-like structure in the shape of PNG. Visitors will be encouraged to walk through the different provinces seeing the orchids from that region. The orchids of PNG will be celebrated as never before.

The Christensen Research Institute in Madang is dedicated to marine biological research. It is a non

profit field biology research institute established in 1985 with the support of the US-based Christensen fund. It shares premises with the Jais Aben Resort on a peninsular some 15 kilometres north of Madang town. Qualified researchers need to clear their proposals through both national and local government committees before being accepted at Christensen. Once there, they have every possible facility at their disposal, good standard accommodation, laboratories,

tanks and rich forest and marine life on their doorstep.

Many scientists have come to Christensen and agree, "The Madang Lagoon is one of the best coral reef systems we have ever seen. It beats any place else we have ever been for finding the kind of animals or plants we are interested in." It is a very young lagoon, geologically speaking. It is 15 kilometres long and 4 kilometres wide. There are more kinds of clown fish and sea anemone in the Madang Lagoon than has been found anywhere else in the world. There are more species of nudibranches - beautifully coloured sea-slugs - than any other place. At least 300 species have been named and there could be yet another 200 to be found. Over a thousand species of fish live in the lagoon. It is one of the world's richest sites for crinoid animals, strange feathery creatures that look like plants. But the lagoon is under threat - from dynamiting, pollution, siltation and industry. The question is: will it survive?

The Wau Ecology Institute is a field station which does much to promote research and education. It has a venerable history since its inception as a field station for the US Smithsonian Institution and the Bishop Museum in the early 1960's. The present director, Mr. Harry Sakulas arrived at the Institute in 1979 and

immediately began to expand both the work and the workforce. There are now a total of 65 staff, half of them with professional and semi-professional qualifications. There has been a shift of emphasis from basic research to applied research, largely as a response to concern from the PNG government to meet immediate needs.

Several important programmes are currently underway at Wau. Many staff are engaged in monitoring the effects of mining, logging and weather. One programme unique to Wau is a study of shifting or slash-and-burn agriculture. One of the project aims is to persuade villagers to maintain their gardens at one site by improving soil fertility. But one of the more exciting developments has been in the medicinal plants programme. A nationwide survey collected herbarium specimens and recorded their uses by traditional healers. Important species have been propagated and in some cases sent overseas for further screening and analysis. At present all these programmes are under threat because of inadequate funding. The Institute has only one road-worthy vehicle. It will not be able to continue its extensive field operations. It has attempted to generate income from its guest house and from the sale of coffee beans and vegetables but this did little more than meet some operating costs. Furthermore the law and order problems in the local area have reduced all opportunities for income generation. Wau must have help from outside donors to continue.

The Department of Environment and Conservation is committed to maintaining the natural resources of PNG for now and for the future but the international community also has a responsibility to help PNG make a full contribution to global environmental welfare.

FORESTS AND FORESTRY

Forests lie deep in human consciousness. In almost every culture in the world they are seen as dark dangerous places. The wild wood at the edge of life's clearing. Inhabited by supernatural beings none too friendly to the locals.

At the end of the 20th century that view is changing. Forests are described emotionally as the lungs of the earth, giving it the oxygen of life. Loggers from the developed North are accused of 'raping' the forests of the South. In turn logging is the target of environmental fascism. No longer are there jokes on the level of 'woodman spare that tree'. Saving forests has become much too serious.

Throughout history forests have been stripped by people seeking fuel. Europe, the Middle East, India all have semi-arid areas which were once thickly forested. Today large areas are still stripped for fuel by poor people who rely on firewood for their cooking and warmth. In certain areas of Papua New Guinea, the forest is endangered not only by firewood collectors but also by slash and burn agriculture. When the logging concessions are handed out these are additional to this 'natural' depletion. What is alarming is the accelerating pace of clearances of both kinds.

Estimates suggest that 21% of PNG's accessible forest has already been logged, including much unnecessarily. 30 to 50 species of tree supply 80% of the market. PNG forests are highly diverse and as many as 240 species are felled. This is terrible wastage. The wastage continues as trees are felled without a care for the direction of fall, excessive clearing is done for access roads, and excessive trimming is carried out once the logs get to the timber yard. If buffer zones are not maintained along river banks water sources dry up or get polluted. Villagers are finding that after the logging is over, reforestation with monospecies like eucalyptus for woodchip badly affects the fertility of the soil. There is no evidence that logging has ever brought permanent development to remote areas.

In PNG people hold 'custodianship' over the land, not ownership. Land cannot by alienated by selling it. People, especially women are becoming more aware of their rights whether environmental, conservational, legal or human. It could be that it will take little more than an proper awareness of the problem for it to be solved.

To travel anywhere beyond Port Moresby and the barren hills of National Capital District is to appreciate the huge extent of intact forest cover in Papua New Guinea.

While much of this is on steep mountainsides or in areas that are completely inaccessible because of the impossibility or undesirability of constructing roads, 12 million hectares - over a quarter of PNG's total land area - has been identified as containing forested

land with potential for some form of timber extraction. The actual area of forest within this which it is believed could be productive adds up to nearly 8 million hectares. One million of hectares of this has already been logged, and permits and entitlements of varying degrees of status exist in relation to up to a third of the rest. It is the responsibility of the Ministry of Forests, working in conjunction with the PNG Forest Authority, a statutory body that replaced the old Department of Forests in 1991, to preserve and manage PNG's forest reserves.

The PNG Forest Authority has one over-riding aim: to promote the management of these resources as a renewable asset for the benefit of present and future generations; in other words to ensure that the forestry industry in Papua New Guinea is a sustainable one.

The main aim of government policy in recent years has been to phase out log exports in favour of processed timber products in an effort to add value and provide employment, but at present 90% of the timber exports in this K600 million industry is still in the form of crude logs. The new emphasis on sustainability, embodied in agreements signed with various international bodies and at the Earth Summit in Rio in 1992, has extended this agenda. Now the Government is faced with the task of setting new standards, for example in relation to the proportion of timber an area which can be cut in any year, and of monitoring the performance of the contractors involved.

White oak, rosewood, kwila, black bean, ebony and walnut are some of PNG's most handsome woods, but the forests contain over 200 species of hardwoods, 70 of which have been identified as of commercial value. There are also softwoods such as klinki pine. Veneers are made from some of the most expensive and beautiful woods and other products include plywood and woodchips. But PNG's forests cannot be valued merely in terms of timber.

It is only in the late 20th century that biodiversity, the separate existence of millions of life forms, has been understood to be such a vital feature of life on earth. Man's economic activity has savaged this diversity in many parts of the world, but, for historic reasons, not in Papua New Guinea. Strong feelings are now aroused in many people by any further threats to the remaining wealth of flora and fauna in the world, wherever it might exist and whoever might be said to own it. The survival of Papua New Guinea's forests, with their huge variety of birds, mammals, butterflies and other species is thought to be of maximum importance by environmentally aware people the world over, and somehow PNG has to live up to these hopes and expectations. This is necessary for strictly commercial reasons also. as many countries are forcing the issue by banning imports from non-sustainable sources.

The Ministry of Forests has responded to this situation by putting in place a series of policies designed to guarantee sustainability. The system by which Timber Rights Purchases used to be agreed has been scrapped and more stringent conditions attached to the new type of agreement, which goes by the name of a Forest Management Agreement to recognize the wider responsibilities involved. An F.M.A. is an agreement between the traditional landowners, usually a group or tribe, and the government. Subsequently the government can lease rights to a contractor, who under the new scheme will only be able to work one thirty-fifth of the permitted volume of timber each year, leaving the rest untouched. This is calculated to permit regeneration of the total area in a period of thirty-five years - a tree 'generation'. There are other conditions also, for instance the need to undertake a certain amount of silviculture, or tree planting, as well as managing natural regeneration.

It is the government's aim to have in place mecha-

nisms for the sustained management of forests by the year 2000, and also by that year to have reduced to zero the proportion of timber that is being exported as logs. These are grand aims and what PNG's magnificent forests deserve.

"The natural forests of Papua New Guinea are not public forests. They are privately owned forests, and, unless this becomes part of a forest management ethic and practice here in Papua New Guinea, it is doubtful there will be any effective base for long term goals of Forestry Policy". Thus the Forest Industries Association sets out it's stall, declaring what it considers to be the main obstacle to the future growth of the industry.

The Forest Industries Association slogan is "Sustained Forest Industries for PNG". It represents the interests of the forest sector at all levels. The need for such an association dates back to the early 1950's.

During the immediate post war period, reconstruction of war damaged centres and programmes to establish new rural centres led to a dramatic increase in domestic requirements for sawn timber. Commonwealth New Guinea Timbers (now PNG Forest Products Pty Ltd) at Bulolo began to manufacture plywood. Their major outlet was the export of prime grade marine plywood. Klinki Ply became a world wide brand name in the plywood trade. In the pre-Independence period a large amount of sawn timber was exported to Australia. The Department of Forests decided that this growing saw-milling industry should have a 'voice' as the industry developed. The ancestor of today's Association was born.

In the early days the Association took an active role in negotiations with the government on

industry development, royalties, infrastructure requirements, marketing and standards. It was also actively engaged with the Australian industry. As land was cleared for large scale agricultural projects, notably the Oil Palm estates in West New Britain, the export of logs began. The government realised that logging had a potential both as a source of revenue, a means of generating rural infrastructure and a means of creating rural employment.

The scope of the original Association was inadequate in the face of the rapidly changing industry. A statutory body, the Forest Industries Council, was created by Act of Parliament. Funded entirely by industry operators the Council was effective in early years but later its function became clouded and its performance declined alarmingly. The Forest Industries Association pressed for an investigation.

In 1987 there was a public war of words in the press and in Parliament over the competence of the Forest Industries Council. The council had just started large scale marking of logs on behalf of the State. A commission of enquiry was called, chaired by Judge Thomas Barnett. Its findings became notorious, un-earthing specific examples of wrongdoing which were much publicised. With the passing of the Forest Act 1991, the Council was abandoned and the Forest Industries Association (Inc) was identified as the body recognised to represent the interests of the Industry. It has a position on the National Forest Board.

The membership structure is very wide, being comprised of many different types of interests including loggers, sawmillers, resource owner companies, equipment and materials suppliers, contractors and manufacturers. All have an interest in the development of a sound industry, based on the mobilization, utilization and management of the identified areas of commercial forest in PNG. Currently the Association represents 85-90% of the commercial forest taken annually and it is always looking to increase its membership base. It is a non-profit organisation.

The Association is currently pressuring for sustained yield management of PNG's forest resource. Forest conditions must be monitored and maintained. Past lessons have taught that the people with the main interest in the secure development of the sector are the resource owners and resource operators. However, monitoring has to be done by trained foresters and at present there are too few and their workload is too great. The current trend is for private enterprise to supply their own foresters and to plan their own operations. There are only 150 professional and technically trained foresters in private enterprise operations, most of them national men and women trained in PNG.

The Association believes that future success for PNG's forest industries could well depend on regulation by the government and implementation by private enterprise.

Commercial activity in the forest industry sector is dominated by log exports. In 1994 a volume of 3.1 million cubic metres of logs were exported, mainly to Japan, Korea and Taiwan. This generated export sales of approximately K490 million for the year. All logging for export is carried out under Government Authority.

As a developing country with a strong resource sector, PNG is taking steps to balance the push for the development of economic infrastructure with environmental responsibility under sustained yield

guidelines. Only a third of the country is estimated to carry forest of commercial potential. Much work is yet to be done to establish the optimum level of log harvest. However, many analysts consider that PNG is well within sustainable levels on a national basis.

Processed timber exports include sawn timber and plywood and scope exists for an increase in investment in processing operations under appropriate conditions. PNG processed products are sought after for furniture manufacture and specialist uses and many more markets could be opened up under appropriate investment conditions.

Manufactured products such as furniture are a growing market, with a number of fine furniture factories using selected kiln-dried PNG timbers. PNG-made furniture is very attractive and has found appreciative markets in Western Europe, Australia and New Zealand. This is one area for likely expansion of demand in the future.

In summary, the member companies of the PNG Forest Industries Association are active in resource harvesting and management, in exporting, pro-cessing and manufacture.

With the further development of the forest industry sector in Papua New Guinea, the FIA looks forward to continuing its representative and liaison function.

Vanimo Forest Products, a company owned by the giant Malaysian WYK Realty Pty, is one of the new generation of timber companies now at work in Papua New Guinea.

Based in forest-clad Sandaun Province since 1990, Vanimo Forest Products aims not only to take out logs but to export processed timber products and at the same time to be involved in a programme of works that will benefit the whole province of Sandaun. To this end it is constructing an integrated sawmill and processing plant at Vanimo and installing the necessary infrastructure. This K40 million project will log timber, cut it into boards, kiln-dry it and then either export it as logs or as sawn timber or process it further, in particular into high-value parquet flooring, hardwood plywood, and quality veneers. Eventually it is hoped to manufacture furniture for the export market.

The Project Agreement spells out a maximum harvest per year of 300,000 cubic metres of logs, of which 80,000 cubic metres is for processing locally, an amount which will increase. It is envisaged that by the year 2000 all logs harvested will

be for local production, thus fulfilling the aims of the national government's forest policy.

At the same time, and in fulfilment of the terms of its licence, Vanimo has been investing heavily in the infrastructure of Sandaun Province. Projects include 80 km of the East West Highway linking Aitape in the east to Vanimo. This road includes the Pual Bridge opened by the Prime Minis-

ter in July 95. When finished, it will pass through Serra, where logging is taking place and a wharf is being constructed.

Vanimo has also built seven double classroom schools, a library, six aid posts and an airstrip in the forest area, which is a concession totalling 326,000 hectares. Vanimo town has nearly tripled in population since Vanimo Forest Products came into the area. There are now quite a number of trade stores and supermarkets where previously there were very few.

"Many people say that this timber project is the life blood of Vanimo and of Sandaun Province generally", says Vanimo's General Manager, Philip Tiong.

All this is because of the thick virgin forests which cover most of Sandaun's total land area.

These forests contain more than 70 species of fine-quality timber trees, with species such as Kwila and Pencil Cedar being two of the most well-known. Sixty percent of these 70 species are hardwoods, the rest semi-hardwoods and softwoods.

The market in tropical hardwoods is heavily affected by environmental considerations and many foreign governments forbid the import of timber from non-sustainable sources. It is probably fortunate for PNG, and for Sandaun Province in particular, that the development of the timber industry here has come relatively late, when the proper management of forests is well understood.

Vanimo is operating a policy of reforestation by regeneration, in which the undergrowth is cleared around young trees which will be saleable in the future. Under the terms of its agreement, Vanimo must manage the regeneration of 1000 hectares of new forest each year.

PNG, by inviting Vanimo to be the concession-holder for this large forest area, has shown its faith in this company to conduct timber extraction in an environmentally responsible manner with accompanying social and economic benefits for the local people. Vanimo is honouring that commitment.

AGRICULTURE AND LIVESTOCK

People were gardening in Papua New Guinea when most of the rest of the world were living in caves. One more amazing fact about this country.

When it comes to gardening, forget the image of stone age man. It was women who did the gardening, they were the cultivators, the subsistence agriculturists responsible for producing food and cash crop surpluses. They still are.

Papua New Guinea is an agrarian society. 80% of the people grow the food they eat. Lowland agriculture is mostly shifting cultivation and bush fallow. In the Highlands, where farming is much more intensive, the planting is done on mounds and every usable area of land is cultivated. Village root crops are highly efficient in terms of time taken to produce.

There is variety. A village in the Eastern Highlands has 87 different food crops under cultivation. Within the last twenty years maize, cassava, pumpkin and 'English' potato have been added to the staple crops of yam, taro and sweet potato. Papua New Guineans are assiduous traders in plants, constantly seeking to improve cultivars. And they also trade. Highlanders trade vegetables for betel nut with the coastal people. Every town has a market. Every roadside has a few stalls with tempting fruit and vegetables.

Almost every subsistence farmer also grows cash crops. One of the big successes of the last twenty years has been small-holder coffee growing. About 40% of all rural households grow coffee. But they also grow cocoa, coconut, banana and spices. Some crops like palm oil are grown by small-holders as well as on big plantations. There are more than 900 plantations in PNG producing tea, rubber, copra, coffee, cocoa, sugar and palm oil. Ownership of plantations has gradually been transferred to villagers and developments such as processing factories have been encouraged.

No ceremony, no feast is complete in PNG without the slaughter of many pigs. Pigs live under the houses with the dogs and chickens. They are a sign of wealth. Other livestock includes goats, cattle and sheep, cassowary, wallaby and deer, though their numbers are comparatively low. Factory methods are now used in poultry and egg production. In the last few years crocodiles have been added to the farmers products. They just lie around in ponds until large enough to be turned into crocodile-cash.

"Papua New Guinea is an agricultural country, our people are rural and agriculture is their life blood", said Bernard Narakobi, Minister of Agriculture during 1994-5. "Why is it that so much of the wealth that comes in from our minerals is squandered on imported food, imported meat, imported fish? Whatever else, the import bill must be brought down, not to the exclusion of trade but to the benefit of every family unit in PNG."

Improving efficiency to become self-sufficient in food, must, Narakobi believes, start with the nuclear family. The unit of father, mother and children forms the basic unit of production in the agriculture sector. He has worked on a development model similar to the Moshab in Israel. It creates a nucleus around which the small farmer can operate. The nucleus might include a factory, a market, support services, fertilisers, transportation, education, health and basic services. The nucleus could be joint funded or even 100% foreign funded. The

farmer remains independent with a choice of selling back to the nucleus or creating his own market.

It could be that Narakobi has a chance to realise his vision in his home province of East Sepik. There is a pressing need to re-settle large numbers of mountain Arapesh who were drafted to work on the coastal plantations after 1945. The Department has surveyed an area of 10,000 hectares and worked on a plan by which the timber could pay for the whole resettlement programme, including roads, bridges, homes, schools and clinics. It is a controversial scheme which will not please the environmentalists, comments Narakobi wryly. But it is a way

forward that will avoid the squabbles over land which have characterised so many PNG developments.

A Ministerial statement in July 1995 set out the department's objectives. The peoples of PNG were amongst the earliest agriculturists in the world but so successful were they that they had no need to advance beyond the digging stick and shallow water fishing. In the last twenty years the growth rate of agriculture is 1.0%, way below the population growth of 2.2%, yet agriculture remains the dominant economic activity for 85% of the population. It makes up 38% of formal private sector employment and it contributes 37% of GDP and one-third of export income. Despite this broad base, agriculture is in recession. This directly affects the living standards of the majority of the people. Revitalising agriculture and restructuring the rural economy has to be a key development objective for PNG.

Some projects are already under way for example the development of the tree crops sector, including coffee, cocoa, oil palm, coconut, rubber and tea. These crops account for over 94% of the total agricultural export value and engage the bulk of the population directly or indirectly. Their value has been declining on world markets. Now there should be some effort to add value before export. There may yet be a future for PNG chocolate, cocoa drinks and coffee ice-cream. PNG has a wealth of tropical fruits, mangoes, guavas, pineapples, pawpaws, bananas, but very little is done with them. The department wants to encourage processing factories to produce juice or canned fruits. Likewise a highly lucrative future can be foreseen for PNG spices, especially chilli, vanilla and cardamom. The prices are high and the weight is low so shipping costs are minimal. PNG should be able to enter the spice market at a competitive level.

Another aspect of the Agriculture Ministry which has been neglected is livestock. PNG has a few large herds of cattle but there has been some expansion recently. Now there is a quota system which should encourage people to farm cattle. A similar scheme is suggested for sheep. At present there are no more than 10,000 head in the entire country. And there are more exotic beasts. The trade in farmed crocodiles is developing, largely thanks to horizontal integration - the chicken bits are fed to the crocs.

The Ministry operates several research institutes. The Bubia Agriculture Research Centre has recently found the answer to taro leaf blight, a disease which almost wiped out the taro crops in Western Samoa. The discovery has already attracted international attention. Bubia works co-operatively with other DAL research stations at Aiyura in the Eastern Highlands, Kerevat in East New Britain, Laloki in Central Province and the Land Utilisation section in Port Moresby. Ultimately every institute, every project will need funding. DAL is looking not just to the government but to developers to put up capital in joint ventures with local landowners. This, they are sure, will be the way forward for agriculture in PNG.

It's an amazing fact that coffee is second only to petroleum in terms of dollar turnover on the world's commodity markets!

In the newly prosperous export sector of Papua New Guinea, coffee follows closely behind petroleum, minerals and timber in terms of export earnings and is the most valuable of PNG's agricultural crops. 70,000 tonnes of fine quality coffee are produced annually, the bulk of the crop being fine quality arabica coffees from the Highlands region.

In one respect, however, coffee can be said to be the most important commodity produced in this country. This is because so many people have a direct cash benefit from it. It is estimated that there are about 240,000 small coffee farms in the country. The sale of the crop from these farms directly benefits well

over one third of PNG's population. Between 70 and 80 per cent of the coffee exported from PNG comes from these small farms.

The benefit from the smallholder sector is not only widely spread, but also, because of the fierce competition for high-quality coffee, highly lucrative. It is not uncommon for a well-organised smallholder to sell his

crop for up to 70% of the export price ruling at the time. It's unlikely that any other tropical tree crop in any other country in the world can demonstrate such a high rate of return to the individual primary producer.

Papua New Guinea's coffee industry is a free enterprise industry. This fits well with the independent outlook of the typical small coffee grower who owns his own land, owes nothing to the banks, and whose only input costs are a few simple hand tools and his own and his family's labour.

Nevertheless, as in any successful industry, there are rules and standards to be observed, some set nationally and some deriving from international conventions as to terms and conditions of sale.

The organisation which administers these, together with other provisions of the relevant Act of Parliament, is the Coffee Industry Corporation. This is a democratically elected industry organisation controlled by a 12 member board, six of whom are

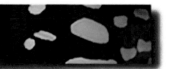

elected by the smallholder and one each by the export sector, the large plantation sector and the small plantation sector.

The remaining three seats are held by the Government Ministers of Agriculture, Trade and Industry, and Finance.

The Corporation's largest operating division is Extension Services, which provides education, hands-on training and leadership to smallholders. The Research Division, which operates the Coffee Research Institute at Aiyura, has been paying Iattention to the problems of Coffee Rust, a disease which made its appearance in PNG a few years ago. The Industry Affairs Division looks after compliance with rules and standards, being particularly interested in quality control and licensing within the industry. It is also responsible for the promotion of PNG coffee overseas.

On a graph showing the annual output of the coffee-producing countries of the world, Papua New Guinea would show as one of a large group of minor producers gathered below the four giants:

Brazil, Colombia, Indonesia and Mexico. Shipping around 1.5% of the world's requirements, PNG is placed between Kenya and Tanzania in terms of exported tonnage. One might imagine that means a low position in terms of bargaining power in the market. Fortunately for PNG, however, the ambient conditions in the major growing areas are such that we produce an intrinsically high-quality arabica, equivalent to the best from any other producer. No matter what happens to the market, we can always sell our crop - so long as we pay attention at all times to quality in preparing the coffee for export.

In this complex and occasionally unruly industry lies the source of great wealth and one which is not a finite resource. Coffee farms can be expanded or reduced according to the needs, desires and capabilities of each individual grower. In PNG coffee is truly the peoples' crop, which even in today's constantly changing, technology-driven world, provides stability and real independence for many tens of thousands of Papua New Guineans.

ANGCO COFFEE

Goroka coffee, a product of Angco, is now becoming internationally known as the brand name of one of Papua New Guinea's most superior coffees. But with annual production at a mere 100 tonnes, it is overshadowed by the other interests of that company - the buying, processing and exporting of more than 23,000 tonnes of best Papua New Guinea Highlands raw coffee to more than 20 countries world-wide.

Angco is at the heart of PNG's coffee business and PNG's largest coffee exporter.

Coffee first began to be produced in the Highlands in 1953. By 1967, when Angco was formed, 5000 tonnes per annum were being produced. Today the national figure stands at 70,000 tonnes and the industry has established itself throughout the Central Highlands where the geographic conditions at around 5,000 feet altitude are perfect for a high quality crop.

'Coffee arabica' is the botanical name of the small tree with dark green leaves and sprays of white flowers which are followed by the festoons of red berries containing the all-important bean. The varieties grown in PNG are of the traditional type, providing the clean distinctive taste that European coffee-drinkers in particular seem to enjoy.

As coffee growing in Papua New Guinea is substantially an activity of small-holders, with 75% of the crop produced in this way coming from holdings of less than 1 hectare, it provides many families in the Highlands with their major source of cash income. More than 1 million people - something like one quarter of PNG's total population - depend on coffee for the cash element of their livelihood, making coffee PNG's single largest source of employment and income.

The future looks good for coffee grown the PNG way. Some of the Goroka brand is organically grown and certified, another very attractive feature in today's environmentally conscious world. "We could sell twice as much coffee as we do at present if only we were able to get it and if the quality was maintained", says General Manager, Craig McConaghy. Quality is all-important in the coffee market and to understand what Craig means by quality you could always try a cup of Goroka!

"Start at the bottom and climb your way up. That is the best way to build a successful career. If you go straight in at the top you miss out on the basics and never fully understand your work."

This is the philosophy of Amnon Ricanati, an Israeli, whose first job was driving a tractor on a chicken farm.

Since then he has scaled his way up the agricultural career ladder, running farming enterprises everywhere from Hungary to Liberia. He is now the general manager of Ilimo Poultry in Port Moresby, one of Papua New Guinea's leading agricultural businesses.

"Initially I had wanted to be a sculptor but I soon discovered it did not pay the rent," explained Amnon. "I was brought up on a corporate farm in Israel and decided agriculture was a more practical career for me to follow. I have no regrets."

Last year Amnon was headhunted to run Ilimo by Agridev, an international company formed by the Israeli Ministry of Agriculture.

This Port Moresby posting is Amnon's most challenging to date. Despite a degree in animal husbandry and a formidable amount of farming experience under his belt, Papua New Guinean agriculture is a whole new world to him.

"The philosophy here is very different," he admitted. "Things move at a slower pace than in more modernised countries but the locally grown products are excellent and the agricultural potential is severely underestimated."

Ilimo Poultry Products, formed in 1971, is spread over an immense area of 1,500 hectares. On this land there are several different enterprises, but poultry dominates. Over 4,500 tonnes of chicken meat is produced each year on the farm.

"The poultry part of the set-up encompasses all aspects of chicken manufacturing," said Amnon. "We breed the chickens, hatch them and deal with the meat production right from the slaughtering stage through to packaging. We also have a separate enterprise for the egg-laying hens. All the poultry products are sold in our farm shop and at food stores all over town.

"Big scale poultry farming is a scientific and sophisticated business. New technology is being developed everyday and we have to move with the times. Innovation is a priority at Ilimo and we are currently building a chicken shed to test out a new feeding and ventilation system."

Another Ilimo innovation is the development of a hi-tech feed mill. The mill, which has only recently started operating, is capable of processing up to 28,000 tonnes of grain a year. In the long run this will help to substantially cut Ilimo's feed costs.

"The feed mill blends different types of grain together," said Amnon. "This way it can produce food mixtures for many different types of livestock - whether chickens, cattle or pigs. It is a very exciting project which I hope will boost not only local employment but the country's economy as a whole. The more products that can be processed in Papua New Guinea itself, rather than being exported, the better."

Despite his degree in animal husbandry there is one creature at Ilimo that Amnon had never encountered before his arrival in Port Moresby - the crocodile. The lush, swampy land that runs alongside the River Laloki is ideally suited to both salt water and fresh water crocodiles .

Ilimo capitalised on this and started farming both types of crocodile back in 1982. They now boast over 1,000 crocs and during the next four years plan a radical increase of up to 30,000.

"The weather and the environment is perfect for crocodiles here," said Kambut Kamon, the crocodile farm manager. "It is tropical but not too dry. Another advantage is we can feed them the chickens.

"Crocodiles are very much an up-and-coming market in this country. The meat is popular locally and their skins make lucrative exports."

Ilimo employs over 400 staff of which only six are expatriates. All the employees receive comprehensive in-house training but those who show particular potential are sent on training courses abroad to develop their skills.

"Educating the national people so they can manage their own businesses is essential," said Amnon. "That is the key to the success of this country's future. Agriculture is full of fertile opportunities and will provide the key to this country's long term prosperity. Ilimo is glad to be part of this. I am very optimistic for the future, both for the company and for Papua New Guinea's agriculture in general."

Mainland Holdings in Lae is a big company, with an extraordinary diversity of interests, but there are plenty of companies in Papua New Guinea with multiple interests, which are just as big. "What today makes Mainland special," says Group General Manager Paul Stobbs, "is the extraordinary vision displayed by its founder just a few years before Independence and the present composition of its shareholders".

Coffee was the foundation of the business and is still very important. The Lae coffee mill was owned by the Goudie family, long term residents of Lae, and was run by Graham Goudie. He persuaded a group of thirteen small-holders whose coffee he processed to form a Marketing Co-operative Company in order to purchase some shares of the coffee mill company. By 1974 the mill was a wholly owned subsidiary of the

co-operative. Since then it has never looked back.

Appointed General Manager to Mainland Holdings in 1976, Goudie was a shrewd and patient adviser to his shareholders. Profits were put by, not spent, and as opportunities arose, other companies were purchased. Seen in the supermarket, Nuigini Tablebirds (2,500 chickens a week) might seem a world away from coffee, but this business too was a rural one, based on small-holder skills. Day-old chicks are now bred and supplied to villagers who may own one or two (or even more) broiler sheds. The mature chickens are bought

adding skilled people to PNG. The work force is well looked after. Employees have free houses, electricity, water, sports facilities, TV, library and schools. The company also has the only doctor and ambulance in the area and willingly makes them available when there is need.

The company is proud of its record in social improvements for the people of Ramu valley. 700 children go to school and achieve a pass rate of 70-80%, the highest in PNG. The level of malaria used to be 95% now it is down to 5%. This remarkable drop has been achieved by issuing health information, nets and chemical repellents, and by getting rid of standing water and encouraging people to wear long-sleeved clothes. It has gradually brought about a change in attitude.

Ramu sugar not only supplies the entire sugar needs of PNG but has begun exporting. Last year it exported 10,00 tonnes of industrial raw sugar to the United States. It is also producing 30% of PNG's beef from 18,000 head of cattle. In just under twenty years Ramu Sugar has justified its investment and is proud of its contribution to the progress of Papua New Guinea.

HIGATURU OIL PALMS

Palm oil is used in cooking oils, margarine, soap, paint, plastics, cosmetics and in many other products. It comes from the fruit of a palm with the botanical name of Elaeis guineensis, a sturdy, upright palm which can be over 50 feet tall at maturity.

Papua New Guinea has had a palm oil industry in Oro Province only since the early days of Independence. The first palms were planted and a mill was built at Higaturu on land that Australian planters had been using to grow cocoa. Higaturu Oil Palms Pty Ltd was a joint venture by the newly independent PNG Government and the British Commonwealth Development Corporation, each of which had a 50% share. Now a steady 45,000 tonnes of palm oil are produced annually in Oro Province alone, injecting an estimated K16 million into the Oro economy in the form of wages, payments to smallholders and increased local spending.

Like coffee, palm oil is produced either by small-holders who sell their crop to the company or the company itself. In Oro 6,000 hectares are owned by small-holders, while a further 6,000 is company plantation.

In each case the fruit of the oil palm is first harvested with a kind of chisel tool, which detaches it from the main plant The whole bunch is transported to the mill. Heating and pressing results in the palm fibre within the fruitlets giving up its oil. The product, in liquid form, is ready to travel to the coast where it is transferred to ships whose destination is likely to be Rotterdam or Merseyside.

1,785 small-holders are involved in the Oro oil palm industry and a further 2,500 work for the company for wages. Taking into account other family members, more than 20,000 people are reliant on palm oil for the cash component of their livelihood – a considerable fraction of Oro's 106,000 population.

The existence of the industry is not untrou-bled. All plantation economies are targets for environmental criticism and subject to labour problems. The oil palm industry is no exception. These aspects of the industry are receiving serious attention in PNG.

For example, the Oro Conservation Project, funded by the World Bank, has been set up to find out if the very rare Queen Alexandra Birdwing Butterfly has been endangered by the loss of forest habitat to oil palms. Its results may affect future planning.

For the present, however, the oil palm industry is a profitable part of the PNG economy, providing a much needed cash income and assisting in the development of infrastructure such as roads.

107

Someone has calculated that there are 1,752 fish species in Papua New Guinea waters with an additional 80 unverified. Most of these fish live around reefs and in coastal waters. PNG has one of the world's biggest fishes, the whale shark, which grows to 13 metres and can weigh 14 tonnes. At the other extreme Dahl's coralfish is only 2.8 cm long and is one of the smallest known animals with a backbone.

All along PNG's 17,000 kilometre coastline there are people fishing in their own traditional way, using small canoes or dinghies, diving, collecting shells, spearing fish, using traps, nets, hooks and lines. They catch fish for consumption, for barter and for a little cash income at small markets. In some provinces, like Milne Bay, men fish everyday. Fish with coconut is a staple diet. Fish is used in a traditional exchange with the people who live in the Highlands for taro, yam and vegetables. Fish has a place in every feast.

With the arrival of Europeans and the introduction of new fishing technology, people started to earn a cash income from various marine products. But the fishing industry was then still small-scale, restricted to communities of clan and family members. Now local fishermen are powering their boats with outboard motors. They fish at night. They have small generators to run freezers and sell the fish at markets and restaurants. One day, they hope, they may own a longliner or a prawn vessel.

Today, industrial fishing is conducted off the coasts of PNG by other nations under licence. Otherwise PNG is not yet involved.

The other foreign groups interested in PNG's fish are the tourists, divers, snorkellers and game fishermen. The most famous destination is the Bensback Lodge near the Irian Jaya border where without boasting even a 20kg barramundi can commonly be caught. Then there are many towns around the coast where boats can be hired for deep-water fishing for sharks or marlin. Diving and snorkelling is tremendously attractive, the water is clear, there is an abundance of reef, soft and hard corals and hundreds of species of fish. One tour guide said that to go to PNG without looking underwater would be like going to Nepal and not looking at the mountains.

Of all the resources that Papua New Guinea has on offer, those in the sea can be considered to be the most elusive. Compared to countries to the north and south, PNG is not a commercial fishing nation. Fishing amounts to less than 1% of Gross Domestic Product. However, almost 80% of its people do some fishing. PNG is an artisanal fishing country where people do their fishing in their own traditional grounds using largely traditional methods. That could be about to change.

We have got one of the richest fishing grounds in the world," said the Minister for Fisheries and Marine Resources, Titus Philemon, in July 1995. "PNG is one of the biggest contributors, in terms of catch, to the world market, even to the canneries that make up tinned fish, but as a nation we have missed out on the benefits of all this activity. Recently we have tried to uphold the of PNG as a maritime nation endowed with a bounty of commercially exploitable marine resources. We have been developing policies conducive to private sector investment. I must admit that it has not been easy trying to create the appropriate investment climate. However a lot of opportunities exist."

The Ministry of Fisheries is working closely with the Department of Environment to develop the resource in a sustainable way. The Department of Commerce and Industry to working to encourage commercial and investment opportunities. Finance and Planning and Idustrial Relations ministries are also involved. Fisheries Minister Philemon said, "I am determined to wake the sleeping giant and to exploit the resources of the millions of hectares of sea which surround the PNG archipelago."

Following the declaration of its Exclusive Economic Zone (EEZ) in 1978, PNG has the third largest marine jurisdictional zone (2.3m sq Km) among the Pacific Island countries. The inland waters of PNG are extensive but, in general, the river systems do not have a rich bio-diversity of fish. There have been attempts to fish farm and to stock rivers but this sector is very much underdeveloped. The present fish production from the trout farm in Eastern Highlands and a carp hatchery at Aiyura is less than 100 tonnes per year. There is potential for expansion but it is the coastal and marine resources which present the biggest prospect for investment.

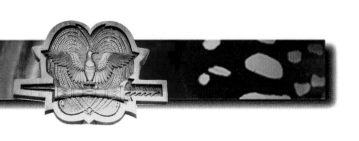

PNG has one of the most productive tuna fishing grounds in the Western Pacific. In the past much of PNG's tuna has been caught in purse seine nets by distant water fishing vessels from countries like Japan, the United States, South Korea, the Philippines and Taiwan. In 1993 there were about 130 purse seine vessels under license to fish. There are no PNG boats. Only in the last two years have there been access agreements which demand certain conditions of the foreign vessels. Access to archipelagic waters will only be allowed to those fleets that have invested in onshore developments such as the construction of wharves, cold storage and/or processing facilities. They must call into port at least once a year to transfer stocks on shore, to provision and refuel. It is one way of checking catch reports and log books. Tougher penalties are being introduced for breaches of agreement.

The other popular form of tuna fishing is long-line - a very long line with thousands of hooks. Access to territorial seas outside of 3 miles is limited to Papua New Guinean owned and registered long-liners, fishing sashimi-grade tuna. This industry requires better access to international air services to Japan or feeder routes to Japan to facilitate marketing. The response of the private sector to the restrictions on external long-liners has been good, creating jobs and bringing confidence to this sector.

PNG has approximately 17,000 kilometres of coastline. The annual subsistence consumption of inshore marine and inland fisheries resources is about 20,000-25,000 metric tonnes. There are many small scale commercial ventures. Some 8,000-10,000 tonnes of reef, lagoon and coastal pelagic fish are traded each year in coastal populations such as Port Moresby, Lae, Alotau, Wewak and Daru. In addition, about 2,500 tonnes of high-value sedentary and inshore species such as prawns, lobster, beche-de-mer, shells, barramundi and other finfish, as well as and dry marine resources, are harvested for export by commercially-oriented artisan fishermen who work together mostly with small-scale private sector processing and marketing businesses.

It is in this context that the current Minister is formulating his policies. For some years the stress has been on the 'biological' aspects of managing the resources of the sea. The time has come, he feels, to concentrate more on the 'economic' aspects. The needs of private investors must be served. The government will stop trying to play developer and instead will play the role of facilitator. Well established private entrepreneurs who have experience in the industry will be targeted to assist them with expert advice in areas such as marketing, business advice, credit access and so on.

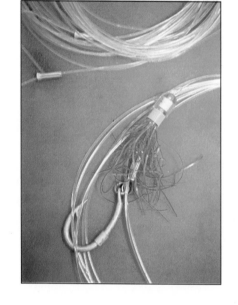

All plans for the next ten years focus on the growth of the domestic fishing industry. The Asian Development Bank is assisting with an investment project in the private sector, especially commercialising the artisan fisheries. The Government will provide venture capital, credit access, necessary infrastructure such as port facilities and other roles necessary to facilitate development. The aim is to increase the contribution of fisheries from around 1% of GNP to over 5% by the year 2005. One specific objective is to increase employment in the fisheries sector from around 400 sea-going jobs to 2,600 sea-going and 400 on-shore jobs by the year 2001. The goal is K80 million of new investment in the domestic fisheries sector and to increase the domestic commercial catch from 8,000 to 30,000 tonnes per year.

Administration is under control but where inter-agency implementation of projects is concerned there still remains a degree of doubt as to whether the concerned agencies can work effectively together and whether they have the manpower to be able to perform their part of the project.

GULF PAPUA FISHERIES

Gulf Papua Fisheries, one of PNG's leading prawn fishing companies, is fully owned by the citizens of Gulf Province through their Provincial Government. The company specialises in the harvesting and processing of natural prawns from the waters of the Gulf of Papua. It owns and operates four prawn trawlers and exports most of its catch to Japan under the Gulf Star brand name.

The trawlers, each with about 17 crew, spend 30 to 40 days at sea on each trip. Using a beam trawling method, the fishermen bring on board a mixture of prawn species with names like 'Black Tigers' and 'White Bananas'. The sorting and packing of the catch is done at sea and the trawler can arrive back with up to 20 tonnes of prawns, frozen and ready for export. Over a year, the total catch is about 300 tonnes, with earnings amounting to over three million US dollars.

Gulf Papua Fisheries' success can be attributed to wise management practices and a dedicated workforce.

Prior to Independence the prawn industry was dominated by foreign operators, mainly Japanese. After Independence a joint venture was set up between a Japanese company and the Gulf Provincial Government. By 1984 it had become clear that this arrangement was not adequately benefiting the Papuan side. The provincial premier decided to terminate the agreement and, under the leadership of Mr Hiro Muramoto, a joint national and expatriate manage-ment initiative was put to the PNG Government, making the case for nationalisation.

Gulf Papua Fisheries started as a two kina company in the same year, acquiring two old boats from the Japanese company. After painful years of re-investment, it has replaced these with new boats and has added others. Now it has paid up share capital of K876,000. The present Managing Director, Mr Sepoe Karawa, sees future development taking the form of co-operative ownership, firstly with company's own 90-strong workforce and then with the resource owners of Gulf Province, those coastal villagers who often, in the past, have not benefited from the commercial exploitation of their waters.

113

TMM operates 7 days a week satisfying requests ranging from a bag of ice to the bunkering of 1,5000,000 litres of diesel fuel.

The ice would come from the Ship's Chandlery. Operating underneath the Royal Papua Yacht Club in Port Moresby, it is the largest in PNG. It carries electronics and other equipment for the boating industry. A wide range of parts for Volvo Penta and Mercruiser marine engines is carried and, if you haven't got your own, a charter boat service is available for game fishing enthusiasts or for those wanting a more peaceful trip to the islands for a picnic in the sun.

At the other end of the scale TMM, in association with Shell PNG, operates a deep water bunkering operation and a fuelling station at the new marina. This includes 2 'dumb' barges which carry from 95,000 to 700,000 litres of fuel. They are used to fuel the fishing fleet out of Port Morseby as well as local container ships, small coastal craft, Navy Patrol Boats and even overseas warships.

A direct pipe feed is available from the main shore storage tanks to a loading platform in the harbour. This pipe is capable of carrying 3,000 litres per minute. It is used by coastal fuel tankers supplying the mining and timber industries.

TMM has been operating for 15 years and has naturally expanded its services over that period to accommodate PNG's development into the world at large. Dalco International, an associated company, has only been operating for 4 years. In that time it has specialised in industrial, marine and electrical engineering. It sells and services engines, generating sets, electronic equipment and the useful Emmerson Liebert range of un-interruptable power supply systems.

Fully qualified technicians find no job too hard for them, whether it is fixing a radio, replacing a bilge pump or carrying out a complete overhaul on a large marine or industrial engine.

The latest development is the Electronic Engineering workshop which is under construction. It will be able to repair HF, VHF and UHF radio equipment and a string of other marine devices such as autopilots, plotters, radar, PLCs, generating set controls and the remarkable GPS (Global Positioning System) which uses satellites to locate itself with astonishing accuracy.

NEW GUINEA MARINE PRODUCTS

New Guinea Marine Products is a wholly PNG-owned prawn and tuna fishing operation which operates a fleet of prawn trawlers and long-line tuna fishing boats in the Gulf of Papua and the Coral Sea.

The oldest commercial fishing company in PNG, New Guinea Marine Products was established by a Japanese corporation in 1973. The first activity was fishing for skipjack tuna off the coast of Madang. This was followed a couple of years later by prawn fishing in the Gulf of Papua. By the time the PNG Government acquired shares in the company in 1983, New Guinea Marine Products had become, almost entirely, a prawn fishing operation. The fleet consisted of six prawn trawlers and the catch was exported to both Japan and Australia. In 1994, K & K Fisheries Ltd, the present owners, bought up all the Japanese and PNG shares and New Guinea Marine Products is now a wholly PNG-owned company.

In the same year, in an exciting development, at present operating on a trial basis, the company resumed tuna fishing.

Tuna are large fish which live 100-250 metres deep in the ocean. They can weigh up to 600 pounds for a single fish. They are caught by either purse seine nets or long lines. New Guinea Marine Products uses long lines. These are a set of baited lines which hang from a 1,000 metre long travel line, 80 metres deep in the ocean. The fish are exported to Japan on commercial Air Niugini flights.

While prawns are a relatively steady fishery, especially since a closed season was introduced at the beginning of this year, tuna, the more valuable fish, cannot yet be regarded as a sure thing. Many problems beset the commercial fisherman in PNG, not the least being heavy PNG government taxes on everything from bait to the final export duty.

New Guinea Marine expects to discover within the next few months whether its estimate of an annual catch of 120 tonnes of tuna.

"There is a huge opportunity for fisheries development in Papua New Guinea", says Maurice Brownjohn. "We are at the centre of some of the richest waters in the world. It is up to us to make sure we use this resource well for the benefit of the nation."

The Net Shop makes and markets fishing gear and equipment. Specializing in all forms of nets, it also includes in its stock a full range of products imported from abroad.

Long lines, fish traps, fish hooks and lures, ropes, floats, chain, fish-boxes and anchors - all can be acquired at the shop at Six Mile in Port Moresby, N.C.D. As for the nets themselves, both nylon and polyethylene nets of all plies and all mesh sizes can be made to order. They can be in the form of prawn nets, gill nets, seine nets and trammel nets. Even knotless nets can be found here.

As well as stocking well-known international brands, The Net Shop sells a range of fishing line and tackle under its own brand name: Strongpela Moa.

The Net Shop's owner, Maurice Brownjohn, has been closely involved with the fishing industry in PNG since his arrival here as freshly-trained fisheries officer at the age of 21. First posted to West New Britain, he quickly learnt the business, spent several years working for various provincial fisheries departments and then branched out on his own.

As founding Chairman of the Fisheries Industries Association and an acknowledged expert, he advises and acts as a consultant to a wide range of people and groups.

"There are three sorts of fishing in PNG", said Maurice. "Commercial, village or 'artisanal', and sport. Commercial fishing except for prawn fishing is still underdeveloped. Village fishing is an intermittent activity alternating with agriculture as part of a subsistence lifestyle. Fishing for sport is popular with individuals and many towns have fishing clubs".

All of the three types of fishing require nets and tackle and "The Net Shop" is proud to be the first of its kind in Port Moresby and indeed in PNG.

The two most significant events in the Papua New Guinean economy recently have been the closure of the Panguna copper mine on Bougainville in 1989 and the devaluation and subsequent float of the kina in 1994.

Unfortunately for the nearly four million people of the country both came within a space of just over four years. The pains being felt now are the direct results of both events. The mine closure took with it 40% of the country's annual export revenue and 20% of direct revenue flows to the national budget.

The hole left in the economy remained, despite government attempts to fill it in. By the end of 1993 it became apparant that public expenditure needed to be reduced drastically. The deficit had increased significantly and inflation rose.

The unprecedented but inevitable happened in late 1994. The kina was devalued by 12% and subsequently floated to find its own value in the open market. Up until then the Bank of PNG set the rate for the kina on a daily basis.

Since independence in 1975, PNG's small and open economy has been the envy of he rest of the South Pacific. In the developing world, the country fared well, being given the "middle income country" status. Within a decade per capita income had reached K500 per year. But being dependent on primary exports – agricultural, forestry, fisheries, minerals and petroleum – it was subject to price fluctuations in the world markets.

The post-Panguna years saw sharp swings in economic performance. Domestic production fell by nearly 5 % between 1989 and 1991. Then it swung back, aided by the mineral and petroleum sector, to record a huge 16.6 % growth in 1993. Speculation in the currency market and concerns over the huge deficits resulted in money leaving PNG's shores.

A new government took over in mid-1994 and made a firm commitment to pay its international debts, thus more money left. The result was depleted foreign exchange reserves. In September 1994 the kina was devalued and a month later it was floated. The objectives were to end the on-going speculation over the currency strength and also to boost exports, which would in return help rebuild the foreign reserves.

Economic indicators pointed to an improvement by the end of 1994, but a major restructure of the economy and policies was needed to lift PNG. Public confidence internationally had been lost. The 1995 budget contained major reforms, both those recommended by the World Bank and those by the government. They were aimed at improving delivery of services to the majority of the people and achieving economies of scale. Controversial as they may be, the reforms and their endorsement by the World Bank are necessary for PNG's standing in the international community.

Moves have also been made towards liberalisation of trade. PNG's membership of international bodies such as World Trade Organisation (WTO) and Asia Pacific Economic Corporation (APEC) require it to free up trade restrictions and protective tariffs and duties. There is optimism that, as soon as the current balance of payment crisis is passed, Papua New Guinea's economy will rejuvenate and rapidly grow.

Start of construction for the Lihir gold mine, the Gobe oil field and a host of other major resource projects, will be the catalysts to the PNG economy's rebounding.

FINANCE AND PLANNING

The success or failure of an economy depends on the outcome of the national budget. The budget contains all the policy initiatives and visions of the government, and so affects all the people they govern. One of the most important functions of government, year in and year out, is planning, formulating and implementing that budget.

In Papua New Guinea, that unenviable task belongs to the Department of Finance and Planning. The Department plans and allocates funds to all the functions of the government and to public investment programs, depending on the priorities set by the government of the day.

Recently, and as part of a World Bank recommended restructure, the planning function of the Departments were shifted. The National Planning Office will now take charge of the initial planning of development policies to be pursued by the government. Finance Department keeps the role of allocating resources and managing the national purse. There have also been other changes in the restructuring exercise. The aid co-ordinating body OIDA (Office of International Development Assistance) is to be merged with the aid co-ordnating Branch. Staff ceilings will also be lowered.

In 1985, ten years after independence, Papua New Guinea's first fully-fledged national development plan was set in place for the period 1986-1990. The objectives of the plan were mainly: economic growth that creates jobs, sustained development in the long term, making PNG more self-reliant, and equal opportunities for all in the country's development. It was during that decade that PNG felt progress.

This year marks another ten years since that plan was set in motion. Ten years ago too, there was a separate National Planning and Development department and Ministry. The recent restructuring of the cabinet and public service sees the planning functions once again separated from Finance. Finance and Planning, together or otherwise, have called on the capabilities of Papua New Guineans to run and manage them. (Sir) Mekere Morauta set the pace. Morea Vele and the current Finance Secretary Gerea Aopi are among those people. Current Prime Minister Sir Julius Chan, a highly regarded leader in the Asia-Pacific region, has also held the finance ministry the most number of times.

Under Finance and Planning fall the other important functions of National Statistics Office, OIDA, the Internal Revenue Commission, the Bureau of Customs and Excise, the Government Printing Office, the Consumer Affairs Council, the Central Government Supply and Tenders Board and a host of statutory corporations.

Some of these functions will be placed under the newly created Planning Department while the others will remain in Finance. The Department has also taken the lead in negotiating numerous loans, the latest one being with the World Bank. The bank has recommended major reforms to fiscal and structural operations of government which are being implemented. The department is overseeing the implementation of the reforms. The success of the reforms will determine PNG's economic advancement.

The 1995 government of Prime Minister Sir Julius Chan and his deputy Chris Haiveta is faced with the toughest challenge ever to win international public support and confidence and to revitalise the Papua New Guinean economy.

The current government took over in mid-1994 amid fears that the economy was near to collapse. Social and economic indicators pointed to a recession and something drastic needed to be done.

The events of the latter part of 1994, including the 12 per cent devaluation and subsequent floating of the kina, the introduction of a tough monetary policy which has seen big increases in rates of interest and the mini-budget of November 1994, are all part of that drastic move that was considered necessary to fix the economy.

Deputy Prime Minister and Minister for Finance and Planning Chris Haiveta, a young politician who is in his first term in Parliament, has had to contend with another major issue: a "structural adjustment" programme.

The programme is the initiative of both the PNG government and the World Bank. The World Bank recommended massive restructures and reforms which the government agreed to implement in exchange for a loan from the bank. The government

also included its own reforms in the 1995 budget.

Endorsement of PNG's reform programme by the World Bank and its implementation is required if PNG is to access funds for both public sector and private sector projects from international financial sources.

"If Papua New Guinea wants to remain in the deep and dark hole in which past government abuses have left us, then our friends in the international community will not be willing to help us," said Mr Haiveta. "Our friends would be quite indifferent to our problems if we chose to show no commitment to correcting the abuse and pulling ourselves out of the hole we are in. We must help ourselves first before asking others to help us."

More importantly, the outcome of the structural reforms will decide whether PNG will recover economically and rebuild stability in its finances and planning.

Mr Haiveta has been vigorous in his pursuit of the reforms. He said he does not want to see a repeat of the failed 1989 structural adjustment programme. The 1989 reforms, also recommended by the World Bank, were abandoned when the government then pushed all efforts and resources into the Bougainville uprising and the effects of the mine closure.

Over the next few years, Papua New Guineans can expect the cost of living to remain high. But in the long term, when the adjustments have been completed and are in place, a more positive outcome is forecast.

"Structural adjustment means changing the way the government operates to make it more efficient and more responsive to community needs. It means providing the country with the right environment to produce more jobs and improve our living standards. This means that government policies, programmes, regulations and laws governing resource allocation must be changed," said Mr Haiveta. In the short term, Mr Haiveta suggested, the government must restore economic stability, with sustainable and balanced budgets, a comfortable level of international reserves, a stable exchange rate, low inflation and internationally competitive interest rates. Standard monetarist policy.

"We must re-orientate our taxation and tariff systems to meet our budget requirements while at the same time providing a good economic environment that will encourage growth in private sector business," he said.

He said that industries must be restructured to be able to compete internationally.

"The changes we are beginning to implement will produce higher growth and higher employment opportunities for our people. The reforms," he said, "seek to increasing the proportion of investment and development spending."

The structural adjustments are in the main areas of expenditure controls: a year-long wage freeze, cuts to the public service, restructuring of government departments, improvements to draw down on donor funds, implementation of projects funded by those donor funds, trade liberalisation and land reforms.

"The benefits of the reforms," Mr Haiveta said, "outweigh the costs. The structural adjustment the government is pursuing is aimed at revitalising the economy, which over the past few years has deteriorated badly. The current state of the economy has

been the result of unplanned and irresponsible spending by governments over the years."

Public expenditure levels in PNG have grown from a mere K330 million in 1975 to nearly K2 billion in 1995. However, these levels of growth, while not sustainable in relation to the revenues earned, are low in relation to population growth and in relation to the much undeveloped state of infrastructure handed over by the Australian administration at Independence.

A review of the past trends suggests considerable variation in past public service levels, compared to the desirable patterns of expenditure. The huge fluctuations in budgeting over the years have had adverse effects, especially on planning.

The closure of the Panguna copper mine in 1990, the prolonged low world prices of commodity exports and the uncontrolled growth in expenditure over the years have resulted in huge deficits being amassed, thus the current major structural adjustments.

The difficulty that PNG faced was in applying a disciplined approach and in resolving the conflicting ideas and initiatives of different governments. Expenditure growth over the period 1982 to 1988 was restrained, averaging 5.2 per cent per annum. This shot up to 12 per cent for the years 1989, 1991 and 1992. In the past governments planned on a five year time frame but because of the lack of continuity, planning objectives have been reduced to three years.

The planning functions have also been moved back and forth according to government priorities. Recent governments have realised the importance of expenditure planning and in the latest (July 1995) reshuffle, the gov-

ernment has again shifted Planning out of Finance and given it a ministerial portfolio.

The traditional approach of analysing expenditure has been to divide it by different departments and agencies into six or seven key sectors. The many changes in the nature and functions of departments and agencies naturally caused problems. Expenditure is analysed by departments and agencies presenting their requirements to the Finance and Planning Department, which then allocates the money. The Finance and Planning Department monitors the expenditure by the departments through regular checks on expenditure records. When Departments keep changing, analysis becomes difficult.

Only recently have governments started acting on the imbalances of budgeting, with new objectives being put in place. Among them were:. expenditure to be planned on medium term resource availability, focus on important areas of public concern, letting go of assets that are not profitable, priority to be given to rural sector development, to education and training, to physical infrastructure, to health and to law and order. That was a lot of priorities. Nonetheless, expenditure was reduced for urban based administration, non-productive investments and subsidies.

Generally, the years

after 1987 saw increased emphasis on the economic and social sectors. When the Bougainville crisis flared in the late 1980's and the Panguna copper mine was shut, taking with it over 40 per cent of export earnings for the country and 20 per cent in direct tax incomes to the national coffers, a new problem arose. Suddenly, expenditure for Defence expanded in order to finance the security operations on the island. Cocoa and copra producers on the island also stopped producing. Also the Australian government decided to reduce gradually its direct budget support to PNG.

With the revenue inflows greatly reduced and expenses still high, the deficit began to grow large.

There are indications that revenue collections are now improving. The Internal Revenue Commission (IRC) said that, in the first six months of 1995, it collected a total of over K500 million in taxes. This exceeded its budget forecasts and its collection in the corresponding period in 1994. The IRC says it will surpass its 1995 budget forecast for collection of K1.2 billion.

The IRC, which comes under the Finance Ministry, has also gone through a major revamp recently, with improvements in collection capacities and more defined tax regimes.

Taxation policies and regimes have also been in continuous change since pre-Independence periods. The main emphasis now is to create a taxation regime that will encourage investment as well as ensuring that the country earned sufficient revenues from the taxes. Personal income tax and company taxes, which are traditional, continue to exist at the same levels while fringe benefit taxes have been introduced, removed and re-introduced.

Import and export taxes have also continued to have changes to their rates made from time to time. Generally, there has been a reduction in the rate of import duties for products needed for domestic production and exemptions from duty on capital imports.

Protective measures aimed at assisting local production, such as bans and tariffs have been created. To encourage foreign investments, incentives have been put in place, including tax discounts, 5 to 10 year tax holidays and special rates of tariffs and import duties.

Tax revenues from mining and petroleum projects and other companies in general have shown increases. The improved capacity of the IRC to collect, has been the main reason for the increases.

Despite the problems, there is widely held optimism that the PNG economy will lift itself and quickly start to grow again. But this once more depends on whether the government is able to control spending over the coming years.

The structural reforms the government is now undertaking will, it is hoped, be the catalyst to the future health of PNG's economic growth and development as a whole.

The return of public confidence in the government at home and by the international community are paramount to achieving the desired goals and objectives.

Information technology is now an everyday part of the efficient running of major corporations. These days most operations involving listing, compilation, calculation or record-keeping will have used a computer somewhere in the process, and government operations are no exception. Most government offices in PNG have computers.

The National Computer Centre, part of the Department of Finance and Planning, was first set up in the early 70's, at a time when big mainframe computers were the order of the day. These computers were the size of rooms, hugely expensive and only for the initiated, but gradually systems were developed on them for various Government departments. The processing of payrolls, the annual national accounts, the preparation of reports and the presentation of data in the form of tables were all things they could do well.

As communication links were established, it became possible to extend the power of the computer to regional centres, allowing government officers in the provinces to connect directly to the mainframe. Criminal records, for example, held centrally, can now be accessed by a police officer in the regions.

As information technology developed, computers became more manageable. Confidence increased and eventually some users felt that

they were able to take control of their own systems. The National Computer Centre then helped them to select appropriate equipment and to transfer systems from the mainframe to their own machines.

A proposed centre of excellence, the National Centre for Information Technology, operating under the Information Technology Board (ITB) will take on the role previously performed by the NCC, while NCC will be given a more focussed role of providing computer services to the Department of Finance in order to strengthen its role in financial accountabi-lity, planning and budgeting.

Certain functions, though, will remain with the NCC, such as the massive task of processing the seven

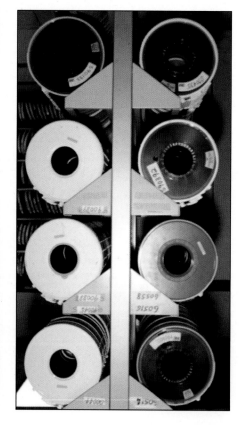

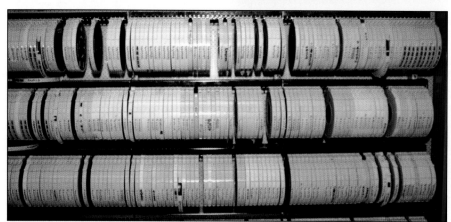

different government payrolls. Every fortnight the salaries for more than 6,000 people working in the government sector, including Finance, Defence, Civil Aviation, Village Courts and Education, together with the payrolls for the University and the NCDC, are processed by the National Computing Centre, so far without fail.

Another centralised function is that of managing the submissions and allocations of the National Budget. Every March preparations for the following year's Budget begin. First a circular is issued giving details of the size of the allocation to each budget holder, for them to itemise and - inevitably! - contest. This they do by returning the itemised budget by the month of June. The government then comes to a decision about the final allocations, which then become available for the financial year commencing in January. The advent of computers has greatly increased the decision-making powers of financial planners. With NCC's computer pro-grammes they can issue spread-sheets, draw graphs, do calculations and forecasts, and apply as sophisticated an analysis as they like - all at the press of a button. The only thing the computer does not supply is wisdom - that still has to come from human sources.

The future shape of computing within the PNG Public Service is still being refined. The advent of Open Systems, the move to small server-based technology, the increasing trend towards data manipulation rather than number-crunching, the availability of off-the-shelf packages, the distribution of control to end users, the explosion of interconnectivity and networking, means there is obviously a need to continue to supply policy advice and training to all users. The transformations that have been caused by the information technology revolution are such that no-one can escape or remain unaffected. Literacy now, especially for a public servant or government officer, includes computer literacy.

According to Francis Ko'ou, General Manager of the National Computing Centre, the NCC sees a permanent and expanding role for itself in training. For in the end computers are only as useful as people choose to make them. So, effective Information Technology management is just as important as hardware and software and it will be a major task to educate all users, from keyboard operators up to Ministers, how to best make IT work for them.

The Bank of Papua New Guinea is the country's central bank. It was established on 1st November 1973. It administers monetary policy, supervises the financial system, acts as banker to the State and to the banks and publishes economic and financial information.

The Central Banking Act, 1973 says: "...the Bank shall, within the limits of its powers, ensure that its monetary and banking policy is directed to the greatest advantage of the people of Papua New Guinea and direct its efforts to promoting monetary stability and a sound and efficient financial structure."

The Governor of the Bank, Mr. Koiari Tarata, is only the third in the Bank's history. A Board is appointed by the Minister of Finance to decide on the policies of the Bank. It includes six to eight members who serve for three year terms.

The bank employs 228 people of whom 222 are nationals. 54 of these are graduates. The International Monetary Fund, the United Nations Development Programme and the Overseas Development Institute provide 6 non-nationals for secondment to the bank. There is only one office - in downtown Port Moresby.

The Bank supervises and monitors the operations of the financial system including the commercial banks. It issues and distributes all notes and coins in PNG. It is responsible for the implementation of monetary policy in PNG. The goal of monetary policy is to support sustainable medium-term growth of economic activity in the private sector, excluding mining and petroleum which are wholly financed offshore. It aims to maintain stable levels of the exchange rate, interest rates, prices and credibility in international financial markets and institutions.

The Bank relies on trade in government securities as the principal tool of monetary and liquidity management. In 1995 the Bank will introduce a monetary management facility, the rate on which will become the key official rate, as it will determine the price of liquidity at the margin. The facility will take the form of a kina auction, in which the Bank can both offer and buy kina.

The Bank has used a Minimum Liquid Assets Ratio (MLAR) raising the total deposit requirement of commercial banks from 11% to 32% but it does not foresee using it as an active policy instrument in the long term.

Although the Bank no longer sets a target for credit growth, it monitors it as a key indicator of economic activity.

On 10th October 1994, PNG moved from a fixed exchange rate to a floating exchange regime. The exchange rate is now determined by the demand for and supply of foreign currency in the market through an auction system held once a day. Exchange rates between the kina and other currencies are set by commercial banks based on the closing rate of the previous days auction.

The Bank of Papua New Guinea looks after the control of flows of money in and out of the country. It does this on behalf of the Government and the main aim is to conserve the country's holdings of foreign exchange. Six commercial banks are allowed to deal in foreign exchange for transactions up to K500,000 per annum. Amounts above that are referred to Bank of Papua New Guinea for approval.

Permission is readily given for payments overseas for imported goods and services and transferring overseas the earnings on investments in PNG by residents of overseas countries. People departing permanently from PNG are free to take or send the entire value of their assets out of the country when leaving. People travelling to overseas countries are able to take sufficient funds to meet their needs while absent from PNG.

The Bank closely monitors all large capital inflows. Approval is required for all overseas investments in PNG.

The Bank acts as banker to the government as a Temporary Advance Facility. It also acts for commercial banks, for stock registry and a small numismatic and collector's currency operation.

Finally it issues the Quarterly Economic Bulletin, which provides a detailed commentary and analysis of current economic and financial conditions, backed by a comprehensive range of statistics on the financial sector, the domestic economy and the balance of payments.

The quarterly employment survey and six-monthly visits, to interview businesses in major regional centres around the country, provide the most timely information available about recent economic conditions and expectations for the short term.

INVESTMENT CORPORATION OF PAPUA NEW GUINEA

The Investment Corporation of Papua New Guinea has played a central role in the economic development of the country for more than 20 years.

Founded in 1971 with the aim of making investments in various business and commercial projects in the country, it is a statutory body and entirely Government owned.

As part of its investment process it provides local equity capital to investment projects where sizeable local equity capital is not readily available. Shares in the Corporation are held by large institutional fund-holders.

The Investment Corporation also manages a unit trust fund which is available for investment to members of the general public, whether individuals or groups. By purchasing units in this fund, an individual or group can earn dividends based on the perfor-

mance of the Corporation's portfolio of holdings. More than 23,000 different shareholders comprising individuals, small groups and large groups and associations own shares in this fund, representing tens of thousands of Papua New Guineans.

The Investment Corporation currently owns equity in a diverse array of PNG enterprises in sectors that range from agriculture, forestry, mining and petroleum through manufacturing and merchandizing to transport services and real estate. On the 20th anniversary of Independence, the total value of the holdings stands at K63,000,000.

The decisions that the Investment Corporation makes about investments are based on both financial and non-financial considerations. However it will only consider purchasing equity in business activities that are deemed to be economically and technically viable and financially profitable.

In keeping with the PNG's emphasis on self-reliance, the Investment Corporation has been entirely self-financing since 1975. Starting with Government equity of approximately K5.5 million, it has grown to its present size in twenty years.

In 1994 the Investment Corporation Fund made a profit of K4.9 million and distributed profits of nearly K4.5 million. In the meantime it has supported, in the most practical way possible, the development of locally-owned and managed businesses in the Papua New Guinean economy.

NATIONAL PROVIDENT FUND
BOARD OF TRUSTEES

The National Provident Fund is a compulsory saving scheme for establishments in the private sector having greater than 25 employees.

The Provident Fund's main purpose is to insure its beneficiaries and their families against loss of income due to:

loss of employment
disability
retrenchment
death
retirement

The Fund also assists with housing advances and emigration.

The National Provident Fund Board of Trustees is financed by contributions of a compulsory 5% employee and 7% employer net salary deduction. Employees have the option to increase voluntarily their 5% salary deduction up to 10%.

The Fund's assets at the 1994 year end were K137 million. That makes it the second largest Superannuation Fund in Papua New Guinea. It is estimated that the total assets of the fund will double by the year 2000, given its current capacity to grow at 25 % per annum.

The National Provident Fund was established by an Act of Parliament in January 1982 and is governed by a tripartite Board of Trustees, consisting of representatives of employers, employees and the government. It is administered by the Managing Director as Chief Executive of the Board of Trustees.

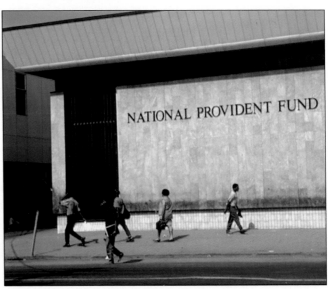

133

The oldest bank in Papua New Guinea, Westpac Bank - PNG - Limited was established in 1910. The parent company is now Westpac Banking Corporation of Australia which is in turn the oldest bank and the oldest public company in Australia. It was established in 1817 as the Bank of New South Wales.

In the last 85 years Westpac has contributed to the development and growth of Papua New Guinea, not just in the provision of Banking services but in terms of community services. It is a major sponsor of the Salvation Army Red Shield Appeal as well as a number of other worthwhile organisations. A little known contribution by the bank is its donation to the National Parliament of a portrait of successive Speakers of the House since Independence in 1975.

The bank has a number of long-time associations with major businesses in Papua New Guinea, most notable of these being historic associations with the Burns Philp Group and the Steamships Trading Group.

Over the years the bank has experienced a number of disruptions. During the war years Wau branch was completely destroyed except for the strongroom. In another incident at Salamaua the banks records and cash were buried by the staff before they fled and have not been located to this day, as far as we know.

The bank survived volcanic eruptions at Rabaul in the 1930's and more recently in 1994. It made a major donation of K75 thousand to the Rabaul Volcanic Disaster Relief Fund.

For years Australian & New Zealand staff have spent a term in PNG as expatriates. There is a thriving reunion each year in most capital cities in Australia when ex-PNG staff get together to re-live their time in PNG. These days the numbers are dwindling as the bank proudly exhibits the results of many years of localisation. Today the bank boasts the highest ratio of Papua New Guinea staff to expatriate staff. At Independence the bank had less than 10% Papua New Guinean staff. It is 96% today.

As it stands today, the bank has a clear strategy which is focused on bringing it up to current-day international best practice under the banner of being "Simply the Best Bank".

PAPUA NEW GUINEA BANKING CORPORATION

PNGBC is known locally as "Nambawan Haus Moni", the bank that is second to none.

The Papua New Guinea Banking Corporation is the largest commercial bank in PNG with an extensive network of branches throughout the country. The bank is wholly owned by the Independent State of Papua New Guinea and it traces its origins to the Commonwealth Bank of Australia. PNGBC was incorporated under the Banking Corporation Act in 1973 and began operations on 22 April 1974 when it acquired the assets and operations of the Commonwealth Bank in PNG.

At that time PNGBC acquired a network of 13 branches, 2 sub branches and 207 agencies. This has dramatically grown to 20 branches and 15 sub-branches employing 2048 staff. The number of agencies has been scaled down to 80.

PNGBC's charter requires that the policies of the Bank "ensure its functions are directed to the greatest advantage of the people of Papua New Guinea". This is a challenge as 80% of the country's population is rural-based. It is achieved by providing a wide but cost effective range of services including deposit, lending and international.

The lending portfolio of the PNGBC is diverse with agriculture, transport and communication, hotels & restaurants and personal lending being amongst the largest components. PNGBC finances a number of large employer-sponsored housing schemes as well as owner-occupied housing.

PNGBC's share of international business has gown in recent years. It is a member of SWIFT (Society for Worldwide Interbank Financial Telecommunications) which has given it access to a sophisticated global telecommunications network.

PNGBC has recently introduced electronic banking services, operating the country's only Automatic Teller Machines and maintaining a network of Electronic Funds Transfer at Point of Sale (EFTPOS) terminals. It maintains its own authorising switch and has interchange arrangements with ANZ Bank (PNG) and MBF Finance (PNG). Through these arrangements customers have access to over 250 EFTPOS terminals. PNGBC has the largest cardholder base through its SaveCard.

The "Nambawan Haus Moni" is a title of which we are proud and a reputation the company intends to keep.

When it comes to breaking new ground, McIntosh Securities make a habit of excelling themselves.

This crusading company is described as the "stock-broker of superlatives". It is the biggest underwriter in the South Pacific, the only publicly listed stock-broker in Australia and, perhaps most innovative of all, the first stockbroking firm to set up in Papua New Guinea.

The McIntosh office in Port Moresby has built up a formidable reputation due to a combination of

reliable service and financial expertise. It has been involved in practically every major project in PNG over the last few years.

The company balances its time principally between co-ordinating capital raising projects and advising private clients, who range from investment seeking individuals to international companies. It is the leading manager of the Lihir gold mining project, which has a projected expenditure of 600 million Australian dollars. Other assignments include the management of the National Provident Fund, valuations for the Post & Telecommunications Corporation, advisory work for the Investment Corporation of PNG and Paradise Bakeries.

For some time the Government of PNG has been preparing the way for the opening of a stock exchange in Port Moresby. John Hooton, McIntosh's forward thinking managing director, is prepared. "We have done all the work to get it up and going. It could start tomorrow if we felt that the climate was conducive to it being successful. It all depends on a turn-round in the economy and that will happen. There is no doubt of it."

Other than the small stock exchange in Fiji, Papua New Guinea's exchange will be the first among the island nations. It will be very much an emerging market. There are always fund managers who want to inject a portion of their funds into the global equity scene. Papua New Guinea will provide a fresh lure.

Much of McIntosh's business is international. They have offices dotted all over the major cities including Hong Kong, Tokyo, New York and London. They are able to offer advice on financial markets all over the world. It is a very formative and progressive time for the Papua New Guinean financial market. McIntosh are at the forefront of this exciting new era.

Most accountants are stereotyped as charmless individuals in grey suits. But Greg Nairn shatters this long standing image. Wearing an open-necked shirt and a relaxed smile, the charismatic Australian's conversation is so animated it is surprising he did not opt for a career in radio or television.

But Greg, the managing partner of Price Waterhouse in Port Moresby, has no regrets. A senior position in one of the world's leading accountancy firms is a job he would not swap for the world. The fact he has been posted in Papua New Guinea for the last year has served to add fresh challenges and a new edge of excitement to his work.

"When I was first told I was coming to Papua New Guinea I was in a state of disbelief," he admitted. "Apart from postings in Jakarta and Wellington I had always lived in Australia. At first I was rather wary about being posted to Port Moresby but now I am simply grateful I have had the chance to experience such a unique city.

"In a sense, accountancy is still in its infancy here. It gives international firms like Price Waterhouse the opportunity to pass on their experience and help the profession in Papua New Guinea to develop and modernise. There is still room for innovation and fresh approaches here, as opposed to countries like Aus-

tralia where accountancy is already heavily regulated."

Price Waterhouse has offices dotted all over the world and was the second international accountancy firm to establish itself in Papua New Guinea. The tiny, initial Price Waterhouse office, set up in 1969, pales in comparison to the new, modern headquarters at Pacific Place in Moresby's central business district.

The company's presence in Papua New Guinea is principally to service its international clients: New Britain Palm Oil Development Company, Chevron Niugini, Indosuez Bank, Shell PNG and Remington Pitney Bowes. The firm has also been instrumental in co-ordinating some major local projects. Ok Tedi, which is based in the Highlands, is one of the largest copper/gold mines in the world. Price Waterhouse were involved with it right from the start, when the idea to develop the mine was sparked over 10 years ago.

"Considering 90 percent of Papua New Guinea is inaccessible by normal means I think the excavation of Ok Tedi mine is a major achievement," said Greg. "We are very proud that we had confidence in the project and gave it our full support and expertise. It will, hopefully, pave the way for further mining ventures in the region."

Greg considers Price Waterhouse's principal role in benefiting Papua New Guinea is the recruitment and training of local staff. Of the 23 staff employed in the Port Moresby office, 15 are nationals. Many of them will be trained in-house and then have the opportunity to transfer to Australia or one of the other Asian offices. This helps them to gain valuable international experience which they can put into practice when they return to Papua New Guinea.

"I still have over three years of my contract to run in Papua New Guinea," said Greg. "The thing I would most like to achieve during my time here is to successfully train the national staff. Seeing them gain in confidence and experience would make me feel I have made a small contribution to this country."

It is unlikely Price Waterhouse will spread its wings into other parts of Papua New Guinea. With its multi-functional office in Port Moresby which deals with everything from tax planning to business consultancy, there is little need for other branches.

Greg accepts Papua New Guinea has its faults.

He feels that haphazard infrastructure means potentially money-spinning ventures in mining and forestry sometimes never get off the ground. He thinks the tourism industry needs a serious kick-start before it reaches its full potential. But he sees Papua New Guinea as a country on the verge of a fresh dawn - about to experience an auspicious and exciting new cycle.

One sector of the business world continues to grow in step with the development of the economy as a whole.

Helandis Management Services was formed in 1991 to meet the needs of the small to average-sized business in Papua New Guinea. According to Isaac Minicus, qualified accountant and Principal of the firm, there is a need for an efficient and cost effective service in this area which is easily accessable to the average PNG businessman.

Helandis Management Services offers a range of services designed to relieve the business person of some of his or her most onerous responsibilities. On a fixed quote basis, Helandis will provide bookkeeping, accountancy and taxation services with prompt preparation of periodic and year-end financial statements.

More extensive business consultancy services are also available, from feasibility studies and public and private sector consultancies, to the preparation of loan submissions and the location of sources of finance.

Helandis can also assist foreign investors in dealing with government agencies and statutory bodies such as the Investment Promotion Authority and the Departments of Industrial Relations and Immigration. Arranging extensions of business, employment or dependent visas and assistance with passport and work permit applications are some of the services offered in this area. An associated company, Niuguini Commercial Debt Collection Agencies, looks after this very important aspect of commercial life.

Isaac Minicus and his fellow directors are able to assist in all areas of commercial management, be it for an individual project or for day-to-day or long-term company operations. As Isaac says "My greatest satisfaction is in assisting clients to create a company, guiding it through the process of establishment and into successful businesses. And there will be a lot more of these to enjoy as Papua New Guinea fully develops into the year 2000 and beyond."

In early 1992 the National Executive Council (NEC) approved a major policy paper called Beyond the Minerals Boom. The paper was endorsed by Parliament and was soon after to become the government's industrial policy package up to the year 2000. PNG would no longer rely on resources dug up from underground.

Over the past four years the Department of Commerce and Industry have facilitated more projects than ever before. Some of these are completed and are in production, while others are in the planning or construction stages. In just three years, a total of nearly K1 billion in new investments were attracted under the industrialisation policy.

The result has been the establishment of several major industrial projects in the country. Some are now producing, while others have been approved or are being negotiated. These include the Halla cement factory in Lae, a number of fish canneries and several oil refinery projects. Battery manufacturing and numerous other small to medium scale manufacturing projects are coming to fruition under the industrial centres scheme. Many other proposed projects have been marred with controversy and others have been delayed.

Because of changing policies and priorities since independence, industry was not allowed to develop at the pace that PNG's Asian neighbours pursued. Numerous governments have seen this department change names five times: Labour and Industry, Commerce and Business Development, Industrial Development, Trade and Industry and now Commerce and Industry.

However, commerce and industry has really moved forward over the last four years, much of the advancement being the result of the efforts of Minister David Mai and his team of public servants headed by Secretary Robert Igara and his successor, Chris Vihruri.

Mr Mai, a former premier of Simbu Province, feels very strongly about his work and especially the policy initiatives he has been involved with, particularly Beyond the Minerals Boom. His strong support of these initiatives has seen him vigorously opposing the World Bank sponsored 'Structural Adjustment' programme, which, among others things, has recommended the removal of the reserved business activities for national or citizen businessmen and women. Manufacturing and construction have been the first areas hit by trade liberalisation. He has also been strongly opposed to de-controlling of prices and privatisation. In a cabinet resuffle in July 1995 he moved to Agriculture and Livestock after being Commerce and Industry minister for four years.

"If I had my way, I would remain with Commerce and Industry. My vision is for Papua New Guinea to achieve some degree of industrialisation," Mr Mai said at his farewell party. "Commerce and Industry is one of the best run departments in the public service. The professionals and staff in the Department have helped me a great deal. I am a better person and minister of government now."

For the future, Mr Mai wants new ministers to the post to carry on from where he left off. "PNG must expand its manufacturing base and move towards import substitution and more value-added exports."

This policy recognises that the private sector is the engine for growth. The department will be the catalyst and partner for development. The targets that were set were:

- Industrial sector to contribute at least 35 per cent of gross domestic product and provide 80,000 jobs or 20 per cent of total formal employment.
- Greater emphasis on an export-driven economy with manufactured exports being doubled.
- Establishment of a strong PNG business sector with increased ownership and participation by nationals.
- Expansion of downstream processing facilities.
- Improved infrastructure to support industries.
- Formation of regional development centres and
- Equal opportunities for women and meaningful participation by them in the workforce, business and industry.

The overall industry policy is to promote domestic manufacturing. The private sector is encouraged to set up labour intensive industries and to relocate industry from other countries to PNG.

The Department's aspirations, policies, plans and programmes are all targeted at taking "bold and pioneering measures to develop new industries," especially those which would ensure a sound and self-sustaining export-driven economy.

The prime targets are the small scale to medium businesses. These are the engines for economic development, not the giant multi-national corporations..

For example, in 1992 the Department and Ministry were responsible for devising the "Beyond the Minerals Boom" policy. It supplies policy guidelines and a vision for year 2000. The policy addresses the question: "Where to after the mining and petroleum resources have been depleted?" The Department's answer is: in manufacturing and exports.

Major projects that the Department and Ministry have facilitated and which are now in production include the Lae (Halla) cement project and Lae mackerel cannery, where a total of K67 million has so far been invested.

Projects under construction in 1995 include the K55 million "ZZZ" tuna cannery in Madang and the Motukea oil refinery project, worth K215 million.

Projects that have been approved are Battery manufacturing for K5 million and the Pacific Fish Cannery to be located in Port Moresby for K8.8 million.

Projects under negotiations in 1995 are Phase Two of Halla cement in Lae worth K170 million and the K75 million Kopi Oil refinery in Gulf Province.

144

Over the past 4 years, the Department and the Ministry have worked on incentives to encourage investment in the manufacturing and industrial sector. These include:

- contribution of 50 per cent to feasibility studies for projects,
- government credit guarantee scheme (now discontinued),
- industrial financing provided through the European Investment Bank especially for manufacturing projects, and
- fiscal incentives which include pioneer industry schemes incorporating tax holidays, double deduction staff training schemes, new product exemptions, rural development incentives, reduced duty on imports for manufacturing, tariff measures to protect local manufacturing, wages subsidy schemes, industrial centres with government subsidised electricity and other utilities and, lastly, free zones where the government permits entry of major consumers of goods to encourage commercial activities to flourish.

Other, nonfiscal incentives are:

- policy intervention where the Department recommends to other service providers to give special rates to investors to reduce their costs,
- organisational reforms to ensure efficient promotion of investments,
- investment guarantees against expropriations,
- bi-lateral investment agreements with other countries to protect those countries' investments in PNG,
- double taxation agreements with Australia, Canada, United Kingdom, Malaysia and Germany, which protect companies from those countries being double taxed and
- special trade agreements.

There are constraints that the Department and Ministry will have to take into account and to work towards overcoming. They include a small, fragmented domestic market, a short supply of skilled labor, high labour costs, high costs of land, housing, transport and utilities, inappropriate technology and persistent law and order problems. All these are attrib-

145

uted to the high structural cost of the economy.

The other major threat to the vision set out in 'Beyond the Minerals Boom' would be the move to free trade and the removal of protective incentives for PNG citizen businesses. PNG's membership of

organisations such as the World Trade Organisation and the Asia Pacific Economic Co-operation (APEC) means the country must pursue free trade policies. Freeing up trade will encourage foreign investors in those areas but will have a negative impact on indigenous businesses.

The Department's target for the next few years are industries based in agriculture, forestry, fisheries, mining and petroleum, textiles, chemical and engineering. Others include waste paper recycling, stationery and automotive parts.

Within the sphere of the Ministry of Commerce and Industry are several important statutory organisations and sections.

The Investment Promotion Authority (IPA) is the most important of them. The IPA has its main objective to promote Papua New Guinea abroad as a location for investment. It has also been actively pushing for joint ventures between PNG businessmen and women and foreign investors. IPA, which succeeded the National Investment Development Authority (NIDA) in 1992, has also successfully updated and improved investment laws and procedures. IPA now has the tag "one stop shop" for investors. IPA has its own act and is headed by one of a growing number PNG women professionals, Aivu Tauvasa.

The Small Business Development Corporation

(SBDC) aims to promote and facilitate the growth of indigenous business sector. SBDC has succeeded to some degree, but funding constraints have not allowed it to venture further.

The others include Industrial Centres Development Corporation (ICDC), Construction Industry Development Authority and National Institute of Industrial Technology (NISIT). These authorities all aim to achieve industrialisation as the vehicle for the creation of employment and economic growth for the country.

The Papua New Guinea Investment Authority is a statutory body set up to promote and facilitate investment in all sectors of the economy.

The idea is that potential investors should contact the IPA for information about the law which governs business in PNG, and to seek out both business and investment possibilities.

There are many incentives for the foreign investor in Papua New Guinea, from tax holidays of five to ten years for 'pioneer' industries or new businesses in certain designated rural areas, to wage subsidies for new manufacturing enterprises and various export promotion incentives. There are also other advantages which have been negotiated by the government, such as preferential access to a number of overseas markets for certain products manufactured in PNG. The IPA can explain the details of these incentives, promotions and trade agreements to interested parties.

While PNG's mining and petroleum industries offer some of the most attractive investment opportunities for any investor, the IPA will offer advice and information on investment opportunities in all areas, and in all business types. Some of the most promising sectors are fisheries, agriculture, manufacturing and forestry. The IPA currently has hundreds of potential investment opportunities from all of these sectors, some with detailed studies already completed, while others have brief marketing reports.

Joint ventures, are one of the many ways in which foreign investors can participate in the PNG economy. A foreign investor can team up with a local partner which may, for instance, be a government department or a locally registered company. The IPA can provide all the information on the process of setting up a joint venture, and can help a foreign investor find an appropriate partner.

The IPA is able to deal with investor applications for certification within 35 days and process company registration and other applications within seven days. With its network of links with various government agencies and departments, the IPA can walk investors through the process of securing the necessary approvals, permits and licences. Its growing database can help businesses find supplies and connect with retailers. The most common enquiry, though, is for assistance in helping to find a business partner, which it is often able to effect using the database of foreign and domestic investors and by arranging introductions.

The IPA deals with several hundred enquiries from the public each week.

It recently completed a nation-wide survey to help counter the chronic problem of a general lack of information in the country, particularly at the provincial level. The results of this survey have proved to be very useful, not only helping to identify investment opportunities in the provinces, but also revealing areas where policy changes were required in order to boost investor confidence.

This kind of information can be fed back to the relevant government departments and changes can be made.

Another major activity currently under way is the review of the Companies Act. Changes are being made in this Act to accommodate changing business conditions and to prepare for the planned Papua New Guinea Stock Exchange. The IPA is helping the government in its efforts to start this Stock Exchange, which, once established, would obviously further facilitate investment and economic development.

Specific services offered by the IPA include: a montly newsletter which highlights Joint Venture business opportunities, the Investor and Promotion Services Division to help approval process in relation to the investment (modest fee is charged for this service) help with the Companies Act, the Business Names Act and the Trademarks Act; there are very few limits on the types of investment that can be entered into.

For an organisation in its infancy the Industrial Centres Development Corporation has already made a substantial impression in Papua New Guinea.

Not only has it helped propel industry to the top of the government's priority list but it has also sparked the interest of both foreign and local investors in Papua New Guinean products.

"We still have a long way to go," admitted Gerald Mwayubu, the organisation's operations manager. "But we have got off to an auspicious start and I am confident that with our help this country's industrial base will go from strength to strength."

The ICDC is especially keen to generate interest in locally processed products and local manufacturing.

The ICDC is a statutory agency of the Ministry of Commerce and Industry. It is a semi autonomous organisation. It is headed by a managing director, Mr. Stanis Bai, who runs it partly as a government concern and partly as a business. "After twenty years in banking, I know how to deal with companies and their needs. And I have a good team here. One of our successes is that we were able to win support from key Government departments like Finance and our own Department of Commerce and Industry."

"The fact that the organisation balances both governmental and business aspects is to its advantage," said Gerald Mwaybu. "To a great extent the two areas compliment each other."

Other than encouraging local manufacturing the ICDC has taken the initiative to establish industrial

centres in specific urban areas. These provide local and foreign entrepreneurs with ready made factory units and multi functional industrial land.

The Mahalang Industrial Centre in Lae, which opened in 1993, has proved a major lure to all kinds of investors. The K10 million development is a multi-functional site comprising factory buildings and worksheds. As much care has been taken over the supporting infrastructure as over the buildings. Roads, surface water drainage, sewerage, water supply, electricity system and telecommunication system are all in place before a single operator sets up shop.

"The beauty of Malahang is that it takes away all the headaches for investors," said Gerald. "Whether they want to use the factories for food processing or simply for storage everything is already sorted out for them."

Major manufacturers with venture capital and small private enterprises are equally attractive targets for ICDC. Now the talk is of encouraging nursery units. Small entrepreneurs can be developed with help from the Ministry of Commerce.

"We will replace import with export. Create jobs for Papua New Guinea. What we have printed on our T-shirts is ICDC - Landlord: Industrial Centres," quips Gerald. "What is crucial is title to the land, there must be no misunderstandings." It is with this caution in mind that ICDC are negotiating for a new site in Rabaul and another in Port Moresby.

The difficulties normally encountered in acquiring land for industrial use under the country's complex land tenure system and the lack of industrial sites with adequate infrastructure are major obstacles to the development of industry, particularly for the private sector. ICDC cuts through those problems.

The opportunities and incentives will be there for businesses. ICDC see themselves as spearheading the industrialisation process in PNG. PNG may be behind other Asian countries like Malaysia, Singapore, China and the Philippines but they intend to catch up. They are encouraged by the support of the Asian Development Bank.

ICDC is itself a business. They too have to maintain efficiency and cost effectiveness. Their commitment to their clients is encoded in their slogan, "YOUR PARTNER IN PROSPERITY".

PAPUA NEW GUINEA CHAMBER OF COMMERCE

Whether you are a self-employed graphic designer or the managing director of a multi-national company, the Chamber of Commerce will welcome you onto its membership list.

The Chamber, which has been running for over 50 years, encourages the involvement of every type of business in order to achieve a wide cross-section of ideas and experience. The current president, Adrian Warupi, sees the Chamber's main purpose as offering its 1000 or so members an opportunity for mutual support and advice. "All the members of the Chamber help each other out," says Adrian, "and the Chamber is especially useful for newcomers to Papua New Guinea."

During his period as President, Adrian wants to highlight the importance of self-reliance to Papua New Guinea. In particular, he wants to see reliance to a greater degree on local, rather than international, investment. He wants to emphasise the value of agriculture. "Of course two of the biggest developments over the last decade have been in mining and more recently in forestry. But while they are lucrative resources they will never provide the same number of jobs as agriculture. It is a grassroots profession and one in which we should increase our investment. There should be more agricultural colleges, for instance. There should be more vocational education of all sorts."

While acknowledging the central role of agriculture, the Chamber of Commerce is keenly interested in increasing the number of people in the cash economy. At present, out of the population of nearly 4 million, only 20% have jobs, professions or occupations that provide a cash income.

"We need to have more local employment generated," says Adrian. "For example, whole timber logs are still being exported from this country. These should be processed in Papua New Guinea."

One of the roles of the Chamber of Commerce is to offer the Government constructive criticism and advice.

"Government spending has sometimes been wasteful and disorganised. For businesses to grow, government must create a positive investment climate. Improvements in basic infrastructure must be a matter of priority.

"This country is rich with resources and we are not a divided nation. No one tribal group could ever be big enough to dominate the rest of society. To that extent we have built-in security. There are also not many of us – only a few million. We should be able to manage our affairs so that our inherent wealth benefits all."

The Chamber of Commerce exists to promote that aim.

PAPUA NEW GUINEA CHAMBER OF MANUFACTURERS

It makes no difference whether you are a self employed wood carver or the managing director of an enormous food factory, the Papua New Guinea Chamber of Manufacturers deserves your support.

This enterprising organisation welcomes all manufacturers to its members list in order to generate the widest possible cross section of opinions and ideas.

The impact of the chamber on Papua New Guinea has been something of a phenomenon. Formed in 1991, it has been propelled from initial obscurity into one of the most influential and respected bodies in the country.

"It is only when all the manufacturers in this country combine their individual strengths that Papua New Guinea can move forward," explained Wayne Golding, the Chamber's straight-talking chairman.

"It is essential PNG starts to process more products locally rather than sending them abroad. Only by doing this can this country graduate to a more industry-based economy."

The role of the chamber is to offer its 2,500 strong members both information and assistance on all aspects of manufacturing and to promote competitively priced Papua New Guinean products, not only across the country, but world-wide.

"The chamber is always pushing to create more export opportunities," said Wayne. "Since 1992 we have been holding an annual trade fair in Port Moresby. Although it is still very much a local event I think in time it will spark interest from abroad.

"Creating a solid manufacturing industry in Papua New Guinea is the only way to combat unemployment and the best way to benefit the long term prosperity of the country."

Although the Chamber of Manufacturers is apolitical it is not without influence on government policy. A phrase the chamber likes to use to sum up its political stance is "negotiation not confrontation." It prides itself on working with the government rather than against it.

The chamber not only airs the concerns of its members with the relevant ministries but offers advice to the government on everything from fiscal planning to customs duty and tariffs.

Manufacturers in this country are becoming increasingly innovative," stressed Wayne. "A new cannery to process locally caught fish is in the pipeline and there are moves to have more timber processed internally.

"While some developed countries have already exhausted their manufacturing base, in PNG we are only just starting to discover ours. I am very optimistic for the future."

153

"There is hardly anything in the world that some man cannot make a little worse and sell a little cheaper. The people who consider price only are this man's lawful prey."

This quote has pride of place at the reception desk of Hornibrook NGI in Port Moresby. It is a fitting thought for a company that has built its reputation on the high quality of its products.

Hornibrook is Papua New Guinea's leading steel fabrication contractor; that is, an engineering firm that makes goods to order by casting, welding and forging steel.

"We can make anything that is made of steel," said Managing Director Mal Lewis, "whether it's a huge fuel tank or small baskets to carry fish. We can make pylons for carrying electric cables and gold processing tanks for mines just as readily as steel tables for commercial kitchens and restaurants."

Hornibrook NGI was formed over fifty years ago through the merger of two existing steel fabrication businesses, Steamships Trading Company and Hornibrook Constructions. This has turned out to have been a productive combination and Hornibrook NGI has comfortably retained its pre-eminent position in the steel industry ever since.

With workshops at Port Moresby and Lae, Hornibrook processes up to 1,000 tonnes of  steel a month. Heavy duty steel is used for making bridges, tanks, processing plants and big buildings, while the lighter 'space frame' steel is used for transportable offices or buildings with up to a 20 metre roof span. Hornibrook is also a shipbuilder - in fact, PNG's only shipbuilder - and last year launched a 30 metre long barge from their slipway in Port Moresby.

"The key to our success is our staff," said Mal Lewis. "We train our 500 national and 22 expatriate staff to international standards both here in Port Moresby and overseas and we keep on training. We are proud of our staff."

With its diverse range of clients and products and its readiness and ability to take on new design briefs, Hornibrook NGI has a large part to play in the continuing development of PNG.

Howard Porter is a long-established Australian company which is one of that country's largest and most diversified motor body builders.

Truck bodies and trailers, waste collection and recycling equipment, fuel tankers and various kinds of giant tipping trucks are all made by Howard Porter and are in use throughout the Pacific region.

Howard Porter (PNG) Pty Ltd was established in 1992 as a joint venture between Howard Porter Australia and Hornibrook NGI, thus combining the expertise of a master motor body builder with PNG's major steel fabrication contractor.

"The in-country manufacture of standard ranges of transport equipment saves on import duty as well as providing employment and training opportunities for PNG citizens," says Managing Director Dave Howard. "It also allows for the customizing of equipment to suit a client's particular need."

Based in Lae, Howard Porter (PNG) Pty Ltd makes and repairs a comprehensive range of transport equipment for PNG's expanding road system and industrial sector, equipment such as standard semi tri-axle trailers and tray bodies, dropside bodies and trays for tipping trucks. Equipment adapted for particular local applications includes trays for coffee trucks and frames for PMV's. Howard Porter supplies a long list of agricultural equipment together with grain and livestock trailers, fire tenders, water tankers, and waste collecting equipment.

As logging and mining have developed as major sectors of the PNG economy, Howard Porter has been able to tender for the specialized equipment they inevitably require, for example: timber jinkers (the trailers for logging vehicles), drop-deck semi-trailers, loaders, dumpers and service vehicles for the mining industry.

Liquids such as palm oil and petroleum have to be transported in tankers. Howard Porter makes tankers in both steel and aluminium.

A retail spare parts outlet was established in 1994 with a wide range of stock from manufacturers around the world.

"Although we are based in Lae, we work closely with Hornibrook in Port Moresby," says Dave Howard. "Between us we can deal quickly with customers' demands from anywhere in PNG."

Howard Porter has a corporate mission to expand even further than PNG, to provide internationally competitive, quality products to the surrounding regions..

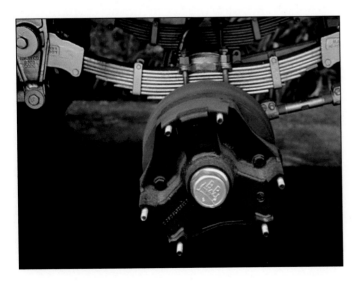

155

Mobil is a household name all round the world. In PNG the company runs a complex distribution and marketing operation of Mobil oil products - some 250 million litres a year.

"Mobil began operations here in 1922, long before I was born!" says Corporate Affairs Manager Namon Mawason. "Twenty six years ago they provided the scholarship money to send me to Australia to school and, when I came back, they found some more to give me three years study at PNG University of Technology at Lae. I studied Business Administration and

majored in Marketing and that fits in very well with the job I have now."

Mobil's ocean terminals were opened after the Second World War in Lae in 1950, in Port Moresby in 1951 and in Madang, Wewak and Kavieng before 1960. Further investment followed at Alotau, Rabaul, Vanimo, Kimbe and Kieta, completing the chain of coastal facilities.

Refined products are imported from Singapore and Australia and then redistributed by smaller tankers around the coast and by truck into the Highlands region. Lubricants are shipped directly from Australia into the various centres where they're needed.

In recent years Mobil has invested in new inland depots, service stations and bulk aviation refuelling facilities. This distribution network is supported by the Port Moresby headquarters where the bulk of the employees work. The staff is smaller now than it was at Independence, 90 compared with 130, and expatriate numbers have gone down from 35 to 10. Distribution and retail sales however are handled by local distributors and dealers, who themselves account for another thousand jobs.

"Mobil dedicates a large amount of time and resources to the development and sales of lubricants and in PNG this tradition continues", says Namon Mawason. "We employ three lubrication engineers to provide technical support to the customers. They're backed by Mobil's technical group world-wide and can therefore provide the most up to date lubricants, including the most modern synthetic ones, and lubrication advice to match."

Mobil plans to continue expanding their facilities and services to meet the growing needs of PNG. Significant effort is devoted to increasing the expertise of local staff and this will continue to ensure that Mobil can deliver what their customers want, maintaining the reputation of Mobil as the No. 1 Team.

"To cut steel you have to burn oxygen and acetylene together at 3000 degrees centigrade", said Barry Burke, Managing Director of BOC Gases Papua New Guinea.

Oxygen and acetylene, like the rest of the 165 chemicals sold by BOC, are gases. They are manufactured at BOC's main plant in Lae, stored in re-useable cylinders and distributed to users throughout PNG. BOC also stocks the welding machines with which the gases are used and even the safety boots and other protective clothing that a welder has to wear.

Their main business, though, is the gases themselves. With a brand new K1.5 million acetylene plant, BOC is one of PNG's major manufacturers and a source of employment and training for local engineers.

"The new acetylene plant was installed by our own local engineers", said Barry. "We import the raw materials, calcium carbide and acetone, and make the gas right here."

Members of the general public not directly involved in activities like welding may be surprised to find how many gases are in everyday use in PNG - and how many of them are supplied by BOC.

"We stock LPG, which stands for liquefied petroleum gas, from Australia. That's the gas that's used for cooking. We also import medical oxygen and nitrous oxides for hospitals, sell helium for weather balloons and nitrogen for inflating the tyres of earth-moving equipment. We have lots of carbon dioxide which is the fizz in soft drinks and is also used in fire extinguishers, and we have just started stocking a new gas with a really nice smell which is made from tea-tree oil. Called 'Bactigas', it fights air-borne fungus and bacteria and can be injected into the air-conditioning units of hospitals and offices."

'Bactigas' is only the most recent of the long list of mostly invisible, intangible but potent substances which are BOC's stock-in-trade and which are increasingly in demand as PNG takes further steps towards industrial development.

Boroko Motors sells motor vehicles, especially Nissan cars, vans and trucks, together with Ford tractors and a full range of agricultural machinery. It also supplies construction and mining equipment, boats, outboard motors, tyres and spare parts. It has been a supplier of Ford tractors for over 30 years and is the largest automotive distributor in Papua New Guinea.

It is also a large employer, by PNG standards, with 340 people on the pay-roll, about 30 of whom are expatriates. Since 1965 it has been part of the W.R. Carpenter group of companies, which has branches throughout the Pacific. The group has investments in many different industries such as coffee, cocoa and other plantations, as well as supermarkets and hardware stores.

Boroko Motors has nine branches throughout the country, in Port Moresby, Lae, Mt. Hagen, Madang, Kimbe, Rabaul, Popondetta and Tabubil. But it aims

to serve customers in the whole of PNG. Because of the nature of the terrain, this is no slight undertaking. The rugged geography and the lack of roads combine to make delivering agricultural machinery, for example, a difficult task. Boroko Motors often has to use aircraft and helicopters to get vehicles and machines to their final destination. Many pieces of equipment have to be dismantled before they can be flown in.

Some of Boroko Motors largest clients are the big sugar cane and oil palm plantations, all of whom use many tractors for their haulage work, and the PNG Government itself, which requires not only tractors but a range of other agricultural machines. The growth of the mining and timber industries has provided another group of corporate customers, this time for equipment like blast hole drills and logging trucks. Individual clients are an equally important market and Boroko stocks small tractors and other cultivators that are suitable for village smallholdings.

As a long-standing and substantial business, with well-understood responsibilities to both clients and staff, Boroko Motors is a familiar feature of the PNG commercial scene.

Ela Motors is an instantly recognised name in Papua New Guinea. Until two years ago it was part of Burns Philp the largest importer of new motor vehicles in the country. Now Ela Motors has entered a new era. It has become part of the Toyota family.

John Dapling, General Manager for a scant eight months is conscious of the reputation he has inherited. "Toyota is possibly the strongest and most reliable vehicle manufactured and therefore ideal for PNG", he says.

Ela Motors has more outlets in more areas of PNG than any other motor dealer. It covers all four geographical regions, owning outlets in 13 separate locations, including all the major towns. It has dealers in four more, making 17 outlets in all. "We sell from the very smallest motor-bike, generator or water pump to the heaviest of trucks and large excavation and earth moving equipment. We have a huge advantage because our customers can expect a similar standard of service throughout the country. Our after sales service keeps all this equipment functioning efficiently."

Training is crucial to their success. Ela Motors is proud to claim that its training school in Port Moresby is the only such school accepted as a Technical College by the Government. Training covers Management, Computers, Service, Parts and Sales. The company sends trainers to regional branches to carry out training in the latest product development. It uses the facilities of the Toyota Motor Corporation in Sydney who have one of the most modern training installations in the South Pacific Region. Also it actually sends people to Japan for training knowing that it will develop a highly skilled staff back home in PNG.

What is the future of Ela Motors? John Dapling laughs and says, "I've been here for 8 months now which seems like yesterday. Three weeks before I arrived the volcano erupted in Rabaul and since then we have had currency devaluation, the foreign exchange has been frozen and many more problems to contend with. But you have to make the most of the situation.

"Basically the philosophy of the company is that we think long term. Japanese manufacturers all make very long term plans and we have probably adopted a little bit of that philosophy from our Japanese parents. We look at PNG and we think: we'll keep on training and see the good times again."

Computers and Communications, with more than 40 employees and offices in both Port Moresby and Lae, is one of Papua New Guinea's leading computer companies.

Started eight years ago by Tony Royle and Gideon Kakabin, its business is to to sell computers and to train people how to use them.

Specializing in Compaq machines, the company provides for the computing requirements of a range of clients throughout PNG. Tony, an Englishman, has been selling, installing and servicing computers in Port Moresby for the last 15 years. As General Manager he is responsible for the day-to-day running of the business while Gideon specializes in applications, software programming and implementation.

One problem that affects the computer industry in PNG is the lack of copyright protection for software, which means that there is little incentive for software designers to invest time and money devising new programmes. The practice of copying software and trying to use it without much assistance is associated with what Gideon perceives to be a rather slack attitude to computer education and training as a whole in PNG. Computers and Communications now runs a whole range of training programmes in order to remedy this situation.

"We were shocked at how ignorant many people were about computers," said Gideon. "And this does not refer to first-time buyers only. We could see that there was an urgent need to help the owners of computers get the most out of their machines."

Computers and Communications' courses last from one to four days and cover many specific computer applications, from a one-day general introduction to advanced spreadsheets, payrolls and ledgers. "Even small businesses are finding that computers can simplify their operations and save them money in the process," says Gideon. "We have clients all over PNG, ranging from the large user with say 20 to 30

terminals in their installation to the owner of a single machine for use in the home."

Experience from round the world indicates that the market in computers is set for expansion for many years to come as their prices come down and the range of tasks they can perform increases. Papua New Guinea will be no exception and it is firms like Computers and Communications who will make that future come about.

When Remington Pitney Bowes set up their first office in Port Moresby back in 1948 - many years before their competitors arrived in town - their products were basic and limited.

Now, in their recently re-vamped offices in Munidubu Street, they market every type of office machine imaginable, ranging from state of the art facsimiles and photocopiers to pocket dictaphones.

Remington Pitney Bowes need no introduction. With 12 offices in PNG they are a houshold name and the Pitney Bowes parent company, worth $3.5 billion, has a high profile world-wide.

Managing Director, Ian McKay puts the company's success down to a combination of professionalism and a continual quest to provide 100 percent customer satisfaction.

Pitney Bowes. Over the last year company turnover has reached an unprecedented high, more than a 20% boost in business despite a stagnant national economy. Ian McKay thinks the future looks even more promising.

"One of the most encouraging signs is the sustained enthusiasm and dedication of the local staff. Remington Pitney Bowes offers extensive training to them and gives them the chance to study abroad so they can return to Papua New Guinea with fresh skills and ideas."

"The statistics speak for themselves. In 1990 there

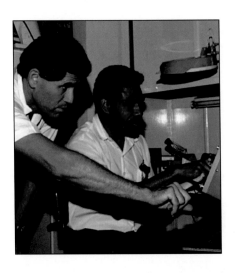  

"Pitney Bowes produce most of our products," said Ian. "This means we cannot blame suppliers or anyone else if something goes wrong. The buck stops with us. We are responsible for every single part of the business. For this reason we have to maintain exceptionally high standards."

"When we deliver a machine we accept that we have an on-going obligation to look after it. Port Moresby is a relatively small place. There are not many new clients to attract, so we make every effort to hold onto the ones we already have. For this reason our company always puts the customer first."

This philosophy has worked well for Remington

were 20 expatriate employees in the company and this year there are only six. This is a very positive indication for the future."

The staff at Remington Pitney Bowes also have talents outside of their work. One salesman plays the blues on his guitar at various Port Moresby venues in the evenings and another is a champion weight lifter. The office exudes energy and Ian insists that staff only produce their best if they're having fun, so he makes sure they do. "Equally", he says, "the sense of community is important to the staff and to their company. That's just one of the reasons why we are among the official sponsors of the Independence celebrations - and a major one at that."

When Bruce Dahlenburg arrived in PNG as a young civil aviation engineer back in 1975, he believed he would be back in Australia within five years. But that is not how things worked out!

Bruce recognised the opportunity for a viable consumer electronics company and opened Daltron Electronics Pty Ltd in 1977. Since then it has emerged as one of the country's leading Information System and Office Equipment suppliers.

"I started Daltron with my car and limited funds. I rented a small office in Boroko and began selling hi-fis and portable stereos," Bruce recalled with a laugh.

"It was hard work but I could see a gaping hole in the market, crying out to be filled, especially in service and repair. At that time it was very difficult to get electronic products repaired in PNG, so I began using the slogan "We Service What We Sell!" I still attribute much of our success to that philosophy. We will always stand by the products we sell."

Once the full impact of the computer revolution reached Papua New Guinea, Daltron took another step forward by introducing photocopiers and facsimile machines to their product line providing complete information management solutions to their clients.

Now in 1995 Daltron have moved into the big time. They are building a K1.6 million manufacturing outfit, including a new showroom and office,

just over the road from their showroom in Waigani Drive.

NiuLogic is the first computer to be fully assembled in PNG. Following their reputation for service Daltron offer a 3 year guarantee. It would not be possible without Daltron's efforts in training.

Training is a vital part of running a business in PNG. At Daltron, all of the 50 staff benefit from comprehensive in-house training and many are sponsored to attend additional technical courses. Daltron also caters to the computer training needs of the general public with a regular timetable of computer courses.

"This is one of the most exciting places in the world to conduct technology-based business," added Bruce. "Papua New Guineans are not afraid of new technology. We do not encounter the resistance to learning computer skills which is common in many other parts of the world. In the future we will do what we have always done: assess the needs of the market and provide the best products available to meet those needs."

It is no idle boast when BNG Trading uses the words "a wealth of experience" as its motto - after all the company has been in Papua New Guinea since 1924.

Current general manager, Uwe Fock, arrived in Port Moresby as a young apprentice from Germany over 23 years ago and has spent the bulk of that time with the company.

Although BNG has been trading in Port Moresby for over 60 years, it is still an expanding enterprise and now has offices countrywide. BNG has its own offices in Lae, Goroka, Mount Hagen, Wewak, Madang, Rabaul, Kiunga and Kevenga. The head office is in Port Moresby.

"We are a very traditional, well established company," explained Uwe. "This gives us a degree of respectability but we also like to show that we are not afraid of innovation or moving with the times."

The company focuses mainly on importing food - especially tinned meat from Denmark, fish from Japan, Fiji and Chile and processed poultry, both chicken and goose, from mainland China. It also trades in a wide range of other items such as electrical goods, agricultural fertilisers and building materials from all over the world. And BNG serves as the local agent for such international names as Macintosh, Canon, Brother, Philips (from Singapore) and Samsung (from Korea).

"Electronic goods have a wide open market in Papua New Guinea," stressed Uwe. "Since the introduction of MTV in the late 1980's, television sales have spiralled and even now show little sign of slowing down.

"Refrigerators are other items that are selling well. A decade ago fridges were a rarity in Port Moresby but now they are commonplace. The public are now becoming more adventurous and willing to buy frozen meat or fish as opposed to just cans. We are responding to these new demands.

"We are always looking at innovative ways of both boosting the local economy and providing employment. The best way to do this is by processing products locally rather than abroad. Papua New Guinea has so much untapped potential," stressed Uwe. "In my opinion this country is the Middle East of the South Pacific. We are sitting on a pot of gold here - it is just a case of utilising it. I am very optimistic for the future."

Sir Dan Leahy came to Papua New Guinea in 1947 as a boy of 17 to join one of his uncles as a farmhand on a farm near Lae. The Leahy family was already famous in the area through the pre-war exploration of the Highlands. Dan's uncle Michael Leahy led the first expedition by Europeans - to discover that the Highlands were already well populated.

Dan himself came up to Goroka in 1949. It was a different place then, tree-less, with scattered villages, and people who had been little affected by European contact. Everything was done by hand. Timber was hand-sawn in the Leahy family saw-mill. Roads, of a sort, were being carved out of the hillsides by hand. Before long the young man saw an opportunity to strike out on his own. Starting in a grass house, he began trading in a modest way, supplying salt, knives, tomahawks and spades to the local people. The currency was shell, which had to come up from the coast by footpath. It was the era of Australian colonial policy. Peace was enforced by the Kiaps. The road from Lae to Hagen was built. Dan sold clothes, matches, tinned fish, bully-beef, hard biscuit, rice. More Europeans arrived. In the early sixties Dan teamed up with his cousin, Edgar Collins, and formed a company - Collins and Leahy.

In the early 80's the road from Lae through Goroka to Mt Hagen was sealed (metalled) and, with electrification, trade increased greatly in the Highlands.

In 1986 Collins and Leahy acquired a one-third share in "Steamies" (Steamships Trading Company) and so got involved in hotels, property, shipping, transport, steel fabrication, timber, automotive and industrial services.

Manufacturing soon followed, the products being soft drinks, ice-cream and such. By 1994 the company listed aviation and road transport as major areas of activity with the 100% ownership of a helicopter company. There is also an agricultural sector specialising in coffee, cattle and cocoa.

Collins and Leahy is a wholly PNG-owned company. It employs 2,500 people of whom all but the odd hundred or so are PNG nationals. It has come a long way since the early days when Dan Leahy traded tomahawks and kina shell in a grass house somewhere

near Goroka but it remains close to its roots, its future closely bound to that of the Highlands.

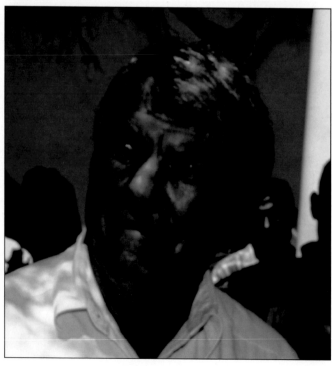

TREID PACIFIC (PNG) PTY LTD

"We make sure that educational supplies, paid for by sponsors or from pubic funds, are delivered right into the hands of the beneficiaries they're intended for," says Wilson David, General Manager of Treid Pacific (PNG) Pty Ltd, "and that means the children, their parents or the teachers."

This nationally owned company provides a unique 'door-to-door' delivery service of basic school materials, text books, office items, science and sports equipment to 80% of the 2,700 community schools in PNG.

It goes without saying that many of these schools are in remote locations. Sometimes the only access is by river boat, or even dinghy. Sometimes a fixed wing plane can use a local airstrip, sometimes only a helicopter will do the job. In the most inaccessible areas, after a jolting, squelchy pass in a 4WD, a team of carriers, often the school children themselves, must traverse the last few miles on foot. Treid Pacific organises, directs, and pays for all of this.

The objective is crystal clear: the educational materials (even if they're only pencils, paper, chalk and paper clips) must reach their target and be accounted for. So the company makes sure that every parent or teacher, or the children themselves, sign a receipt for the materials supplied. There's often a little ceremony when the supplies arrive at a school or a provincial District centre, but even when there isn't, there's always a receipt!

Administrators are delighted at this solution to a very real problem. They know that materials have arrived and they know that their calculations as to how long the materials should last have been acknowledged and accepted by teachers and parents alike. What's more, delivery is comparatively quick. Detailed packing lists may be sent direct to suppliers, even when these are far away overseas, and large consignments delivered to PNG ports by container. From these centres, Treid Pacific's staff have considerable expertise in hiring transportation, from mining company choppers to locally owned canoes, and in the process forging links with the Provincial and District officials who help to administer the system. In other words, teamwork.

"We're already planning to extend the scheme to the delivery of school and university text books," says Wilson David, "and some of our satisfied clients in remote areas are asking why we can't go further, and apply it to packs of basic medical supplies - antibiotics, malaria tablets, antiseptic ointments, bandages, things like that, for the aid posts in these little communities." Well, why not?

If you buy a T-shirt in PNG and find the brand name 'Kumul' on the label, you could reflect on the success story of the Woo family from Rabaul, now fifth generation in Papua New Guinea.

Fifteen years ago they joined the ranks of the country's clothing manufacturers. Today they are leaders in the field. Out of a total of twenty seven, "Woo Textiles" is one of the handful of PNG clothing manufacturers who are capable of competing in the overseas market-place.

Beginning from scratch, the firm pursued the conviction that local advertisers would be glad to see their names in bright colours on the back of the ubiquitous T-shirt. To exploit this idea, they launched Woo Textiles.

The entire range of plant for the manufacture of the shirts was brought in from Japan. Technicians from

were trained to operate and service them. Months of "hands-on" training for seamstresses followed.

"We were right about the T-shirts," says current managing director Murray Woo, son of James. "They were immediately accepted in the market-place. But then we needed another idea."

It was not long in coming. PNG-ans are fanatical about sport - rugby league for the boys, net-ball for the girls, as well as tennis, volley-ball, basket-ball, softball, golf and darts. Teams for all these games need their own individual 'strip.'

"We're proud of the fact that we manufacture specifically to the requirements of our customers -

Hong Kong were commissioned to install the machines in the new factory at Gordons in Port Moresby. Selected group of Papua New Guineans

colours, logos, stripes, whatever, " says Murray.

And the quality of the product was up to scratch too. So much so that Woo soon won the right to manufacture rugby uniforms under licence for Westmont Active Sportswear of Australia.

Now the product range has encompassed the flags for the 9th South Pacific Games and sports uniforms for the Commonwealth Games in Canada. The company's school, corporate and leisure wear is available at retail outlets nationally. Woo Textiles employs and trains many Papua New Guineans in skills which not only equip them to earn a living, but also enable them to design, cut and sew for their families! A double advantage for them!

167

There is a familiar logo on household shelves in PNG. It shows a man with a strong arm saying "Bikpela na Strongpela". It is the logo of the Lae Biscuit Company, affectionately known as just Lae Biscuits.

PNG consumes tonnes of Lae Biscuits everyday. Lae Biscuits are so popular they are virtually one of the basic food items in PNG. They are called 'navy bis-

cuits' because they were a standard fare on ships in the old days. They're basically a hard long lasting biscuit made from flour and sugar.

Biscuits are one of the most easily portable food products for a rugged and widespread country like PNG. They can be carried into the most remote villages or islands and still be fresh and intact. They do not go stale or soft like normal sweet biscuits and can be eaten anytime without cooking or preparation. All people have to do is open the packet. Lae Biscuits are better than tinned meat or fish. Weight for weight a carton of biscuits will feed and satisfy more people at less cost compared to any other food in PNG.

It could be that this is PNG's first convenience food. There is now a beef flavoured Lae Biscuit which looks like taking over as the biggest selling biscuit in the country.

Director Ian Chow says, "I just grew into biscuit making. I had always been interested in cooking. I started baking and that's how we got into the bakery side". From there began the French Bake House chain of bakeries making all types of breads, cakes, pastries, buns, rolls and pies. French Bake Haus supplies all the major hotels, airlines, government institutions and all supermarkets and shops in PNG.

The 'navy' biscuits are transported to the islands by "Coastal Shipping" a company which operates from Rabaul and Lae, plying the islands with general cargo, bulk fuel and passengers. It operates PNG-designed barges which can deliver to any harbour, without wharf facilities. The company is a nationally owned company and operates as shipowners, shipping operators, ship and fishing agents and stevedores. It has comprehensive wharf and workshop facilities and a shipbuilding and repair slipway in Rabaul.

On April 21st 1995 Wills (PNG) Ltd opened a new cigarette factory and office complex in Madang at a cost of K6.8 million. It was evidence of long term commitment by British-American Tobacco Company, one of the largest tobacco marketers and manufacturers in the world, to investment in Papua New Guinea.

Wills ties with PNG began in the 1960's with Players Gold Leaf cigarettes. In 1971 Wills became WD & HO Wills (PNG) Ltd and began locally manufacturing five different brands. In 1972 Wills established depots in Port Moresby, Rabaul, Lae and Goroka. A year later they began manufacturing Benson and Hedges in Madang. Twenty years later they had been taken over by BAT and changed their name to Wills (PNG) Ltd. The whole operation was moved to Madang and celebrated by the opening of the new cigarette factory.

In 1994 Wills (PNG) Ltd. contributed over K90 million in excise duties to the PNG tax coffers - 7% into PNG's revenue budget. Recently the Company has begun substituting imported material with local products underlining its support in promoting its investment in the country.

The re-location to Madang marked the start of a major reinvestment drive totalling over K10 million. "We are one of the companies who are taking a leading role in promoting investment in line with the country's aspirations," said General Manager, Mak Mokaddem. "Our reinvestment in Papua New Guinea in paid up capital amounts to K5 million but by the time we finish, it will be about K18 million."

Wills (PNG) Ltd, with over 270 workers, is one of the largest private employers in Madang Province. Business and employment opportunities extend to real estate, shipping, hotel conference facilities and accommodation and the employment of local residents through the engagement of security companies and other tradesmen including catering services. The whole of Madang's small economy has benefited from the Wills relocation.

Within the new plant Wills produces leading international cigarette brands Benson & Hedges and Kool, as well as a range of tobacco, the most notable of which is the range within the Spear Brand.

The new factory is a state-of-the-art fully air-conditioned building including the latest technology in network fibre-optic cabling which enables the Company to link all its productions departments and depots. It incorporates an office complex which includes a clinic, a consultation room and an Intensive Care Unit for its employees. The staff canteen has a 60-seat capacity. The designers included a water reservoir with its own treatment plant in preparation for Madang's notorious dry spells, and at a cost of K220,000, an effluent treatment plant which takes an 'environmentally friendly' approach to dealing with wastes from the factory.

Wills have always been a safety conscious company. The Madang factory has been designed to the highest international standards and includes many safety features. In addition they conduct frequent checks and run courses to maintain a high safety record.

Since the move to Madang, a programme of nationalisation has begun with a huge recruitment drive to employ highly qualified Papua New Guineans. "To be effective, the Company is going to get the best talent, who we will then train and develop", stressed Televika Faite, the Personnel & Corporate affairs manager. Over the last three years the drive has already resulted in the employment of 11 qualified nationals at management level.

The benefits of Wills (PNG) relocation to Madang include various sponsorships in social, community and sporting activities, especially a K10,000 donation to assist the Madang Rugby Football League Association. Probably one of the best known promotions is the Golden Music Club which reached a record 15,000 members last year. "The objective is to promote Papua New Guinea music as well as form a home grown music club", said brand Executive Gabriel Laka. In addition to the fan club Wills also sponsors local talent on TV and offers prizes through a weekly radio programme.

Wills (PNG) is a major international company which has brought investment to Papua New Guinea and important benefits to Madang.

For a company that has access to hundreds of gallons of neat spirit, Fairdeal Liquors has a remarkably clear-headed approach to business.

The idea of setting up a liquor business in Port Moresby, now one of the best known in all PNG, was sparked by the father and son team of Terry and George Lee, linked in a joint venture with Papua New Guineans. The enterprise took the town by storm.

One reason why Fairdeal has managed to dominate the spirits market so successfully is that the company holds the franchise for a wide range of top quality, international brands of spirits which it sells at highly competitive prices. So whether you drink whisky, brandy, gin, liqueur, rum or even vodka, Fairdeal can provide it.

The company also has its own brand of liquor, Gold Cup, which is produced solely at Fairdeal's Gordon-based factory. Although no alcohol is distilled at the factory, selected essences together with other ingredients are blended with top quality imported spirit to give each product its own distinctive flavour.

"We make everything from Gold Cup whisky to Gold Cup vodka," said production manager, Micky Josiah. "I think it is important to have our country's own local brand. America has Jim Beam, Scotland has Bells and PNG has Gold Cup. We are proud of that."

Of the 60 employees at Fairdeal, most work in the factory. Their loyalty is unquestionable and a number of them have stayed with the company since the day it opened.

Innovation is always encouraged, but Fairdeal's latest venture is surprisingly uncharacteristic for a company that concentrates on alcohol - a brand of water called "H2Only".

"H2Only, both from the point of view of taste and sales, has been excellent," said Richard Lee, the present Managing Director. "It's also considerably cheaper than bottled water from abroad."

Richard is confident Fairdeal's future in Papua New Guinea will be rosy but wants to make sure the company gives to the country as much as the country gives back. "I want to see us grow along with the country," he said. "The business potential here is staggering and we want to be part of that. Fairdeal is in PNG to stay."

One of the principle issues of policy planning in Papua New Guinea has been the creation of employment opportunities.

Since independence, governments have made and changed many policies directed at achieving this goal. Among the important policies have been the Commerce and Industry Ministry's drive towards the creation of middle to large scale manufacturing projects and the 1992 scrapping of the urban minimum wage. The idea was that lower wages would allow companies and the government to employ more people.

Another important policy was universal education at primary school level. This aims to educate the majority of the children, who would then be able to find work or use their knowledge to employ themselves in their villages.

The trend of employment has however been worsening. Rates of unemployment have risen to about 16%. Out of over 50,000 youths coming out of schools every year, only 10% find formal employment. The rest get sucked into the informal sector or return home to join the 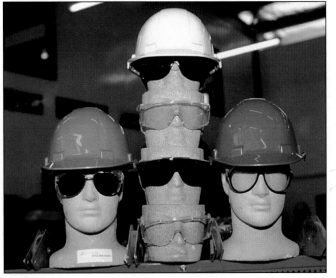 subsistence sector. The government is by far the largest employer, followed by the private sector. Recently, PNG has exported skilled personnel and nationals have taken up executive positions in major resource firms. Despite this PNG is still heavily dependent on skilled expatriate labour. About 10% of the labour force is expatriate.

In PNG the employment statistics vary, depending on the source. The government uses the indexes or figures supplied by the National Statistical Office and the Bank of PNG's bulletins, produced every quarter. In the private sector the Employer's Federation of PNG conducts a survey amongst its members to calculate the actual changes. The federation's employment survey is produced half yearly. Unfortunately for analysts and policy planners, the statistics vary quite a bit, making calculations difficult, although generally they all point towards a decline in jobs.

Employment trends are also led by the seasonal factors, especially in agriculture. Harvesting seasons for coffee and other cash crops fall at around mid-year, thus causing a temporary increase in employment. The numbers fall again soon after.

The 1991 Employer's Federation survey indicated that employment levels in its 137 member companies (one third of the total formal private sector) fell from 55,000 people in 1989 to 47,000 in 1990 and went further down to 45,000 in 1991. Since then employment trends have either been static or have declined marginally The Rabaul volcanic eruptions, which destroyed the entire commercial activity of the town, have had adverse effects on employment statistics.

Recent government decisions also have some bearing on employment The 12% devaluation of the kina in September 1994 and its floating a month later has meant that imported skilled labour is now more expensive. The 1995 budget also re-introduced the fringe benefits taxes, raised the ceiling for provincial sales taxes and increased tariff measures. Employers are restricted in employing new workers as a result.

In the public sector, the government will over the next two years, abolish a total of 4,500 positions in the public service. This will have an effect on general employment trends, although the start-up of Lihir gold mine and the Gobe oil field may counteract that..

175

The Labour market in Papua New Guinea is only a small fraction of the total population, most of whom are self-employed or maintaining a subsistence lifestyle. However, this relatively small number of people is an important part of the development process.

The labour force is defined as 'All Papua New Guineans who are currently employed at going rates of pay, as well as those who are currently unemployed but actively seeking work'. Twenty years after Independence it is said to stand at 250,000. The usual allowances must be made for the quality of the statistics in PNG at the present time. It is always being said that 20% of the population of 4 million are in the cash economy. This amounts to 800,000 people. Assuming that some of these are self-employed, say 100,000, which is probably a low estimate, this seems to mean that every employed person has only 1.8 dependent family members. This could be too low a figure as family sizes are large. Therefore possibly the numbers employed are even fewer than 250,000.

We can approach the available data from other sources. The Employers Federation (q.v.) believes that its members, constituting one-third of the private sector, employ a total of 45,000 people. indicating a total for the private sector of 135,000. The Government, in one form or another, employs 60,000. This gives a total of 195,000. The Government has targeted a 4,000 cut in its numbers, which will bring the numbers down to 191,000.

Whatever the exact size of the labour force, the men and women within it are the backbone of the country's move towards industrialisation and their welfare is the legitimate concern of the old Ministry of Labour and Employment, now renamed the Ministry of Industrial Relations.

The problems that face the labour force are
- insufficient jobs,
- insufficient training for those jobs and
- insufficient pay to keep yourself and others when you do get a job.

There are also specific problems related to the conditions of work in various different places, especially as more specialised kinds of work develop. Each really needs health and safety audits and inspections. In recent years the Department of Labour has not been able to establish or maintain these.

Problems in the labour market (which often derive from problems in the wider economic situation) eventually surface as strained industrial relations. One of the main functions of the Ministry is to keep relations harmonious by helping settle disputes quickly. To this end the Department of Industrial Relations includes a conciliation service.

The protection of local workers from foreign competition is the other main task of the Department. They deal with it by framing legislation. For example, nearly 600 types of job are in a category known as prohibited occupations, for which work permits are not issued to foreigners.

While these are the traditional concerns of any Labour Department, the incoming Minister for Industrial Relations, Samson Napo, MP for Bulolo, is keen to look beyond the problems of the local labour market. He wants to liase with international employers, actual and potential, whom he hopes will do more for their employees in the future, especially in relation to training.

There is already a work-permit related training scheme which aims to make the training of local counterparts a condition of acquiring the permit. Samson would like to see this scheme strengthened.

Samson is also anxious about the low levels of wages that are being paid in PNG's increasingly deregulated labour market. Echoing the concerns of the TUC on this issue, he says that some of these, especially those for unskilled labour, are simply unjust and must be looked at.

There is no dole or welfare system in Papua New Guinea and workers who lose their jobs have to rely on their 'wantoks', friends and relatives, or go back to a subsistence life-style. This is not likely to change. However, the seeming 'buyers market' for labour that this implies is no reason for inaction. The role for the Department of Labour in this situation, says Samson, must be to support every initiative that will strengthen the capacity of the individual worker to contribute their labour in an effective manner, and to obtain full recompense for it.

EMPLOYERS FEDERATION OF PAPUA NEW GUINEA

The Employers' Federation of Papua New Guinea provides a point of contact for newcomers to the country, whether investors or managers, who seek information and advice on the contemporary labour scene.

The operations of the Federation are funded by its members. In return, they receive access to labour information and industrial support services.

The Federation also provides training for employers and represents their interests at forums in Papua New Guinea and all over the world - not bad for a non-profit organisation set up in 1963 with only three full-time staff.

Since its foundation the Federation has gone from strength to strength and now boasts some of the country's most influential businessmen on its 160-strong members list. In fact, between them, its members employ over one third of the national workforce.

"The industrial relations set-up here is quite muted in comparison to some other countries," says Graeme Hogg, the Secretary General of the Federation. "We rarely suffer full-scale strikes and, if we do,

they do not last for long. The trade union movement is not too radical."

Nevertheless the Federation is far from complacent and plays a vital role in creating smooth relations between employers and employees. Consultation rather than confrontation is a phrase Graeme Hogg likes to use when describing the Federation's philosophy.

The long serving Executive Director, Tau Nana, thinks the secret of the Federation's success in Papua New Guinea is its emphasis on offering solid, professional advice. "The number of disputes that go to arbitration is a good measure of how successful a country's industrial relations are," said Tau. "We have remarkably few."

One of the most positive developments within the Federation is the number of its staff who have secured overseas fellowships. This has given them

the chance to visit and learn from other employer organisations in places such as Singapore, Malaysia and New Zealand. Some of the staff have also been on courses in Europe.

"There have not been many changes in the industrial relations field over the years," said Tau, "although three years ago minimum wages swung away from automatic indication and are now based more on productivity and capacity to pay.

"Some recent developments in Papua New Guinea have been in copper mining, petroleum extraction and forestry. These changes have been absorbed without significant shifts in the country's labour practices or conditions."

"In a country like PNG where the labour force is small to start with, it is difficult to make the voice of the worker heard," said the General Secretary of the Trades Union Congress, John Paska.

There have been labour unions in Papua New Guinea since 1963, but more than 30 years later finds only a small proportion of the paid workforce as signed-up members of a functioning union or staff association. This is a situation that disturbs John Paska

"The attitude of employers towards the unions is not serious, and injustices go unchecked. The continuing deregulation of labour over the last year has seen wages for unskilled workers go down to as low as 22 kina a week, while at the same time the devaluation of the currency and the high level of imports have caused prices to rise. Yet where is the effective opposition to this situation?"

The Public Employees Association, the PNG Teachers Association, the Transport Federation and the Communications Workers Union are the main unions in PNG. It is significant that conditions of employment in those areas are consistently better than, for example, for non-unionised shop workers, truck drivers, security guards or agricultural labourers. Of all the plantations in PNG, only the oil palm industry is unionised to any degree.

"This is the problem," says John Paska. "We seem to be dominated by a get-rich-quick mentality which is as destructive as it is ineffectual at promoting widespread economic well-being. Despite impressive growth figures and profit margins, poverty is increasing. High interest rates mean that capital investment is beyond the reach of many, while crime and illegal activities are spreading. This is due to the contagious effect of trade liberalisation policies dreamt up abroad and transplanted into our fundamentally non-cash economy where big-man politics and an incompetent bureaucracy are quite unequal to the task of safeguarding the livelihood of the people."

One of the solutions, according to John, is to strengthen the informal sector of the economy by promoting the growth of small-scale development in the rural areas. "Instead of taking the subsistence economy for granted as a sort of free safety-net, we should realise that it is our only hope. How long is it going to take us to learn the lessons of Bougainville? We should seriously promote all local enterprise. For example, the domestic market for fish should be developed and more businesses should be organised as co-operatives. This will give many more people the chance to earn the small amount of cash they actually need, which is out of their reach at present."

This is not to ignore the plight of the formal sector, for which he also has a remedy to suggest. "If you are a worker, join a union. If you are an employer, start taking unions seriously for the positive benefits they can bring to the workplace."

The transport and communications system of PNG has been shaped by the country's unusual and complicated geography. Air, sea and river are the main links, with road networks only in certain areas. It has never had a railway system, but plans to develop one are being considered. In such mountainous country it would be all tunnels and viaducts, very expensive.

Although there are almost 25,000 kilometres of roads, most of the rainforests and mountainous regions remain unapproachable except by air or on foot. Road building continues but only at a functional minimum, less than a fifth of it being sealed. A quarter of the population live in areas that have no road access whatsoever. The country's main road is the Highlands Highway, which starts on the northeast coast at Lae and services the interior where nearly half the population resides. Smaller systems branch off from this central highway, going to various regional capitals to where trucks carry industrial goods and raw materials. The national capital, Port Moresby, has no road link to the rest of the country. By international standards, very few Papua New Guineans own cars.

Future planning is determined by the National Department of Transport, who have employed the services of international and regional agencies to assist them with development. The need for expansion is obvious. Without it, neither commercial nor domestic needs can be properly handled. Health, education and local government

will all enjoy the advantages of an organised infrastructure.

The history of PNG is inextricably linked with sea transport. Many of the country's first inhabitants came here by sea, traded with one another by sea and built a range of sophisticated vessels of which the most famous is the 'lakatoi'. European navigators, traders and whalers sailed into the same waters thousands of years later. Copra, the kernel of coconuts which was PNG's main crop for many years, was totally dependent on sea transport. The plantations themselves often purposely located close to the coastline. A number of large shipping companies developed the nation's domestic and international sea links and even brought in some of the first tourists. Today, the shipping industry in PNG is dominated by Steamships Trading Company and the Century Group of companies.

Aviation has a long and eventful history in PNG. It began in 1921, when a certain Captain Lang of the Australian Flying Corps set out from Port Moresby in his seaplane to become the first man to fly over New Guinea. A decade later aviation became vitally linked to the economic development of the country in a way that could not have been envisaged when that first flight was made. The discovery of gold in PNG, in the Wau-Bulolo area in the early thirties, sent a thrill through the country, but without aviation transporting the gold would have been impossible.

In April 1927, the newly established Guinea Airways flew from Lae to the goldfields of Wau in a De Havilland DH 37. The following year they acquired two Junkers W34 aircraft which had a much greater payload. In 1932, Guinea Airways actually carried more freight than all the aircraft in England, France and the United States combined! The aviation industry had revolutionised transport in PNG, opening up the country for large-scale communications for the first time. Airstrips were laid all around the nation and light planes carried people and goods to some areas which had previously been labelled as the most remote in the world.

In 1973, two years before independence, the national carrier Air Niuguini was formed, providing a sophisticated domestic flight service and an essential link with the outside world.

181

The Ministry of Transport has recently been subsumed into the Ministry of Civil Aviation and Tourism. This may signal a change in thinking about roads and ground transport in general.

In Papua New Guinea, today as in the past, most people make their journeys by foot or, if they are in an area of rivers and waterways, by canoe. These simple facts can sometimes be forgotten by those developmentalists and transport planners who seem only to be able to think about capital-intensive projects such as airports and highways when they agonise about the lack of 'infrastructure' in the country.

A transport infrastructure does exist in the country. It is an infrastructure of walking tracks and waterways.

These tracks go from house to house, from a house to its vegetable garden or plantation, from one cluster of houses to another, and from village to village. Walking tracks connect villages with market places and larger towns. In the towns, walking tracks cut through the back ways to make shorter, more convenient journeys out of longer ones. Out in the country, long-distance trails, leading over mountain ranges between mighty

rivers, provided the walking and waterway routes for traders carrying goods between the inland areas and the coast.

Many of the tracks are in daily use. Men, women and children pass sure-footed over the soft or rugged ground. The gradients can be steep. People go to church along these walking tracks. Children go to school. Women are the main load carriers. Always with a bilum, they bring firewood down from

the forests, taking produce to and from the gardens. Physical anthropologists have said that women's skulls can sometimes be distinguished from men's by a groove at the front, the result of carrying heavy loads. Easing this load could be a main aim of transport planners.

Motor transport and motor roads are not necessarily the best solution.

The statistics on car ownership and per capita income suggest that planners should start to think in a different way about road transport - and, indeed, about air transport - in Papua New Guinea. For the foreseeable future, travel in motor vehicles and flights on planes will be only an occasional experience for many of the citizens of this country.

When a road is cut through an area, sometimes on the route of an old walking track, it is engineered for vehicles, not walkers. While the hard surface, unlike tracks, may remain dry after rain, the experience of walking on roads is often more tedious. In fact, anyone walking for any distance on main roads feels alienated and ill at ease, only too aware that they are not riding in a car or truck. Roads can also be dangerous places, full of strangers. The walker may sometimes wish for the clock to be put back.

At the same time, the people have transport needs. Their daily journeys pass over streams that need bridges and along tracks that could be improved. Rivers and lakes could benefit from permanent jetties, as well as ferries and taxi canoes. In the islands, more boats would make sense. On flat land, bicycles are an inexpensive form of transport that could be encouraged.

When a new road is the appropriate solution, smaller roads are more desirable as well as cheaper and a network of small roads more desirable still. Highways leading straight to urban centres tend to drain all the young people out of an area as fast as they drain the treasury's coffers. Networks of local roads would strengthen community links. That would be a truly useful infrastructure.

183

In the past sea transport was always linked to exploration. Now it is linked to trade and to the economic growth of PNG. The coastal regions of PNG were, the first to be developed. Whalers and traders in sandalwood, beche de mer and mother of pearl shell were the first to use PNG's natural harbours. The colonial administration developed plantations on the coastal plains close to harbours to allow easy export to foreign markets.

There are now over 50 public ports in PNG of which 17 are administered by PNG Harbours Boards. The total traffic at the Harbours Board ports has grown at an average of 5% per annum reaching over 3 million tonnes, of which 67% is overseas cargo. Dry general cargo accounts for 83% and liquid bulk for 17% of total traffic. The main export commodities handled are copper, copra, coffee, palm oil and timber. Imports consist mainly of manufactured goods, food grains, fertiliser, chemicals and petroleum products.

The Harbours Board is a Statutory Body under the Minister of Transport. It is responsible for the administration and control of all activities associated with the movement of ships and cargo handling within the limits of the ports in its jurisdiction. It is also respon-sible for the control of pilotage services and the maintenance of certain navigational aids. It is not responsible for registration, licensing, surveys or manning.

The Board is financially autonomous but is subject to Government tax regulations. There have been frequent charges that the Board constitutes a monopoly. Managing Director Charles Punaha would like to correct this impression. "In 1976 we were handling 95% of the traffic but now we are down to 60-65%. The rest comes from the private sector. They offer stiff competition. For example since the private wharves opened in Lae in 1989, 15% of the traffic has diverted there and we have been forced to become more customer oriented." At present the Board is not handling any cargo from the big

resource developers - mining, petroleum or timber. They all have their own wharves. The Board is out to tempt them with concessions.

The 17 ports are grouped into regions centred on Port Moresby, Lae, Rabaul and Kieta. Trade comes in combo or multi-purpose ships averaging 12,000 tonnes dwt which either carry part of their container shipment as deck cargo or are pure container ships of around 400 TEU capacity. Copra and coffee exports are generally handled as break bulk. There are no on-shore cranes at PNG ports, or at most other ports in the South Pacific region. All ships are self-reliant.

A berth reservation system applies at the main ports. Passenger vessels, foreign naval vessels, tankers and cargo ships which have given advance notice and have paid fees are allowed to berth alongside.

General warehousing facilities are not provided. All covered and open stacking areas are for transit purposes only. Most of the larger ports have bonded warehouses to which undelivered cargo can be consigned. Only those stevedoring organisations licensed by the Board are allowed to handle cargo within the Board's operating areas, with exceptions at certain smaller ports. However, the Board has no control over charges and cannot be blamed for the high labour costs at PNG ports.

The Board currently has difficulty in meeting its corporate objectives. "They will always be in conflict", says Charles Punaha. "How can we attain a 10% profit on investments as well as fulfil our requirement to be a social provider of services in the outlying areas? Only two of our ports show a profit, Moresby and Lae. They subsidise operations at all the rest".

There seems little chance of the private sector taking on expensive, unprofitable harbours. But without their port some small places would be without food. It could affect the economy of an entire province, like Milne Bay or Gulf for example. It is a dilemma which faces almost any Ministry concerned with infrastructure. Meanwhile the Harbours Board has to maintain an acceptable balance between its financial and social objectives.

The name Steamships is as much a symbol of Papua New Guinea as the bird of paradise or the kundu drum. Since its formation over 70 years ago as Steamships Trading Co Ltd, the company has managed to propel itself from a tiny enterprise, whose sea-captain founder, Capt. Algernon Fitch, once sold goods through the bathroom window of his Port Moresby bungalow in Douglas Street, into the country's leading trading firm.

Although "Steamies", as locals affectionately call the company, now has a finger in nearly every trading pie imaginable, its roots were in shipping. It has stayed true to them to this day. In its infancy the company only owned two ships but this small fleet soon grew into a regular and reliable flotilla which traded successfully all along the Papuan coast. Nowadays the Shipping and Transport division of Steamships operates a multi-functional fleet of 19 ships - tugs, dumb barges, landing craft and survey vessels, all of them kept in pristine condition and equipped with state-of-the-art technology.

"We are constantly up-grading our fleet," said general manager, Captain Duncan Telfer. "Shipping is an area where continual modernisation is essential. It is the only way to stay competitive.

"The company also tries to be innovative and think on its feet. Although Steamships is a household name, we make sure we never get complacent."

Steamships transports everything from minerals and metals to bags of rice and containers of chicken feed. It always keeps an eye open for goods that will whet local appetites.

Although it is based exclusively in Papua New Guinea, Steamships has strong links throughout the world. A steady stream of imports and exports is transported not just around Asia and Australasia but to many parts of Europe. Predictably, Steamships Shipping and Transport has branches at all PNG's major ports including Port Moresby, Lae, Madang, Rabaul and Kiunga on the Fly River.

Another string to the company's bow is Steamships Shipping Agencies. This ever expanding division co-ordinates all the waterside functions of the company and acts as agent for dedicated regional services such as Chief Container Service from Australia, New Guinea Pacific Line from Asia and Pacific Forum Line from New Zealand. In addition, Steamships also looks after the interests of such renowned shipping companies as P and O, and Maersk Line.

"Well co-ordinated shipping control at each of the ports is essential," stressed Terry Hudson, Agency Manager. "Too much time wasted in port can mean a major loss of money. Stevedoring operations have to be very efficient. Fortunately Steamships owns stevedoring companies in the four main ports of PNG."

Steamships' stevedores handle thousands of tonnes of cargo every year and also operate a significant road haulage operation around each of the ports.

Of the 370 staff employed by Steamships Shipping and Transport, 98% are nationals. Steamships puts great emphasis on developing the skills of its employees. Many attend the nautical college at Madang and specific courses overseas. Recently one of Steamships' sea cadets became the first Papua New Guinean trained seaman to achieve a Class 1 foreign-going Master Mariner's certificate.

One third of Steamships is owned by the internationally renowned Swire Group. Swires has bases in every corner of the world and provides Steamships Shipping and Transport with a valuable web of contacts.

"Papua New Guinea has great potential, from a shipping perspective," says Duncan Telfer. "It is a country rich in minerals and timber, both of which make valuable exports. It also has a strong agricultural base.

"Although PNG will always rely largely on imports, I think there will be an increasingly dynamic export trade with more products being processed locally rather than abroad. I am very optimistic for the future of shipping in this country."

187

TOURISM

Fly into Port Moresby the capital city of Papua New Guinea and within an hour you can be walking in upland rainforest looking for birds of paradise. There are a lot of overworked words in the tourist brochures. Paradise is one of them - but the Raggiana bird of paradise is the PNG national emblem. It has a splendid reddish plumed tail and a 'wah wah' call which echoes through the forest. It is a bright metaphor for the variety and difference that is PNG.

The dilemma that faces PNG, is how to exploit its natural beauty, its culture and tradition without destroying them. Compared to its neighbours in the Pacific and in Indonesia, PNG has barely begun to engage in the tourism market. Even the figure of 38,000 tourists is admitted to be optimistic, for it includes many 'business people' dodging their high visa rate. Many provinces can count their tourists in hundreds per year rather than thousands yet they all look to tourism as a source of revenue.

PNG can learn from the experience of other destinations. Mass tourism which brings the tourists in by jumbo jet and deposits them in resort complexes rarely benefits the local people and barely benefits the national economy. The money tends to stay 'out there' in the global network of wheeler-dealing which benefits those who are already rich.

Eco-tourism is another overworked term. It can benefit local people but needs careful nurturing before the costs are truly won back. It is only a very few inveterate travellers who will put up with poor transportation, accommodation and food. Even eco-tourists have limited time. They want to get to their destination and out with the minimum of delay. They want clean water, clean toilets and sustaining food. The PNG villagers can provide all of these requirements but only with help.

At present PNG is a very expensive destination for tourists. It is expensive to get to it, expensive to move around, expensive to stay in hotels. Those tourist operations that are successful are geared to up-market travellers. Opening up the market base will mean reducing costs. It is possible that eco-tourism operating in an improved infrastructure will be the answer.

189

"Foreign tourists come into this country only by air," said the new Minister for Tourism and Civil Aviation to explain his dual ministry.

Minister Michael Nali was somewhat aghast at the size of his task, "they are really two different animals. Each is an industry on its own. But it makes sense to keep some overall link". Whatever plans there are for tourism will involve civil aviation.

"It doesn't matter where you bring the tourists in, whether it is Lae, Port Moresby, Mount Hagen or Rabaul, the tourist will always want to go to the Sepik because of the art and the river. We should be able to

fly them straight in. They don't want to see some semi-desert when they arrive. They want to see an attractive environment, fast flowing rivers, green fresh grass, nice gardens and the beauty of the people living in old 'primitive' houses." Such a plan for tourists would have to involve extending the runway at Wewak or one of the other northern centres. But the minister has other ideas for improving the infrastructure for tourists.

"The first thing to do is to publicise the good things about PNG", says Michael Nali. "We have a problem with the media, especially certain Australian media, giving us a bad press." PNG should not be a fearsome place for tourists. The law and order problem is generally restricted to inter-clan or inter-gang disturbances. The high hotel prices and the high cost of airfares are much more likely to keep the tourists away.

Amongst the Minister's other ideas are training schools for waiters and licences for taxi drivers. The taxi drivers should have their own school. Every taxi should have a meter and they must use them. "We must have some controls, get the fares like those in America or Europe. But also, right throughout the world there are things that tourists like. We have Big Rooster here, but the tourist, if hungry wanting something quick to eat, wants something they already know, like MacDonalds or Kentucky Fried Chicken. We must have them here too." The future of tourism in PNG must, it seems, involve some international standardisation.

And the future for civil aviation? "Really Papua New Guinea has scarcely opened up. There is no road to the Highlands from Port Moresby. We have four regions who do not even know each other very well. I think there are a lot of people living in isolation and civil aviation has a job to do providing much needed services. There is no way that civil aviation should be totally privatised," thinks Minister Nali. "If we try and privatise aviation, communities in the remote areas will be neglected. People are desperate for airstrips. They are still building them, legally or illegally. In Morobe Province there are two airstrips only 8 to 10 miles apart. That is how desperate people are. The country is rough. People have to take to the air."

There are 459 aerodromes in PNG. The Ministry is responsible for them all, though only 47 are operated and maintained by the Department of Civil Aviation of which 7 have full air traffic services. The provincial governments maintain and operate about 160 aerodromes and the remaining airports and airstrips

cial governments maintain and operate about 160 aerodromes and the remaining airports and airstrips are owned, operated and maintained by community and private authorities. For operational safety and compliance with established standards, the Department inspects every one of the 450 airports or airstrips twice a year and issues applicable licences and certificates.

There are facilities for night landings at Port Moresby, Madang, Wewak, Kavieng, Momote and Nadzab. Port Moresby, has, since April 1995, a state of the art instrument landing system on the main runway. System 4000 comes from Italy. It is the most modern procedural control system in the world, only Malaysia and China have it at present. Papua New Guinea nationals went to Rome to train on the system and are now beginning to train the people under them.

In co-operation with Germany, modern navigational aids (VOR) have recently been installed at Nadzab, Gurney, Kavieng and Wewak . There are a number of less sophisticated navigation aids and distance-measuring equipment which have been replaced under an on-going programme and with Australian grant aid. The Department hires an Australian Civil Aviation Authority aircraft twice a year to maintain, calibrate and flight test the navaid equipment.

Air Traffic Services, Search and Rescue and Aeronautical Information Services are provided within the PNG Flight Information Region (FIR). This airspace extends from the equator, along the Indonesian border, halfway across the Coral Sea and to the boundaries of the Solomon Islands and Nauru. PNG also provides aeronautical meteorology with the FIR's of the Solomon Islands and Nauru. Air Traffic Control Radar is not yet available.

There are 275 aircraft on the PNG register. A

great proportion of these are operated by third level operators. Currently Air Niugini operates international services to Hong Kong, Singapore, Manila (Philippines), Honiara (Solomons), Jayapura (Indonesia) and Cairns, Brisbane and Sydney in Australia. These operations are carried out under Bilateral or Commercial Arrangements in most cases based on a 50/50 profit sharing agreement with reciprocal rights. Air Service negotiations are under way with several governments which may result in additional destinations from Papua New Guinea.

On the domestic market, Air Niugini is the only licensed airline operating Regular Pubic Transport (RTP) to 21 destinations while the major third level operators, Milne Bay Air, Islands Nationair, Air Link and MAF provide scheduled services on the same network with a few additional feeder routes. In addition there are a number of charter operators and specialised services such as helicopter operations in support of the mining industry. The domestic market has seen an average 30% growth for passengers and 7.8% for cargo in the last ten years. Passenger traffic is forecast to increase at the past rate but cargo traffic is expected to increase more substantially because of additional demands generated by the mining and petroleum industry.

All the companies do their own training and the Department checks them out and issues licences. The only place in PNG where a young person can learn to fly, get a private license and then progress to a commercial licence is with MAF (Missionary Aviation) in Mt. Hagen. MAF is proud to have a second woman candidate on the commercial course. Hagar learnt to fly on MAF's dual control Cessna and she is now ahead of the men on her course. Like all the students at MAF she will have to complete her licensing exams at the Department's centre at Port Moresby. If successful she will join the other 522 pilots in PNG, of which 69 are nationals.

As passengers gather in the departure areas of airports around PNG they frequently look up at the sky and comment on the weather. At Independence Papua New Guinea became the 131st member of the World Meteorological Organisation. The Department is responsible for the National Weather Service. Pilots and airlines are given constant updates of the weather situation.

Given the rugged topography, the number of islands and the low density of population in PNG, civil aviation is the most natural and essential mode of transport. Minister Michael Nali could well be right when he declares: "For PNG, aircraft are the only key to civilisation right now".

It wasn't until Independence was in the air, in 1973, that a new national airline was inaugurated with the name Air Niugini - Niugini being the accepted Pidgin spelling of New Guinea. Initially, the Papua New Guinean government took a 60% stake, with TAA (now Australian Airlines) and Quantas taking a 12% stake each and the remaining 16% being accepted by Ansett Airways. Top management was originally provided by Qantas with the new airline absorbing all Ansett and TAA staff in PNG who wished for employment.

Air Niugini's inauguration marked the beginning of a period of rapid growth as the demand for traffic, both passenger and cargo, far exceeded all prior estimates. In its first year alone Air Niugini carried 350,000 passengers - 85,000 more than the task force had forecast and more than the number carried in the previous year by TAA and Ansett combined. That same year Air Niugini's fleet of eight Fokker F27s and 12 DC3s flew more than 27,000 hours - some 5,000 more than was projected.

Demand for more international services was not long in coming. By the end of 1975, Air Niugini began leasing Boeing 727s from Ansett and TAA for services to Brisbane. It also leased a Boeing 707 from Qantas for a weekly service to Manila and Hongkong. In 1979 new routes were opened up both east and west, to Honolulu and to Singapore via Djakarta.

PNG is a developing country, and a comparatively small one, so you might well expect to see the national flag carrier flying a few big jets to neighbouring countries a few times a week. That's a common pattern. But would you believe 70 flights a day to 20 internal airports? Would you believe regular international services in an A310 Airbus to Sydney, Brisbane, Manila, Hongkong and Singapore? Would you believe a profit-making record which has been continuous since 1973? Well that really is a national flag carrier - and the name is Air Niugini.

And because one of the A310's isn't quite busy enough, they've already filled ten charter flights for 1995 for Japanese tourists from the new airport at Osaka to Port Moresby's Jackson's Airport, which, some enthusiasts claim, is only fifteen minutes from some of the best scuba and snorkel diving on the reat Barrier Reef.

However this tourist potential is not what makes Air Nugini into a successful and sophisticated "niche" airline, as the jargon calls it. With no road linking the capital to places in the central Highlands, nor one linking up the north coast, with the

very considerable time and distance constraints associated with shipping, few airlines in the world play such a crucial role in the country's economy and basic transport needs as Air Niugini. Fewer still have played so significant a part in opening up previously inaccessible areas.

The gold rush of 1922 was a real one and an extraordinary story in itself. An Australian prospector discovered gold on Koranga Creek in Morobe Province. A further more important find followed four years later at Edie Creek. The subsequent demand for transport to the area could only be satisfied by commercial aviation and, by 1927, long before major world powers had really woken up to the importance of the aeroplane, four air transport companies were servicing the gold mines from Lae, using a bi-plane, six pilots and six engineers. Gradually the skies filled with the planes of one company after another right up to 1973 and the inauguration of Air Niugini itself.

The early eighties saw the purchase of new and more efficient aircraft, including De Havilland Dash 7s which, because of their short-take-off-and-landing (STOL) capability, were particularly suited to operations in the Highlands where short airstrips are the rule. The route network was extended to Tari in the Highlands, to Rabaul in New Britain and later to Hoskins.

In 1987, the position of General Manager was advertised world-wide and Dieter Seefeld was appointed, after 18 years marketing experience with the German national carrier Lufthansa. Not surprisingly he was soon the driving force behind the airline's modernisation, introducing a new corporate image which included an up-dated and stylised version of the country's national symbol - the Raggiana Bird of Paradise. It has been adopted as the company logo and now perches unmistakably on the tail planes of all the corporation's aircraft.

Over the last six years, Air Niugini has once again expanded its services and added additional F28s to its fleet, which now comprises eight of these Fokker

jets, two Dash 7s and two Airbus A310s. Recently the airline unveiled its new reservations, ticketing and departure control system, known in the field as 'Gabriel'. This computer controlled network, used world-wide by many airlines and travel-related organisations, provides improved, direct control of the management of flights, as well as offering information on fare quotations. Basic rates at nearly 10,000 hotels world-wide are quoted and there's a detailed data-base reference to entry and health requirements (that is passports, visas and vaccinations), for more than two hundred different countries.

Looking back over Air Niugini's record since Independence, Dieter Seefeld says that major events really stand out, like the introduction of new aircraft and new equipment and the opening of additional routes. "But there's also the steady success of our annual profits, our safety record (unblemished), and the training of our pilots. We spend over K3 million each year on training to ensure we meet international standards."

"The pride of our people in their airline is obvious," he says, "not just in the way they watch aircraft arrive and depart, but in the competence of staff behind the traffic counters at numerous terminals, at the controls of high technology equipment, in sales offices, in cargo terminals, in catering depart-

ments and engineering workshops."

"The pride is unmistakably there, throughout the airline and the country. Air Nuigini is looking towards the 21st century equipped with experienced staff to continue its success and service, and to continue a job well done."

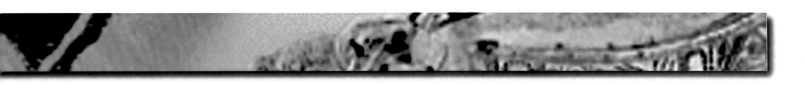

197

When in Port Moresby there are few better places to sit and relax with a drink than the pool-side Alfresco bar & grill at the Airways Hotel and Apartments. This unique setting, high on a hill over-looking the runways at Jacksons Airport, offers a splendid panorama of the green foothills of the Astrolabe escarpment where they run down into the blue seas of Bootless Bay south east of the capital.

Putting this vista on one side, however, the hotel itself is widely regarded as one of the most prestigious venues in the country - the sort of place where the Prime Minister might choose to make a speech, or a prominent couple to hold a wedding reception. Yet its glowing reputation makes it in no way elitist - the Alfresco's 20 metre pool and its eating and drinking facilities are open to everyone.

However there's much more to the Airways than a commanding location. The hotel has over 140 beautifully furnished bedrooms catering for individuals, couples or family groups. The fact that these rooms have a ninety per cent occupancy rate throughout the year only serves to confirm the Airways popularity.

The hotel has three function rooms for business events or private parties plus three restaurants, including the award-winning Bacchus, one of the most sophisticated eateries in Port Moresby. Guests who want to keep fit have the use of a multi-functional gym, two tennis courts and a spacious sauna. Squash courts are currently on the drawing board.

"I think part of the Airways' success is that it's always looking at new ways of improving," says General Manager, George Constantinou.

"When the hotel was set up in 1986 it had only 38 bedrooms, but by next year we should have over 200 and be able to host functions for up to 400 people. We will also be expanding the sporting facilities, and all of this shows the progressive and positive approach of the hotel."

The Airways employs a total of 160 staff of whom only four are expatriates. The management puts great emphasis on in-house training for employees and any who show particular promise or need specific knowledge of new equipment or systems are sent on courses overseas.

The Airways also includes 75 long-stay, serviced apartments which emphasises the need for tight security. So the extensive grounds are unobtrusively but effectively fenced and patrolled, and guests can be confident that their privacy is being scrupulously guarded.

"The Airways is one of the most forward-thinking enterprises I have managed," says George. "The fact that the hotel trade has such unfulfilled potential in Papua New Guinea makes the job that much more exciting and challenging. I am sure the Airways has a very promising future."

"Our business is spiralling all the time. For a car hire company there can be few places more exciting than Papua New Guinea - the road network is growing everyday."

There are few people who know the roads of Papua New Guinea better than Jon McMullen.

John is the General Manager of Avis, the country's leading car hire firm. He travels continually between the company's ten branch offices which are dotted everywhere from Manus to Madang.

"In Port Moresby it is fine to drive a car like a Toyota Corona," he explained, "but if you need to get around the steep hills of Mount Hagan a four-wheel drive Land Cruiser would be much more suitable.

We have cars to cater for every type of customer and every type of terrain. Whether it be a smart executive model like a Mazda 626 or simply a Hilux utility, we will be able to provide it. Whatever the vehicle we always pride ourselves on making sure it is 100% safe and reliable. Avis puts enormous emphasis on customer service."

Avis's head office in Port Moresby, which boasts a selection of 90 cars, is only a stone's throw from Jackson's airport. This is a tactical location as the airport is the place where the bulk of car hire business is generated.

The business has been running successfully for the last 20 years and now has over 50 staff. Despite its many offices throughout the country, Avis has plans to spread its wings even more and another branch is soon due to open in the Milne Bay area.

The company offers an extensive training scheme to all its staff, which helps them get to grips with every aspect of the business. Avis is well-known for looking after its employees and as a result secures their loyalty.

"I think seeing the staff develop as they gain in experience is one of the most rewarding aspects of my job," said Jon. "Obviously knowing that the business is going from strength to strength is also very gratifying."

"The principal reason I came to Papua New Guinea was to face fresh challenges. This country has certainly provided that. We have to rent out cars to everybody from politicians to tourists. The amount of businessmen hiring vehicles has also increased, especially with the expansion in mining and forestry.

"Papua New Guinea is my home and I never want to leave it," Colin Ritchie exclaimed, "I will continue to make any contribution I can to the local business scene. It is important to put back in what you take out and especially to pass on skills and experience to national people."

At 58, an age when most people want to put their feet up and enjoy a leisurely retirement, Colin Ritchie decided to set up his own business.

The dynamic Englishman, whose visa and passport processing enterprise has been running in Port Moresby for only six years, is living proof that anyone can achieve their dreams - whatever their age.

Colin arrived in Papua New Guinea in 1964 and served in the police for many years, ending up in the special branch. He finally hung up his uniform during the mining boom of the early 1970's and landed a job as a site construction manager/expediter on mining projects all over the country.

In 1985 he became a Papua New Guinean citizen and three years later took the plunge and formed Colin Ritchie and Associates. The influential web of contacts he had already established provided him a useful business base. Initially the company's work focused on expediting for mining companies, but now it organises passports and visas for anyone.

Colin puts the secret of his success down to a sustained emphasis on efficiency, honesty and always putting the customer first. He can cater for even the most unusual demands, whether it be organising a birth certificate or securing a visa for Nepal. Other

than the passport and visa enterprise, Colin's company also provides a cable television service to 200 homes in two different suburbs.

His six associates are all Papua New Guinean and play an integral role in maintaining the prosperity of the company.

Mrs. Vivien McArthur, Manageress of the Visa Services Division, has recently joined the organisation bringing with her considerable experience and an established network with the Department of Foreign Affairs and Overseas Consulates in Australia.

Mrs. Raka Tau, Government Liaison Passport/Visa Services, has for the past five years been controlling passports and visas for a number of statutory bodies and is familiar with all aspects of the processing procedures.

Mr. Gorua Dagia manages the Cable Television Division. Being the Director, Mr. Dagia has been trained in all facets of the companies operations.

Mr. Pala Leva has been with the company for five years. He commenced as a courier dreiver and has graduated to the position of Work Permit Consultant.

Mr. Gerega Ravu is in charge of the Property Maintenance Division. Gerega's son Colin is a courier driver and Mr. Tapas Sene heads the Administration and Accounts Division.

Chris Robertson can reel off stories ten to the dozen about his hotel management career which has taken him everywhere from mainstream cities like London and Perth to more offbeat destinations in the Middle East.

This engaging Englishman is now based in Port Moresby as the general manager of the Coral Sea group of hotels.

"Coral Sea is the most widely distributed group of hotels in Papua New Guinea," said Chris. "We have a total of eight different sites dotted all over the country including Port Moresby and Madang."

Over the past year Chris Robertson has personally supervised the refurbishment of every hotel in the group. He is aiming at a group identity offering visitors an assurance that their expectations of high standards will be met whenever they stay in a hotel that bears the Coral Sea Hotels logo.

"We are constantly looking at new ways of improving each hotel and upgrading the facilities," stressed Chris. "Some people hold the view that Papua New Guinea is still very much a third world community. This is wrong, the hotel trade here is maturing very quickly and I would say some of our suites comfortably outclass many of those in the hotels along the Queensland coast of Australia."

Stay in a Coral Sea Hotel and you can be nowhere else but Papua New Guinea. Chris Robertson has re-designed the interiors to reflect the colours and textures of this "natural paradise". Soft furnishings are uniformly in the rich browns and dark greens of the tropics. Chairs and tables are made from South Pacific rattans and wood. Bamboo mats on the floors shine a golden yellow. These colours create a mellow atmosphere in which to relax and enjoy any free time. The spacious work zone, big desk, good lighting, IDD phone, fax and secretarial facilities, now characterise Coral Sea's concern for its business customers.

Of the eight hotels in the group The Gateway in Port Moresby and the Melanesian in Lae are more geared up to serve corporate clients, whereas the picturesque Smugglers Resort in Madang is more suited to tourists who want to escape from work.

"The Gateway and the Melanesian both have multi-functional conference rooms whereas somewhere like The Smugglers puts greater emphasis on leisure pursuits" says Chris. "But most hotels have swimming pools and extensive sporting facilities. We like to be sure everyone enjoys them-

selves even if work is their dominant reason for visiting."

No two hotels are the same - each enjoys its own sense of innovation and originality. The Smugglers, for instance has a swimming pool shaped like a sea-horse. The Highlander in Mount Hagen gives guests the opportunity to step back in time and visit traditional tribal villages. The Gateway has a business centre. The Coast Watchers (also in Madang) has golf, tennis, bowls and squash on offer nearby and The Melanesian has a superbly equipped gym and the highest standard of accommodation in Lae.

Each hotel also has a variety of restaurants and bars to satisfy the most demanding palate. Whether a guest is after a poolside snack washed down with a cold beer or a four course feast accompanied by a fine bottle of wine, Coral Sea hotels will have it on one of their mouth watering international menus.

Between them the hotels employ hundreds of staff. Each employee whether waiter or receptionist receives comprehensive in-house training. At least four times a year a specialist instructor from Australia comes over to teach the staff on specific aspects of the hotel trade.

"Over 98% of the staff here are nationals," says Chris. "We like to give everyone a fair share of responsibility whatever their post. There is a very healthy team spirit among our staff and if any of them show special potential we like to nurture that. Recently we sent some of our chefs down to a competition in Brisbane. They came back with a bronze medal.

"Papua New Guinea is a country proud of its past history, proud of its villages which live the same way they did hundreds of years ago but it is not afraid of modernising and embracing the future. From a business and a tourism perspective Papua New Guinea is maturing all the time. Coral Sea Hotels, which are solely based in PNG, are glad to be helping this country receive its share of the international limelight.

Blue skies, hot sun, a gentle breeze, waving palms and a glittering sea are the basic requirements for a tropical island dream holiday, but rather more is required to make most people's dream come true. Sometimes, for example, the dream involves rather too much uncomfortable travelling, but visitors to Port Moresby can rest assured that, only fifteen minutes drive from Jacksons Airport, a ferry is waiting to transport them across two kilometres of the blue waters of Bootless Bay to Loloata Island.

Simple but comfortable colonial-style bungalows, with wide verandahs, stand on stilts over the shallow tides which lap the sandy beaches. Food is abundant, barbecues frequent and the bar well stocked. Scuba diving and snorkelling are arranged without fuss.

For the enthusiast, the diving potential of Loloata may be its most powerful drawing point. At present up to ten resorts in PNG claim at least some good diving, but none is as reasonably-priced as Loloata's and before long none will be as extensive. Snorkel trips to nearby Lion Island and scuba trips to Horseshoe Reef Marine Park and its wrecks are arranged daily. Spectacular coral growths of strange beauty, fish of uncountable varieties, shapes and colours, welcome the viewer from above or the underwater explorer from below.

Not all of Loloata's guests will be divers, but the sea provides for other skills. Facilities for wind surfing, kayaking, and surfskiing are immediately available. For some an hour's walk around the island will be a simple delight. For others, especially the very young, safely-sloping sandy beaches will beckon. For the romantic, evenings filled with sunsets, barbecues out by the sea wall, a last drink under the stars, will stay in the memory.

And the food! No-one, and that includes frequent conference clients, leaves disappointed with the cuisine.

Islands Nationair is a national Papua New Guinea company, owned by Sir Julius Chan, Prime Minister of Papua New Guinea, and Captain David Pidduck from New Zealand.

Islands is the major helicopter operator in Papua New Guinea. It began operations with one Bell Jetranger which supported gold exploration in the New Guinea islands region. It was involved in the preliminary assessment studies for Kennecott's Lihir goldmine in the New Ireland Province.

In 1985 Islands Aviation brought the first Bell Longranger Helicopter to Papua New Guinea. The additional seating and lifting capacity of the Longranger made it an ideal craft for PNG.

In 1988 Islands became involved in supporting oil exploration and in seismic surveys. August 1990 saw the completion of the most ambitious seismic survey ever carried out in PNG. Three Longrangers based in the Strickland River area of Western Province flew 7,500 incident-free hours over a two and a half year period. It marked Islands' importance for future oil and gas exploration.

Islands Nationair now operates nine Longrangers, three in Mendi in the Southern Highlands, two in Lae in Morobe Province, two in Port Moresby, one at Rabaul in East New Britain and one in Mt. Hagen.

In 1990 the company expanded into fixed-wing, regular public transport (RTP) operations. It is now the second largest third level carrier in PNG transporting passengers on routes over East and West New Britain and New Ireland with its scattered smaller islands. It flies the popular Twin engined Otters, Kingairs and several other smaller aircraft including a Cessna 206.

Since 1987 maintenance has been carried out by Aircair Pty Ltd of Lae. In 1989 a new hanger/workshop was built at Rabaul. Unfortunately the volcanic eruption in September 1994 totally destroyed the entire Rabaul facility. It was a major setback. The company set up a temporary base at Tokua and moved the engineering facility to Port Moresby. Meanwhile maintenance of B200 and Bandierante aircraft is being carried out in Cairns, while Twin Otters and piston-engine aircraft are maintained in Port Moresby. All helicopter maintenance is conducted at Port Moresby or in the field. The company owns and operates a small hangar at Mendi in the Southern Highlands.

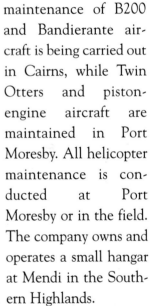

Key personnel are Captain John Thomas, General Manager and Finance Controller and Working Director Ken Trezise. Previous Managing Director David Pidduck is now employed as special consultant and is involved in client liaison, promotional activities, and co-ordination of helicopter operations.

Currently Islands Nationair is operating a full RPT, Regular Passenger Transport, schedule and is working to consolidate that position. Helicopter activity may increase. Islands Nationair has grown in well-planned stages and this policy will continue into the future.

Papua New Guinea is an outdoor sportsman's paradise, a primitive and generally unspoiled frontier. Niugini Adventures will plan and safely guide you for an adventurous hunting or fishing trip to the most remote and scenic locations throughout PNG.

The company is the only one registered in PNG with its own vehicles, boats, planes, helicopters, and hunting and fishing equipment.

Imagine yourself arriving by helicopter to a remote village, accepting the genuine hospitality of the people making you comfortable in a traditional bush hut, then setting out on foot accompanied by the local village guides, by 4WD vehicle, boat, hovercraft or by air to seek your quarry.

It could be some troublesome crocodiles or the famous fighting Papuan black bass or barramundi lurking in the roots of the lushly forested serpentine coastal river systems. it might even be a big tusker feral boar. Deer and wild cattle roam the rugged mountains and the dangerous and powerful buffaloes abound in the extensive lowland areas. In the clean, unpolluted, coastal waters, it might even be big game marlin, mackerel or plentiful tuna, if that takes your fancy. Or you might just want to dive and photograph the famous reefs and undersea marine life.

As keen sportsmen, you now have an opportunity through Niugini Adventures to pursue your sport responsibly under truly unique "last frontier" conditions. This is an experience which has been lost to the developed world.

We are a village-based tourist operator, so your visit will be a bonus to the local villagers because they receive income for their services. Plus you also help protect their village lifestyle by assisting them to exterminate the feral animals which destroy their gardens and natural environment.

The history of civil aviation as it has developed in Papua New Guinea couldn't be more extraordinary. On first encounter it sounds like a sequence of Amazing Facts, which you might stumble on only in popular magazines. Some of the elements, which indeed date back to the '20's, are stories of enterprise, endurance and even heroism. But a little study makes it crystal clear that this is classic country for using the aeroplane as a specialised form of transport and that those who see this and grasp the opportunity it offers, reap rich rewards and deep satisfaction.

The founder of MBA (in full, Milne Bay Air, after the province where it began) was a private architect who happened to be a flyer and to own an aeroplane. John Wild, a naturalised citizen of PNG since Independence, happened to fly an amphibian. Milne Bay Province governs many island communities scattered over thousands of square miles of water, just the place for an amphibian, so they asked him to provide a service to remote villages.

In the eleven years that followed, Wild built a business which is today a fully-fledged commuter airline, operating 22 aircraft, flying 25,000 kilometres a day to 170 destinations each week and offering a charter helicopter service to corporate clients. A jet Medevac service run by the company was used 26 times last year and the comfortable, indeed luxurious, Cessna Citation Jet used for this service is also available for internal and external flights by senior executives and VIP's.

Lady Luck, in the shape of the sudden closure in 1993 of another, similar airline, played her part. The presence in PNG of large corporate clients like oil and mining companies makes for a steady demand for charter flights. But, without enterprise, serious hardwork and a passionate addiction to efficiency and service to the customer, the airline just would not have happened.

Every plane stationed at a base outside Port Moresby is recalled to MBA's hangar there every 50 flying hours for special maintenance. And outstation air-

208

craft are also rotated regularly.

PNG's rugged terrain and harsh climate and its adventurous, short runway airstrips make great demands on the planes and on the men and women who fly them. To increase passenger safety, MBA operate dual-pilot flights with one captain and one first officer. All newly recruited staff start off in the co-pilot seats of the six Dornier 228's and the 328, before they are promoted to captain one of the eight Twin Otters. Pilots accumulate experience steadily, but the difficult flying conditions and the rigorous commuter schedules provide ample justification for the old saw - one year's flying in PNG is worth ten in any other country in the world!

Of course you can fly for fun in PNG. MBA is seriously concerned with tourism via the office it maintains in Cairns, Australia. MBA runs a weekly 'Mountain Explorer Tour' of remote airstrips. In addition

there's a growing number of package tours run in conjunction with various guesthouses and lodges round the country.

Corporate charter work, however, is the backbone of the company and looks likely to increase, as mining and oil-drilling gather momentum. During the construction and development of the Kutubu oil field MBA was solely responsible for the movement of no less than 70,000 passengers and 620,000 kilos of cargo.

The regular transport of commuters and cargo to southern ports and to central highland destinations, as well as to many of the island provinces, now means that the general public sees MBA as an accomplished second level airline. It will not have escaped their notice that 15 of the 68 pilots are PNG nationals, nor that the first woman national to become a First Officer in PNG, works for MBA.

"Experience Papua New Guinea culture as the first explorers found it", says the brochure for Karawari Lodge, just one of four locations offered by Trans Niugini Tours.

Thirty years ago a young engineering graduate, Bob Bates, arrived in PNG. He worked for the government building roads and airstrips. It took him all over the country. He liked what he saw. He decided to stay and began a business showing visitors around. By 1986 he had 30 vehicles running tourists out from Port Moresby. He saw a need for accommodation. "Not", Bob thought, "the standard international hotel but something more characteristic of the country." He built his first lodge. It was the start of Trans Niugini Tours.

From reef to rainforest Trans Niugini Tours offers visitors a unique experience. Ambua Lodge near Tari in the Southern Highlands, Malolo Plantation Lodge on the north coast near Madang, and Karawari Lodge and the expeditionary vessel Sepik Spirit on the Sepik River and its tributaries, have all been carefully positioned to allow the inquisitive or specialised traveller the best locations to see and experience all the incredibly diverse natural and cultural wonders this country has to offer.

"We take our visitors from hot to cool, from high to low, by air, by boat, by canoe. Most of our clients go to all four facilities. They have come to see the people and nature", explains Bob Bates. Accommodation in Ambua Lodge is a series of 40 round thatched cab-ins nestling in lush tropical rainforest. After a day of crossing vine bridges, spotting elusive tree kangaroos or birds of paradise and meeting the flamboyant Huli people, visitors can relax with a drink by the huge fireplace and enjoy fine cuisine amidst massive Sepik carved pillars. Everything is built from traditional materials. Electricity comes from a mini-hydro plant which called on all Bob's engineering skills to develop. Ambua Lodge won the Pacific Heritage Award as " a superb example of culturally sensitive and ecologically responsible tourism".

Malolo Plantation Lodge is of a different style. Originally a coconut plantation, the lodge retains its colonial architectural charm. It has 14 air-conditioned rooms each with a balcony or garden patio overlooking the ocean and flanked by magnificent gardens. This is where the rainforest meets the sea and the emphasis is on the natural environment - blue lagoons, remote island cays and colourful coral reefs with exotic marine life. Expert guides offer a range of activities including walks, bird watching, snorkelling, diving and sea kayaking. Or you might just want to relax by the fresh water swimming pool and sleep to the sounds of the sea.

Karawari Lodge is more of a challenge. It is cut out of the jungle on a ridge above the Karawari river, a

tributary of the great Sepik river. Traditional style houses offer all the comforts of a first class hotel in a location about as far removed from international as you can get. You can dine and enjoy a drink in the 'haus tambaran', a Sepik spirit house complete with stunning artefacts and hand carved furniture. This is Arambak country, a country of craftsmen. There's a thousand miles of jungle in every direction with only two ways in and out, the air and the river.

And if the river beckons you can take a few days on the Sepik Spirit. It is the ultimate 'floating lodge'. A river boat of revolutionary new design which accommodates a maximum of 18 passengers in fully air-conditioned comfort. The Sepik Spirit cruises the middle reaches of the river, with the prolific traditional wood carving of the Latmul people, up to the seldom visited Blackwater Lakes.

Trans Niugini Tours encourages the fully independent traveller as well as small tour groups. It is the very best in eco-tourism. Bob Bates says, "Papua New Guinea is something of a 'last frontier' for that small number of international travellers who visit our country each year. We're a destination where mass tourism has no role to play, a land where the conservation of the wetland, bird habitat, rainforest, rich flora and fauna and the traditional cultural lifestyles of the local people should always be paramount."

Tourism in Papua New Guinea is on the verge of taking off. Despite the country's acknowledged potential, tourism is still a relatively under-exploited industry in PNG. But the scenario is changing rapidly. The national government now regards tourism as one of its key priority areas for the generation of income and employment.

"Unity in diversity" accurately describes the diverse terrains, cultures and people which make up the country. From the point of view of geographical setting, the country is a vast, primitive and sensationally beautiful destination for travellers. From a tourist's viewpoint it is the "last great frontier on earth". This diversity offers a potential for tourism development in PNG far in excess of that for other countries.

Due to the existence of rich mineral and forest resources, little political attention was focused on this service industry in the past. In 1980 the number of short-term visitors to PNG was 38,823. By 1994 it was still almost at the same level at 38,739. More than half of these visitors are from the neighbouring Oceania region, especially from Australia. The majority are here on business (with a steady increase from Asian countries). Only a third are holidaying visitors, though numbers fluctuate wildly over the years.

This poor performance can be attributed chiefly to a number of factors: restrictive aviation policies, governmental disinterest, high internal travel costs, lack of consistent promotional efforts and adverse and often misappropriate press coverage about law and order problems in certain parts of the country.

All these factors are currently being addressed as part of the country's new active drive for tourism growth.

The government established a new and specialised body, the Tourism Promotion Authority (TPA) in early 1993 to change the nature of tourism in the country. It is to operate as a stimulus for the private sector by encouraging overall demand for the country as a destination and by encouraging the development of facilities and infrastructure. The high potential in this area has been widely recognised by the World Bank, the Tourism Council of South Pacific and other international institutions.

The TPA's objective is to market Papua New Guinea overseas and domestically as a tourist destination, thereby stimulating strong economic growth in the sector. At the same time, it is committed to improving the standard of tourism products, facilities and services within the country.

Tourism products include adventure tourism such as diving, surfing, trekking, kayaking and white water rafting. Special interest tourism include bird watching, butterfly watching, game fishing, nature photography and botanist's studies and culture oriented tourism products. For interested and serious travellers, cruise trips through scenic and culturally vibrant regions such as Milne Bay and Sepik provide a memorable lifetime experience.

One of the major problems for tourism growth in PNG was lack of knowledge about its tourism products in the international market. No country was as largely absent from the tourism map of the world. In the past, no concerted effort was made to improve the situation. Since its inception in 1993, TPA has been very actively engaged in promoting the country's tourism image in identified markets. It has taken part in all major trade and consumer shows in Western Europe and Australia, in specialised shows in the USA, Japan and Singapore, and has also organised

213

several road shows in Australia and Western Europe. As supportive measures TPA organised familiarisation tours of journalists, photographers, film and television crews and travel industry people from targeted markets. Advertising campaigns in specific product magazines are also ongoing activities of the TPA.

Along with promotional activities TPA has organised several educational and training workshops in sustainable tourism. It has placed high emphasis on training various segments of the industry such as tour guides, tour operators, accommodation units, provincial tourism offices etc. A large, very optimistic tourism awareness campaign for all sections of the people of the country is likely to be initiated shortly.

TPA assists local entrepreneurs with advisory, technical and administrative support. The country is not looking for large-scale urban oriented tourism. It is encouraging small and medium-sized facilities, village-based, in traditional style guest houses and resorts.

Conservation of the country's ecosystems (land and water) and its traditional culture is the key for developing its tourism future.

Papua New Guinea, with its vast untapped resources for tourism development, has now reached the stage of take-off for fast growth. The TPA's efforts are already paying off. Of the specific products where the country has a tremendous competitive edge, diving has already attracted considerable attention of the international experts and enthusiasts.

However the number of visitors to any destination cannot increase overnight. International tour operators plan their tour programmes and destinations well in advance. PNG is now being promoted actively by both government agencies and the industry as an exciting tourist destination. With a usual gestation

214

period of about two years, these concerted efforts are likely to yield results from 1996 onwards.

TPA expects there will be a significant upsurge of visitors in the near future, the great majority of them being holiday-makers. It is essential that the momentum and direction initiated by TPA be maintained. At the same time structural bottlenecks in the areas of aviation and other infrastructural areas need to be eased.

Development of a viable tourism industry in PNG can ease many of the economic problems the country is encountering today. It can offer effective solutions to social problems through the creation of employment and income generating opportunities for the unemployed and under-employed youth. PNG has all the prerequisites and potential to develop itself as a major tourism destination within a short period of time. It only requires a concerted effort by all the concerned parties to make it a reality.

215

people
and cu

ulture

Papua New Guinea is famous for its wide diversity of languages. With well over 700 indigenous languages (a figure of 846 is sometimes claimed), it has nearly two fifths of all those spoken in the world today. It has proved a veritable goldmine for linguists.

This large number may be broadly divided into two groups: Austronesian, which has about 200 languages, and non-Austronesian, or Papuan, which has about 500 languages. The former are mostly spoken in the coastal and island regions, while the latter can be found in the highland interior. Most of the Papuan languages are complex and spoken by very small groups of people, the main exception being Enga which has over 150,000 speakers. For a long time it was thought that the Papuan languages were unrelated to one another, but they have since been divided into much larger groups. Only seven languages remain isolated from the main branches.

How these people came to speak so many tongues is a fascinating subject for speculation, but more significant are the lingua francas they use to communicate with one another. In effect, there are only three principal languages: Tok Pisin (New Guinea Pidgin or Neo-Melanesian), Hiri Motu (or Police Motu) and English.

The first of these emerged as a trading language, but was developed when trade turned from goods to people in the nineteenth century when many New Britain and New Ireland men were abducted and forced to work on Samoan sugar plantations. Today, Pidgin has a much higher status and, despite its clear associations with colonial times, it is used freely by most people all over Papua New Guinea. Hiri Motu, mostly used in the Port Moresby area, is also a pidgin. It originated in village Motu and was spread by Sir William MacGregor's police force in the late nineteenth century. The press use only Pidgin and English and the latter is the language of government and the education system.

There is a real risk of many local langauges dying out, as has happened in South America. A change of thinking in education policy, to teach the first years in school in the local language, reflects a desire to keep them alive - as another of PNG's amazing treasures.

OVERVIEW

Papua New Guinea as a nation identifies itself more with Melanesia than with any other group of nations and that probably goes for the majority of its people. It is, of course, more complex and much more related to geophysical features. To the west of the Owen Stanley range are the Papuans, to the East those closest to Melanesia. In the outlying islands are some who would feel closer to Polynesia or Micronesia. Then there are the Highlanders. Within each group there is a wide range of physical types.

Papua New Guineans can usually classify their fellow countrymen to within a few hundred miles of their birthplace, often much less. Genetic analysis of a small sample of people from the Highlands has established that there could have been little marriage outside local areas, for the DNA is very consistently different from area to area.

Over the last twenty years PNG has been one of the fastest growing nations in the South Pacific. In 1995 the population is estimated to have reached about 4 million. In PNG indigenous people are always known as 'nationals' and Western or Australian residents as 'expats'. There is still a large expat population, though it has fallen considerably since

its peak of around 50,000 in 1971. Today it is more like 20,000 and that figure includes many from Asia and Oceania.

PNG is usually described as being rural in character, about 85% of the total population living in villages or scattered settlements. The highest proportion of population (36.7%) can be found in the five Highlands provinces, second highest in the northern coastal region (27.4%) followed by the southern coastal region (20%) and finally the islands region(15.7%).

The average age of both the male and female population is 22.7, a figure that has remained fairly constant since the mid-sixties. Just over 7% reach the age of 60 years or above, with a slightly higher longevity record in rural areas. The average age of marriage has increased slightly over the past twenty years and now stands at about 24.5 for men and 20.8 for women. Many marriages are arranged at a young age, but wives do not usually take up residence with their spouses until they are in their late teens. For those who can afford the bride-price polygamy is still an option but it has showed a marked decline in recent years.

This is the context in which the agencies and ministries who deal with communication, education, home affairs, health, housing and public works have to operate. It is a challenge and it has stimulated a diversity of original objectives and solutions.

The Department of Works (DOW), is a technical agency for implementing government schemes for roads, bridges, schools, hospitals and housing. It deals with new works and with maintenance, either undertaking the work itself or assuring quality control on contracted out projects. In 1994 alone, the DOW implemented over 1,000 capital works projects to the tune of K410.5 million. It exists primarily to serve other government departments and agencies and has to reflect their medium and long-term plans. However it is anxious to develop a proper plan of its own which will enable it to operate efficiently.

In 1992 DOW realigned its organisational structure in line with National Government policy initiatives in the Structural Adjustment Programme. It now has two deputy secretaries, six first assistant secretaries and 25 assistant secretaries divided between two functional areas, Policy & Administration and Technical. It currently has a total staff of 3953, of which 114 (3%) are expatriates. Of the national staff, 130 are professionals including 83 engineers, 19 architects, 21 surveyors, 4 land managers and 3 quantity surveyors. Only 20% of these staff are based at the Headquarters in Boroko, the remaining 80% are actively engaged in field operations in all the provinces of Papua New Guinea.

DOW's main function involves the planning, design and implementation of capital projects but it also does feasibility studies, provides professional and technical advice to both Provincial and local governments and ensures that foreign-funded projects are completed within specific terms and conditions. It maintains a procurement and supply service for stores items, vehicles, plant and machinery throughout the country. It provides technical advice to building boards and research into local building materials. PNG nationals are given on-the-job training. There is special attention given to the management of the environment in rural-oriented programmes such as water and sewerage, roads and low cost housing.

It has long been recognised in the DOW that skilled and highly motivated labour force is essential. In 1971 a Works Training Centre was established in Boroko. A second centre was opened in Konedubu in 1974 and a Civil Engineering centre was opened in Madang in 1978. All three are financed by the DOW and provide sub-professional training to DOW staff in technical, financial and management disciplines. In order to keep

abreast of new technology and modern construction techniques DOW is seeking to upgrade the Boroko Centre to an Institute of Technology. It would provide highly specialised and practical courses to PNG and be open to other South Pacific countries at reasonable cost.

One of the few areas where DOW is not happy with its record is in the operations of Government Stores. This Department seems to have been dogged by problems not least of which was being transferred from one Department to another over the last 20 years. Efficiency and output have suffered. Unprofessional work habits have been developed and manpower is drastically short of skills, management experience and numbers. DOW is determined to do whatever is necessary to resolve these problems and to bring efficiency and high productivity back to the branch.

Much of DOW's work is done in relation to the needs of other agencies. For example the Department of Education has a High School Support Programme. It hopes to create up to 3,440 new student places in the next six years. The capital works component involves the provision of student's dormitories, kitchen/mess, staff residential accommodation, office blocks, laboratories, libraries and other infrastructural facilities.

DOW is also completing programmes for the Department of Agriculture, Health, Civil Aviation and Transport. The roads building programme alone involves several massive projects over the next few years. To this end a National Roads Authority is to be established to be responsible for the development and maintenance of major highways. DOW has a busy future.

It is the belief of NHC that housing should last more than the owners lifetime with normal mainte-nance. Modern housing is the most expensive thing that most people will own and most buyers seem to expect to leave the house to their children. If housing is constructed to standards below the level of the conditions it is expected to endure, it is actually a great disservice to the owners and a waste of resources. NHC believes affordable housing can be constructed to last and anything less is really defrauding the people of PNG.

The National Housing Corporation is the sole Public Housing Agency in Papua New Guinea.

Before the Europeans came, PNG was a country of home owners. All citizens were home owners. How-ever, the country went through rapid changes as it developed. As citizens were uprooted and moved to the urban centres and other areas to work they typi-cally lived in employer-provided housing.

After Independence it was thought it would be best if the citizens again became homeowners and the var-ious governments implemented programmes to pro-mote this. Most of these programmes were to allow the people living in government homes to own them. These programmes were successful and now most of the government houses are now privately owned. However, no successful schemes were developed to provide a new supply of housing. This, combined with the rapid growth in the urban centres, has given us the current severe housing shortage. The onus of provid-ing housing was passed on to private industry.

In the late 80's it became obvious that the delivery of adequate new housing units was not working and the government responded by combining the agencies responsible for housing into the National Housing Corporation. The NHC was formed by Act of Parlia-ment in 1990 and operates as a commercial statutory authority. Thus NHC took on a very large percentage of the existing formal housing in PNG, mostly built before Independence and the movement towards pri-vate ownership of housing.

Undeniably, turning housing-delivery over to pri-vate industry has some very positive aspects. Howev-er, where NHC was responsible for providing housing, the citizens were much better housed. Private indus-try has focused on the areas where the most profit is, housing for the very well-off, leaving the normal citi-zens feeling lucky if they get to share an over crowded house. In providing housing to Papua New Guineans, private industry in the most part has failed miserably.

In most developing and developed countries the construction industry plays a significant role in eco-nomic well-being and success. Housing is a major component of this industry. Also various studies have shown that citizens without adequate housing have low productivity. In most countries one can judge the success and well being of the country just by looking at the way it houses its people and PNG is no differ-ent.

The National Housing Corporation has gone through a major restructuring assisted by the World Bank and as a result is embarking on ambitious programme to give direction to the admittedly fractured PNG housing industry. It believes that the best solution to PNG's housing shortage is through a combined effort by private industry and government. As part of this NHC is in the process of developing a comprehensive programme of incentives to encourage development of housing for all citizens. For example, construction has begun on the Waigani Hostel, new self-contained low-cost units from bedsits to 3-bedroom walk-ups. In Port Moresby work has begun on a 4-phase 1,000 unit project providing up to 4-bedroom units. NHC is in the first phase of an all-nation housing construction programme, including replacing destroyed housing in Rabaul, and it is putting together an aid-funded package of 1,000 low cost rural houses. It also has its own housing construction programmes in progress. In these programmes NHC provides the direction and expertise and private industry constructs the buildings. In all of its programmes it favours those contractors who have the largest PNG-sourced component of materials and labour.

When somebody falls ill in Papua New Guinea they are just as likely to look round for a sorcerer as a doctor. Traditional and 'western' forms of medicine run in parallel, each tolerates the other, though Government does not officially recognise traditional healers. Every market in PNG sells medicinal herbs.

PNG has a National Health Service which is provided by both government and non-government (mainly Church) sources. Health services are arranged in a pyramidal fashion with aidposts at the base, health sub-centres and health centres in the middle, provincial hospitals near the top and national referral hospitals at the apex. The hospitals receive over 50% of the funding.

With 87% of the population living in rural areas the provision of those services is most important. The Churches operate almost 50% of all rural health services and employ 16% of health workers in PNG. They are a vocal, political and very important pressure group in health matters. The Government provided just over K13 million as quarterly grants to Church Agencies for providing health services. However, to quote from a recent (1995) report, "The Department cannot issue Grants by cheques to Churches if Department of Finance and Planning cannot give us Warrant Authority." Health has got caught up in a cash-flow crisis.

There are a number of International and Bilateral Agencies who contribute to the Health budget. The World Health Organisation (WHO) provides about K3 million and a deal of technical assistance. UNICEF assists in Child health programmes. AIDAB will be contributing tied-aid to certain projects under the PNG-Australia Bilateral Aid Agreement. Japan has been helping with hospital development. The Asian Development Bank ADB has made loans for improving rural services. Nonetheless there is still much concern over the health of the Nation's people.

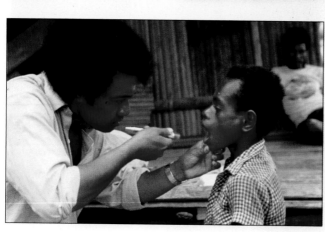

Too many women and children continue to die from preventable causes. PNG has the highest child mortality rates in the West Pacific Region. 24 babies die every day in PNG. To the dismay of all who work in the health sector, clinic attendance has declined since 1986. The causes are identified as lack of funds, poor quality of services and law and order problems. Clinics have been vandalised and medicines and equipment stolen. There has been a decline in the number children immunised and a gradual increase in medium level malnutrition especially in urban areas. The minimum urban wage is K26 per week, whereas food prices have risen by 150% in the last 5 years. Some children are simply not getting enough to eat. The Department fears an epidemic of malnutrition if there is a further rapid rise in food prices following the adoption of free market policies.

On the positive side there are good reports of dental health. Every child at school receives oral health treatment. In the last few years leprosy has been on the decline. While the dedicated efforts of health workers must be acknowledged, there is a general despair that ground is being lost. Hospitals, health centres and even aidposts are cash starved and struggling. Diarrhoeal disease, pneumonia and tuberculosis are on the increase. Malaria control had suffered a setback even before 108 people died in Simbu province in the summer of 1995.

The first case of AIDS was diagnosed in PNG in 1987. The spread of HIV/AIDS was slow until 1993 but is now increasing.

There is an acute awareness of the problems and an effort is made to put forward solutions by the Department of Health. Sweeping reforms may be the only way to avert a crisis. The reformers are asking for more emphasis on preventative medicine. Concerted efforts are needed to educate the rural populations in health matters, utilising women's groups and village councils. The establishment of a radio network would link all health facilities with District and Provincial services. All recognise that access to safe water and proper sanitation is a basic health need. Progress is needed in improving management, cutting wastage and making every 'toea' count. Nobody wants to slip back to a situation where the sorcerer is the only doctor left to consult.

CITY PHARMACY

Whether you need to combat serious diseases like malaria or simply shrug off a persistent cold, City Pharmacy is bound to have a remedy on one of its shelves.

Since its formation in 1987 the go-ahead business has been propelled from relative obscurity to one of the most respected and best known names in Papua New Guinea.

Although the main office and shop is on Waigani Drive, City Pharmacy branches are dotted not only all over the town but all over the country.

"We have expanded at an incredible rate, in fact business doubled last year," admitted Mahesh Patel, the charismatic managing director. "We now have pharmacies in places as far afield as Manus and Madang.

There is so much potential for development we have set up a shop in Kavieng and another started in Bougainville in December 1994. Each one needs to be manned by a qualified pharmacist."

There are now 12 City Pharmacy outlets in Papua New Guinea, five of which were opened in 1993. This boom was partly due to a clinched agreement with Steamships JV Collins and Leahy. Other outlets where City pharmacies are based include Andersons, Stop 'n' Shop and the Family Store.

The rise and rise of City Pharmacy is down to a combination of aggressive marketing, excellent customer service and its capacity to

provide an extensive, high quality range of medical products at competitive prices.

"All our staff have a basic knowledge of first aid and of all the products we sell," said Mahesh. "Some who show particular promise or who need specialist training will be sent off on courses to Australia.

Personal service is very important. Not so long ago Papua New Guinean people would go to a hospital if they had a headache but now they have the confidence to use pharmacies. Our stores are all very well laid out and user friendly."

The fact City Pharmacy is such a young company also makes it thirsty for innovation and fresh ideas. Not only does it boast several of its own in-house brands like antibiotic ointments and antifungal powders, but it now has a range of herbal medicines.

"We always try to be broad minded and prepared to take on new products." said Mahesh. "Also it is important for us to educate people especially about preventing serious diseases like malaria. Papua New Guinea has a very progressive, positive attitude towards health issues and City Pharmacy is glad to be part of it. The future looks optimistic, both for our business and for health-care throughout the entire country."

229

When he took over the Ministry of Home Affairs and Youth Nakikus Konga had been a logger and had spent twenty years in agriculture. He confessed he knew almost nothing about the department. But he soon learnt that this was one of the most complex and crucial areas of government. It is the primary avenue for social development and implements policies concerning women, youth, the handicapped, sport, civil registration and the special needs groups like non government organisations

The Department's mission is to "promote integrated human development with an emphasis on the social needs of individuals, families and communities." A new policy approach has been adopted which reflects a major shift away from individual programmes to an emphasis on the family as the basis or core of society. The Sports commission has developed a 'Sport for All' policy that would cater for all regardless of sex, age, physical ability etc.. Nakikus Konga wants to see "small children, big children, father and mother all participating in sport together. That would be family unity".

The Social Development Policy seeks to promote and maintain harmonious family relationships consistent with traditional family values and Christian principles. But how to get the message across? Literacy, functional literacy, is seen as the answer especially for the bulk of the people who live in rural areas. "People need to understand the world around them, especially those things that are important to improving their lives. For example; a Mini Credit scheme, or awareness of health risks, the right food to eat, general housekeeping, toilet hygiene or how to calculate profits from vegetable marketing."

The department is actively encouraging community based activities. It is working to strengthen and support available resources within the community for settling disputes, handling offences and the village court system particularly with concern for the custody of children and jailing of juveniles.

"Youth is causing about 80% of the problems in the country now. We spend a lot of money on them, treat them when they're sick and then toss them out on the street because there are simply no jobs they can do." Says Nakikus Konga with some passion. "What we offer is non-formal education that will provide them with the basics of how to run a business or how to build a house. We have to do something about the 30% who don't finish their schooling and even the 70% who drop out. Without a literate base there is no chance of a reformed Papua New Guinea people".

One such scheme is at Hohola in Port Moresby. Centre 2000 provides boys and girls with some basic training. The boys, mostly school drop-outs aged 16 to 22 learn metal-work and woodwork. They learn to measure, assemble, weld and, at the end of the course, are given a certificate which they can show to a potential employer.

The boys made the bread oven which the girls are using in their cookery classes. In PNG all the cooking is in one pot. At Centre 2000 the girls have successfully learnt the rudiments of international cooking styles and are skilfully producing pizza, mince-meat balls, bread and bread rolls. They sell their efforts at lunch times and are sold out every day. The girls do a one year training, six months cookery and six month sewing. Again it is basic sewing, six stitches, a little embroidery, tie-dye, rag rugs and simple costumes. Many of the items are for sale. There is only one problem. Currently there are fourteen girls on the course and this is the maximum number.

As in most other countries women are the home-

makers in PNG. Women make up 58% of the population. They produce and process over 80% of the country's food much of which is done with limited technical assistance. They are acknowledged as the backbone of PNG society but as Nakikus Konga says with some force, "in Papua New Guinea, unlike other countries and totally different from western countries, women are always regarded as the lower order."

Molly Daure of the Women's Division does not disagree with this assessment but she and her staff are intent on creating a National platform on which to discuss women's issues such as violence, particularly domestic violence, transport and communication, health issues and education. The disadvantaged position of women in PNG was recognised at Independence in 1975 and actual policy measures were implemented. Ten years later in 1984 the National Women's Development Programme was introduced which aimed to mobilise women and build up a strong network of women's organisations from districts to national networks. Unfortunately it was consistently under-funded.

Current indicators reveal that the literacy status of women, for example, is lower than that in other Melanesian countries. In employment very few women occupy managerial positions. The majority of young women do not receive adequate training either

to participate in the formal sector or to function productively in their own villages. The health status of women is low. Papua New Guinea has one of the highest infant and maternal mortality rates in the world. The life expectancy of women is 47 years and most women die of preventable diseases.

In the late eighties and nineties there has been a decline in the number of women engaged with the decision making process. Although the National Constitution provides for the equal rights of all citizens women have not been able to fully understand and exercise their rights. This has been due to ineffective government mechanisms advocating and promoting the rights of women.

1995 is the year of the Fourth United Nations World Conference on Women. As the Independence celebrations begin in PNG, a group of Papua New Guinea women will be in Beijing discussing sustainable development for the next decade. The Beijing forum and the National Policy for women are raising awareness of women's issues in PNG. Efforts are under way to establish a Women's Information and Data Base System. Whether these measures alleviate the condition of the majority of women in the rural areas of PNG remains to be seen.

The Home Affairs Ministry is also responsible for liaising with Non-Government organisations. There are thousands of NGOs in Papua New Guinea. Church based NGOs run schools, health clinics and other humanitarian projects.. Large-scale NGOs run by international organisations like the Red Cross or Red Crescent and Salvation Army do charity relief work. Indigenous NGOs, some of which are community-based, do development work and others, including advocacy groups, deal with social justice.

ICRAF, the Individual and Community Rights Advocacy Forum was founded three years ago by lawyer Powes Parkop. Based in Gerehu in the outskirts of Port Moresby, it is a resource for any group interested in issues concerned with human rights, women, land and the environment. Funding comes mainly from international aid including the Germany-based Bread for the World and the Dutch ICCO (Interchurch Group in Development). At present there are 9 full-time staff and 5 part-time workers.

ICRAF has three lawyers and a number of staff with para-legal training. It sees one of its functions to monitor the law, lobbying for or against proposed or existing laws and checking whether new laws are being complied with. It runs campaigns. One is the campaign to protect forestry law which involves press publicity, petitioning government and running workshops to make people aware of their rights. ICRAF declares that the registration of customary land is not necessary and could well result in the alienation of land which has sustained the people of PNG for thousands of years. This is a controversial position.

When asked why the NGOs play such an important role in PNG today Powes Parkop answered that they had filled a vacuum. There was a need for a critical perspective and a need to reassure people that a sustainable model of development could work. In Papua New Guinea today the NGOs, the media and the Judiciary are doing a grand job of keeping us sane with our eye on the future.

RUGBY LEAGUE

On every little space in Papua New Guinea you will find people playing rugby. It came with the discovery of gold and it's now PNG's most popular spectator sport.

Australians who flocked to Wau-Bulolo during the 1930s gold rush played rugby as a distraction. It was only a very short time before the game was put on an organised footing by staff from business houses in Port Moresby. The first two clubs, Paga and Magani were founded in the mid-1940s from supporters of rival Australian states, New South Wales and Queensland.

For twenty years rugby was an expatriates game. In the 1960s it suddenly picked up as a national game, some say because the Highlanders got involved. It suited their aggressive natures and was more respectable than fighting! Papua New Guineans immediately showed a natural talent for rugby. An annual Papua versus New Guinea match provided some great moments until it was phased out in 1973 in favour of a four-zone competition, Southern, Highlands, Northern and New Guinea Islands.

In 1974 the Papua New Guinea Rugby Football League, the controlling body of the code in the country was formed and PNG became an associate member of the International Board. PNG has to fulfil its share of international commitments, including hosting Test matches and touring abroad. It also plays 'friendlies' with its nearest neighbours Australia and New Zealand and other South Pacific Ocean neighbours such as Fiji.

Since 1991 the 'in' competition has been the semi-professional Inter-City Cup competition. It has proved a showpiece for the best talent from clubs all around the country. For the future there is a plan to put rugby back into the schools by maintaining a schoolboys competition and helping administer local fixtures.

The national team is dubbed the KUMULS - pronounced Coomools - a Pidgin word for a black Bird of Paradise. The Kumuls have bested all other International board countries except Australia. But as one official pointed out "We're working on it".

RELIGION

Christianity has had such a profound effect on Papua New Guinea that perhaps no traditional beliefs and practices remain unaffected by it. The 1990 census recorded just over ninety thousand people (2.6%) who claimed they followed no religion and a mere ten thousand people (0.3%) who declared themselves to be non-Christian. The other 97% are, at least nominally, followers of the Christian faith.

OVERVIEW

This has been a rapid conversion. The first substantial missionary efforts were not launched until the late 19th century and only 7 of the nine churches currently at work in PNG have a history that goes back to before the end of the Second World War. The Roman Catholic church, which is the largest in the country, began to send missionaries rather earlier than the rest, but with little success and it returned to Europe within a few years. In the 1880s and 1890s, further missions of a variety of denominations arrived and began to work earnestly at converting the country to Christianity.

In that period, and right through until the 1970s, many of the missionaries were extremely insensitive to the cultural and religious rites and practices they found in PNG. They often destroyed, or persuaded their converts to destroy, artefacts, images and even the haus tambaran, the important spirit house in the village, because they were regarded as inappropriate in the light of the new faith. Some missionary work produced even greater trauma, reorganising and realigning the hierarchy and values of the societies they intruded upon.

At the same time, the missionaries and certainly the churches have done a great deal to promote education, health, welfare and transport and may be regarded as the pioneers of the PNG's contemporary infrastructure and social services. By crossing clan lines, they have also encouraged the varied peoples of New Guinea to think of themselves as a whole nation and have played a major role in that aspect of Independence.

The latest grouping of Christian denominations shows that the 30% of the nation is Roman Catholic, 23% Evangelical Lutheran, 13% United Churches (Baptist, Brethren, Church of Christ, Congregational, Orthodox, Presbyterian, Protestant and Jehovah Witnesses), 9% Evangelical Alliances, 8% Seventh Day Adventists and 7% Pentecostals. The remainder are divided between traditional beliefs, Salvation Army, Bahai, non-Christians, other religions, agnostics and atheists.

BIBLE SOCIETY

The first Bible work began in PNG with a translation of the Motu gospel in 1881.

In 1945 an Agency was established by the Bible Society in Australia. Ten years later, in 1955, the first Bible House in the Pacific Islands was opened here. Now it is a national society, a registered not-for-profit organisation serving all Christian denominations.

In the early days traders came with goods to exchange for land or other resources, but the missionaries came with the Gospel. Papua New Guinea is a Christian nation thanks to many of them spending years translating into the vernacular.

There are thought to be more than 864 languages spoken in PNG and even today less than a third have translations of their own. However, the Bible Society has tried to ensure that all the major languages are covered. It currently has 8 full Bibles while many more New Testaments and selected books of the Bible have been published. The complete Bible is available in both the national languages Tok Pisin and Hiri Motu.

The Society has about 50 active projects at any given time. Some projects might only involve corrections, revisions or small reprints but every publication has an important place in the Society's work.

In 1991, designated International Year of Literacy, the Bible Society worked with the Summer Institute of Linguistics and the Seventh Day Adventists to create a series of booklets, "Tok Bilong God" which developed reading skills with Bible stories. They have been a great success, more than two million have been distributed. Many children buy their own copies in addition to those supplied through the schools.

Now the Society is using new technology to produce audio cassettes in Tok Pisin and Motu. It is producing Braille editions for the blind and scholarly editions for seminarians as well as scriptures for the Corrective Institutions throughout the country.

Today the head office and administrative centre are still located in Port Moresby. It relies on co-operation with other translation organisations, Churches, Christian Bookshops, volunteers and a small number of staff.

As a major publisher the Society has produced well over four and a half million scriptures in the past ten years. In addition many more thousands obtained from other publishers in English have been distributed.

The Bible Society of Papua New Guinea celebrates it's 20th anniversary together with 50 years of Bible Society work in the country during this 20th anniversary year of independence.

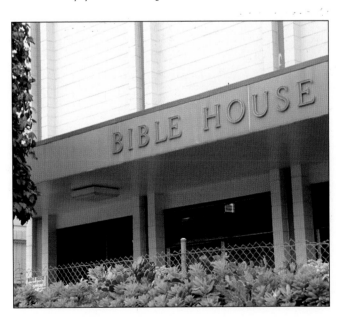

Education did not begin in Papua New Guinea with western contact. All societies have methods to deal with the transmission of knowledge from generation to generation, including knowledge of the right way of doing things. All societies are diligent to ensure that young people learn what is necessary to enable the society to survive and prosper.

Many of the ritualistic practices of traditional society in PNG, in pre-contact times, can be understood in terms of the preservation of knowledge, skills and power and their transmission, at specific times, to selected members of the younger generation. The ten years that young men in parts of Gulf Province used to spend in seclusion in the Haus Elavo, learning the duties expected of men, was education. So were the practices in women's houses that communicated to all young girls what the society thought they should know about the very different expectations their societies had for them. The pattern was repeated in every part of the country. Even today the Wigmen of the Huli people in the Southern Highlands Province go to Wig Schools where they live in seclusion for a year and half while they learn sacred dances and grow the hair that they will later cut off to form the wigs that they need to wear during their rituals.

The first shift in this world view came with missionization and the simultaneous encounter with Western technology and Western forms of social organization. With total confidence in their own view of immortal life the missionaries replaced the old gods with their own. Missionization was the first Western educational process to affect people in Papua New Guinea and it is an on-going one. Converting people to Christianity requires schools, preachers, and literacy. It requires progress through a curriculum or body

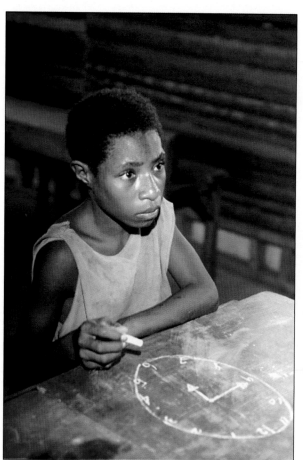

of knowledge and the passing of a test or some form of examination to check the understanding achieved. It is only the subject matter and the degree of faith involved that makes missionization different from the secular processes we normally know by the term 'education'.

As educationists, the missionaries performed one vital function, which even those who deplore their single-mindedness must acknowledge, and that is to have democratized the idea of education. If knowledge was highly valued in traditional society, it was only the few who were allowed access to it. In fact much energy went into the elaboration of rules which were designed to prevent all but a self-perpetuating class of individuals from participating in it. Christianity, with its proclamation that God's word was intended for all, changed this basic social premise. At a stroke, the acquisition of the most important knowledge became a theoretical possibility for everyone, a matter of pragmatic issues such as the provision of schools, teachers, books and the simple opportunity to learn.

Of course what has been discovered subsequently is that, in practice, providing an effective, worthwhile, relevant and valued education service is a far from simple matter.

OVERVIEW

This is true for any country in the world, no matter how 'developed'. It requires endless care and attention to ensure that the experience of schooling does truly reach out to all, that the curriculum is up-to-date and well thought out, that inequalities do not get built into the system, and that those who are particularly successful at it do not fall into the same patterns of behaviour as those earlier shamans and magicians who tried to keep all the benefits to themselves.

Some of these concerns have yet to surface publicly in PNG, which is still struggling with some of the more basic problems that prevent education being the powerful force it might be for both individual and national development. But after these have been solved, when all the school buildings have been built and are being well-maintained, when the teachers are all well-trained professionals who are happy with their status in society, and when all children are attending school, they will remain as tantalizing questions which have to keep being asked.

"Education is the key to everything", says Education Minister Joseph Onguglo. "Without education the country cannot progress, or take its place in the wider world, or even understand what its own problems are. We must give top priority to education - and do it now. Every delay weakens our future prospects. Papua New Guinea is full of talented people but without education and relevant technical training they will not be able to be effective."

Papua New Guinea, like other countries in the world. strives to provide education for all its citizens, first through universal primary education and then by other means. To achieve this aim, successive governments since independence have set different targets, the latest being the year 1999. By 1999 all children of primary school age are suppos'd to have access to and receive at least six years of primary education.

At present primary education is provided by 3,000 community schools, approximately half of which are government schools and half are those organised and run by the missions, of which the number of Catholic schools, 850, slightly exceeds the sum of the other church schools combined. While the church schools are run by the missions, most staff salaries and some other costs are met by the provincial governments, assisted by grants from the national government, with the national government taking responsibility for the core subjects of the curriculum.

Various obstacles stand in the way of achieving the stated aim of universal primary education for all. What educationists call 'attrition rates' are high, so that even though some 92% of the target population are known to enrol at some point in their lives, only 55% of those who start do actually complete their education to Grade 6. A serious 15% drop out of school very early, between Grades 1 and 2. The government believes that language policy may have something to do with this, the language of instruction being the country's official language, English, while the language spoken by children of 7 or 8, especially in the rural areas, may be any of the 700 – 800 for which PNG is famous.

Consequently, language policy has been a feature of the latest educational reforms. "Tok Ples Pri Skul" is the pidgin title of an existing pre-school movement in which young children receive their first experience of schooling in their own vernacular tongue. From 1995 this language policy is to be extended to the first three years of primary education as part of a set of policies designed to recognise the crucial importance of a strong community base to life at all stages but particularly for young people.

A further big loss of numbers occurs at the transition from primary to secondary school. Only 35% of those who complete primary school go on to secondary school and there is much local variation in the take-up rates, with young people in the Highlands, for example in Enga Province, participating in far fewer numbers than those in the coastal districts and urban areas.

Education is supposedly free in Papua New Guinea, although some schools have been forced to re-introduce fees, but it is not compulsory, That is not because the government does not wish to insist that all children should attend school, but because of the practical difficulties of enforcing such a law in a terrain so formidably opposed to visitations, or even communications, from the centre. It must also be admitted that the government is itself defeated by some aspects of the situation. There are areas where schools are closed for one reason or another, and there is a general need for more resources.

"I am worried about the priority accorded to education", says Joseph Onguglo. "To my mind it is the most important of all Government's responsibilities because it relates to the future ability of this country to look after itself, or even survive. I am determined that our education system should progress."

241

The history of Higher Education in Papua New Guinea is closely related to the move towards Independence. In 1966, almost a decade before the cessation of the Australian administration and as part of a drive to establish a cadre of professionally educated men and women who would be able to run their own country after Independence, the first students enrolled at the new University of Papua New Guinea. There were just 58 of them. Three years later, most of them had graduated.

By its Silver Anniversary year in 1991, the University of PNG had granted 4,000 Bachelor's Degrees in 12 different subject areas as well as nearly the same number of Diplomas, A number of students had gone on to achieve Doctorates at Universities overseas. Today students are enrolled in six faculties: Arts, Creative Arts, Education, Law, Medicine and Science. The University also runs a number of shorter courses. With its associated activities and institutions, the University, in its large main campus at Waigani in Port Moresby, occupies a prominent place in the public life of Papua New Guinea.

But now there are two Universities in PNG. The second, the University of Technology at Lae, was formally inaugurated as a fully-fledged university in 1973. Specialising in engineering, mining, business studies, forestry, surveying and land studies, it is now a vibrant academic community with functions that go far beyond the education of its 1,800 students. Most students live on campus. Recent years have seen the setting up of a number of specialist centres (the Management Development Centre, the Heritage Centre, the Land Studies Centre, for example) which are associated with the research and teaching functions of the

university and serve the wider community in a number of ways, for example by interacting with policy-makers in the worlds of government, business and industry.

Topping the list of functions of a modern university, in the opinion of the University of Technology's Vice Chancellor, Misty Baloiloi, is that of being a sort of intellectual ombudsman to society as a whole, with the task of bringing knowledge, scholarship, research capability and technical expertise to bear on the real-life issues of Papua-New Guinean society.

That is also the opinion of Joseph Onguglo, Minister of Education.

"I am anxious to see the development of all forms of education that will empower our people to face the future on competitive terms with others in the Asian-Pacific region and in the world as a whole," he said.

"We need all forms of higher education and training and we need plenty of vocational education also."

Higher education is about to undergo an explosion with the increasing demands of the extractive industries (mining, the oil industry) and the management of forests and fisheries. The growing professionalism of all forms of business and commerce requires a big surge in the numbers of qualified personnel. There is also the matter of the planned expansion in the number of secondary schools which are able to offer Year 11 and Year 12 education,. This is projected to cause something like a five-fold increase in numbers entering higher education by the year 2004. At present 900 students graduate from Grade 12 each year and apply for places in higher education. Within the decade this could be as much as 5,000. This will expose even further the huge need which has to be met.

INTERNATIONAL EDUCATION AGENCY OF PAPUA NEW GUINEA

The International Education Agency of Papua New Guinea (IEA) is a private, non-profit making company which has the responsibility of managing 21 schools, ranging from large urban campuses to small rural schools. The IEA offers an international standard of education to both national and expatriate citizens residing in PNG. It employs approximately 300 teachers to educate the 5,600 students enrolled in its schools.

The IEA is governed by a Board of Directors which oversees all aspects of the IEA and consists of elected representatives of member schools. While schools are accountable to the IEA, many aspects of school management, such as selection of teachers and financial management, have been devolved to the local school level.

IEA schools are characterised by a broad range of nationalities amongst both students and teachers. "In some schools we have pupils from up to 35 countries and also many different nationalities of teachers," said Steve Mead, the IEA Secretary. "It provides a valuable cross-section of individuals, all of whom can learn from each other."

Since Steve joined the IEA 15 years ago, he has seen many changes to its function and structure. "Perhaps the most interesting shift has been in the ratio of expatriate to national children," he explained. "Twenty years ago IEA schools were filled almost solely by expatriate children but nowadays over half our enrolment is national children". In recognising this shift the IEA's latest initiative has seen the employment of a number of qualified citizen teachers. Many of these will be enrolled in a teacher development programme in co-operation with an Australian University leading to a B.Ed. degree.

The IEA maintains a high level of professional development for its principals and teaching staff to ensure that its educational outcomes are comparable with international standards. Students enrolled through to Year 12 have the opportunity to complete an Australian tertiary entrance qualification and, if in Port Moresby, the International Baccalaureate. Leaving students have been accepted at highly-rated institutions throughout the world.

ARTS AND CULTURE

What is meant by the term culture, which is used so frequently by so many different writers and speakers, especially those extolling the tourist industry in places like Papua New Guinea?

The culture of a society, or even of a small group of people within a society, is the combination of ideas, behaviours and beliefs which give meaning to the identity and history of the group. In the traditional cultures of PNG these are embodied in the dress, dances, ceremonies, stories, songs, dramatic performances, and magic practices of a group. They are also in the taboos relating to status, gender, genealogy and the spirit world.

Unfortunately there is a tendency for powerful western ideas and technologies to wipe out any beliefs or techniques that do not seem to be as immediately effective or efficient as the western ones.

The confusion of modern western ways with long-standing local traditions is not helped by commentators who refer to the diverse and complicated technologies, and the arcane spiritual beliefs of societies in PNG as 'stone age'. The term 'stone age' refers to a stage of human technology which, in the Middle East and Europe, took place over a period from 50,000 to 2,000 years ago, after which metal became available. It tends to be a somewhat derogatory term applied to groups living now just because they did not happen to use metal tools until recently.

There is an accurate position to take on these matters in the late twentieth century. It is that all human societies are much more alike than they are different and every scrap of diversity should be prized.

This is why the cultures of Papua New Guinea are so important.

There are more separate tribal cultures with their associated art forms in Papua New Guinea than anywhere else in the world. From the spirit masks worn in initiation ceremonies and dance rituals and the big, basket-weave shrouds donned by elders at that time, to the huge, supernatural representations on the gable ends of houses and the ancestral boards which ward off evil spirits, arts in PNG are evidence of the powerful beliefs of each different group. Tribal fighting occasionally takes place today in some areas of the Highlands and weapons such as bows and arrows, together with spears, axes and shields, are still made with their original purpose in mind. There is a whole range of domestic items, different in each area, from string bags (bilums) to woven baskets, food hooks, knives, spoons and scrapers, all the tools required for hunting, fishing and agriculture, and all the means of mak-

246

ing music and sounds, from flutes and bull-roarers to beaters, whistles and drums.

Art of people in traditional societies is not something to hang on the wall and look at because it is beautiful. It is an essential tool required for the carrying out of ritual, something necessary to wear or carry while dancing, for example, or to use in divination or sorcery or when communicating with spirits. The fact that many of these artefacts are still made today is either because they are still needed for some version of those purposes or because both tourists and local people value them for a whole variety of quite different reasons - for the quality of the workmanship involved, for example, or the startling and unique designs, or the way they will contribute to the decor of a house in another part of the world. Some people, but a minority, can perhaps imagine what kind of experience the original ritual was for the persons involved. Most foreigners, however well-informed, would not be able to do this, and for many local people also, especially young or educated city dwellers, this increasingly appears to be an impossibility.

New kinds of tourism, which count on tourists being willing to learn and to be sensitive to local ways, can go some way to minimizing the impact of foreign life-styles on local cultures. It is a difficult process to manage. It is somewhat naive to hope that all tourists will turn themselves into anthropologists and art historians, especially as the trend within PNG itself, officially encouraged and promoted by government, churches, the education process, development agencies and the world of international business and industry, is towards Westernization. So it is within that framework that the traditional practices of ancient cultures must find their place.

The traditional method of broadcasting information in PNG has been the garamut drum. Modern media have much the same advantages and disadvantages.

The beat of a drum can travel for miles and be interpreted by all who know the code. Drums can convey quite detailed messages. Apart from calling someone by pre-arranged signal, drums can summon people to gather together or can announce a death. The beat of a drum can act as a guide if someone is lost in the bush. A caller in a distant village can announce his presence by the use of his own particular call sign - a pattern of drumbeats. Drums can also ward off evil spirits.

Messages on the modern mass media can also travel for miles and be interpreted by all who know the code. Quite detailed messages can be conveyed and announcing a death is not a problem. A convincing programme may even counteract evil spirits. However the expansion of both print and the electronic media into traditional societies brings complicated problems in its train.

First there is the problem of access, which is not just about having the money to buy a daily newspaper, a radio and its batteries, or a television set, although getting hold of any of these is impossible for many in PNG. Access is also about provision: are the newspapers and books available? Is the radio audible? Is there an electricity supply to run the television? For many areas in PNG the answer to all these questions is 'no'.

Access also means having access to the code: that is, understanding the language which the message is using and the cultural context to which it refers. In the case of print, this requires literacy in either English or Tok Pisin, the two lingua franca of PNG. In the case of radio, knowledge of one of these languages is still likely to be necessary, as even at its best NBC never managed to broadcast in more than one or two local languages in any area. Other stations never even tried. But it is in relation to the visual media of television and video that there is the most glaring discrepancy between the cultural context of programmes and audience. This is a problem that has not been solved anywhere in the developing world.

There have been postal services in Papua New Guinea since 1885, so the 20th anniversary of Independence is actually the 110th for the Post Office! Papua and New Guinea were separate entities at that time, but postal services started in the same year.

In Papua, the service was an adjunct to that of Queensland in Australia, with mail being taken from Port Moresby by sailing ships to Cooktown. Queensland postage stamps were used. At Cooktown the mail was sorted and then sent on to its destination. Much of the correspondence of the early missionaries which can be read today in the archives and collections of libraries and museums around the world would have come out of Papua New Guinea in that way.

In 1901 the Papuan government issued its first postage stamps, and continued to do so until the war years. It began issuing pictorial stamps, which were to become a huge success with collectors, in 1932.

After the war, Papua and New Guinea Post Offices came under one administration. The present-day Post Office in PNG dates from that time. The first PNG stamps were issued in 1952.

Since then, the Post Office has gone from strength to strength. From its early days of being administered by Posts and Telegraphs the number of Post Offices in the country has increased from 42 to 87, of which 35 are official Post Offices fully owned by the Post Office, while the remaining 52 are agencies operated under contract to a local business firm or Government Department.

The services offered by today's Post Office are extensive. It is possible to send a letter to even a remote address in PNG. First it will go to the nearest Post Office, from which it will be collected by contractors who come in to the Post Office from the remote areas. Often this service is performed by missions and other responsible organisations.

'Salim Moni Kwik' and 'Kwik Piksa Leta' are the titles in pidgin of two of the most popular modern services.

Salim Moni Kwik is the fastest way to send

money to anywhere in the country. Money paid in at one Post Office can be paid out minutes later at another. Usually the sender will have phoned the recipient so that they are waiting, ready to collect. This ;method is generally preferred to that of sending postal orders through the mail, although these can still be purchased.

Kwik Piksa is the Post Office's public fax service, ideal for documents, certificates, bills, letters, photographs, maps and any other form of paperwork. Kwik Piksa has transformed business operations in PNG just as the fax technology has everywhere else in the world.

While new services are appreciated by businesses and individual customers alike, some of the original services go on being extremely popular. Papua New Guinea stamps have been a great success with philatelists since the first pictorial issue put out by the Papuan Government before the war. There are 14,000 philatelists who are known collectors of PNG stamps, served partly by direct sales from Port Moresby and partly by agents, mainly in Europe. There are six new issues every year, featuring the work of many artists from PNG. The Independence issue has been designed by Banian Masiboda.

Information and communications services are often grouped for convenience under one administrative unit, although they consist of essentially different kinds of people and serve somewhat different functions.

In Papua New Guinea one ministry and one department has been overseeing policy relating to postal and telecommunication services as well as such technical matters as the allocation of wave-lengths. At the same time it deals with radio and television broadcasting and printed media like newspapers, books and government public relations material.

TELIKOM

At Independence there were hardly any telephones outside Port Moresby and communications with the provinces often took the form of radio links. Twenty years later finds Telikom, one of PNG's most up-to-date corporations, with a customer base of 45,000 subscribers, a full range of services and products, a dedicated and professional work-force and an agenda for future development that could provide a model for other public corporations.

The telecommunications system in Papua New Guinea is 100% automatic, with international links to most countries in the world. While the main use of the system is people calling others in PNG itself on the ordinary direct exchange lines, telephone users can, if they wish, avail themselves of wake-up calls, international direct dialling, fax services, ring back price information on long distance calls, call control, call waiting, call forwarding, enquiry calls, a "ring me back when you are free" system, abbreviated dialling and an operator service. Detailed call information in the form of itemised billing is about to become standard.

The underlying technology which makes all of this possible is a network of microwave radio links with repeaters on mountain tops, now backed up by an alternative satellite transmission system, operating through an earth station at Gerehu in Port Moresby. For subscribers beyond the reach of the exchanges, a high frequency service exists which they access by a radio call to an operator who connects them to the network. Digital technology is gradually replacing all of the analogue circuits, resulting in clearer reception and an increased number of possible services.

The success of Telikom is as much due to human resources as it is to technology and the deployment of people is a matter of fine judgement on the part of management, for Telikom employees are both valuable and expensive.

2,000 people work for Telikom and the cost of their services includes not only their salaries, but also the operating costs of maintaining the expanding network in a country with few roads. Engineers have to fly to their work-places and sleep in hotels if they stay overnight. Many visits to transmitters require the use of helicopters. Human resource managers have to facilitate all of this activity.

The actual establishment of the transponders and relay sites has to be the result of negotiations with the customary land-owners - a whole area of activity which is a world away from the technological image which first springs to mind when one considers modern communication systems.

Special problems exist in Papua New Guinea in relation to the establishment of a telecommunications service. These range from outrageously high demands for compensation from the owners of mountain top land to excessive use of telephones by persons who may or may not be able to pay the bill. The first of these problems, now somewhat mitigated by the existence of satellite systems which do not require repeater stations, has sometimes been solved by offering the customary landowners free telephone services. The second problem does result in rather a large number of disconnections.

Telikom is an example of modern corporate management thinking being applied to a situation many would consider to be more complex than equivalent telecommunications situations in other parts of the world. Its rather interesting that the ideas do transfer.

In the opinion of its General Manager, Mr Stan Basiou, the way forward is by association with similar corporations overseas, to benefit from their technology, their research and their management skills. At the same time as it delivers the service to the subscribers, Telikom can, he feels lead the way in modern corporate management thinking in Papua New Guinea.

Radio is a marvellous way to engage with a mass audience. It has been called 'the lively art', because it, of all the means of mass communication, can make the listener feel as if he or she is being addressed personally, rather than as one of a crowd.

Radio broadcasting has been in Papua New Guinea since the mid-1930s, when 4-PM Port Moresby began broadcasting to the Australian community residing there. After the war the Australian Broadcasting Commission took over the station and their idea, itself adapted from the BBC, of broadcasting as a public service became the accepted policy. In the 1960s Radio Rabaul was set up. For most of the subsequent years there has been a regional service, the Kundu service, as well as a national and a commercial service, with National Broadcasting Commission stations broadcasting in local languages in all 19 provinces.

However NBC is living through the same financial crisis as everyone else and in this 20th anniversary year not all of the stations of the Kundu service are on the air. However, the national service, Karai, has remained intact so far, as has Kaland, NBC's popular advertising and entertainment programme. Many people also listen to the foreign-owned commercial station, NAU FM.

The Karai Service and the Kundu Service operate on short-wave, with the Karai Service also transmitting on easy-to-find medium wave in the Moresby area as well as in some provincial districts. Kalang goes out on FM.

The three services have distinct aims and functions. Kalang's job is to carry advertisements and entertainment. Karai has to educate and inform listeners with programmes that create awareness of political, social and economic issues, especially those relating to PNG, and to reflect public views on these matters. The Kundu Service (until recently the biggest service) does the same for the provinces. It also carries all local and community news, and sports, religious and

cultural programming in the main local languages, paying particular attention to the development needs of rural people.

Chairman of NBC, Sir Alkan Tololo, says that, of all the means of mass communication that exist in Papua New Guinea today, radio is the most effective and the most democratic. "Radio does not discriminate between rich and poor, between the literate and those who can't read, between men and women, between villages with electricity and those without. Radio supplies food for the mind - for everybody, and at no personal cost. It is both a vehicle for new ideas and the way in which the listener's own personal and tribal existence can be acknowledged. It can also contribute to national unity."

This is not to say that broadcasting in Papua New Guinea is an easy task. Only a fraction of the total number of local languages were accommodated on the Kundu Service, even when it was fully operational. High quality  radio requires adequate funding. There are always problems of editorial responsibility. The hilly terrain makes reception difficult in some areas.

NBC has been confronting these problems in its day-to-day operation, and in occasional major re-organisations, one of which has just occurred. With the stated aim of putting maximum resource into programmes themselves, not into layers of management, it has shed some staff, and arranged others into central departments serving all services. It has a number of aims for its staff, one of which is to look into the possibility of public service television. This would run in competition with the commercial station, EM TV, which broadcasts a mixture of programmes and advertisements. Although, as Sir Alkan observes, the merits of television as a democratic medium are not as easy to establish as they are for radio. For the immediate future radio will remain the only source of local programming.

pective

An often quoted fact about Papua New Guinea is that it is the second largest island in the world after Greenland. As a description of PNG this is not very helpful. Firstly PNG shares the island almost equally with Indonesia - along a ruler straight line drawn by European colonialists in the nineteenth century. Second there is much more to PNG than the mainland. There are many large islands both to the northeast and east and these are surrounded by smaller islands.

It is geography which first determines the regions of PNG. The mainland is divided by a great mountain range which makes a natural break between Papuans to the west and the New Guineans to the East. Geography also marks out the islands region. But it was an early colonial land-grab which drew a dividing line across the mountain range to give the Dutch, the Germans and the British a share of the territory and defined the four regions.

Papua comprises much of the south part of the mainland, stretching from Western Province out to the islands of Milne Bay. It was first under British and then under Australian rule until Independence. New Guinea comprises the provinces of West Sepik, East Sepik, Madang and Morobe, annexed en mass by the Germans. The five Highland provinces were the last area to be penetrated by Europeans. The New Guinea Islands from Manus in the Northwest to North Solomons in the east have always taken an independent line. It is no surprise that this

'regional' structure is barely in use today. But it has left a residue, a rich sediment of cultural and traditional difference which erupts from time to time.

A rugby game had to be suspended in 1973 because a Papuan woman referred to the New Guineans as 'kaukau' eaters. The resulting brawl spilt out of the pitch and continued for three days. Papuans express considerable fear of 'Highlanders' fierce disposition. Morobe, Madang and Sepik have formed a loose association called Momase. Secessionist movements break out in the Islands. But overall PNG has succeeded in uniting itself into one Independent modern state - a State which has a provincial structure to represent the interests of difference.

No sooner had Papua New Guinea established itself as a single state than it was threatened by secessionist movements – one answer was to add a layer of Provincial Government.

For two years before Independence Josephine Abaijah led a highly visible and vocal Papuan separatist movement. Bougainville had just seen the opening of its huge copper mine and some saw an opportunity to fund an independent future for the North Solomons. While PNG opted for a unitary state with political and bureaucratic power centralised in Port Moresby, there were some even on the Constitutional Planning Committee who favoured a more decentralised system. It was Bougainville which forced Prime Minister Somare's hand. In order to keep them and their revenue in PNG, he had to write Provincial government into the Constitution.

Provincial Government was effective in North Solomons and, as it turned out, in several other provinces but, looking back over the last 15 years, it was in the main a chaotic failure. The big problem was financial mismanagement. A typical case was Sandaun. In 1984 the Auditor-General's office began to go through the files in the provincial headquarters at Vanimo. They found total disorder: three sets of figures for end-of-year cash balances, illegal loans, a deposit bag for K1,000 which had 31 toea in it and many other serious breaches of financial discipline. The Provincial Government was suspended forthwith.

The provincial governments began to fall like skittles: Enga, Manus, Simbu, Fly, Western Highlands, Central. Then in 1987 Sandaun suspended again for gross financial mismanagement. Morobe suspended in 1989 following a breakdown of law and order. The catalogue of suspensions and re-instatements continued. It became clear that in many cases the Provincial level of government was at best incompetent, at worst fraudulent and that rural communities in particular were suffering for it.

Looking back commentators suggest that some of the blame can be laid at the door of the Australian Administration pre-Independence. There was a dearth of trained administrators. Those that were trained were used to a centralised system not one where power was devolved into 19 separate, provincial administrations. The country's public service was simply not ready.

With some foresight the Constitutional Committee suggested that the system be reviewed after 15 years. And so it was that the present government set up a bipartisan committee to make its revue and come up with some recommendations. It concluded that there had been a lack of proper channelling of financial resources, manpower, facilities and a lack of politically-set priorities. They recommended that the system be changed. In March 1995 Premier Sir Julius Chan stood before Parliament and requested a change in the Organic Law of the Constitution. The identity of the second tier government would remain but the new law would give dual emphasis to both Provincial and local-level governments enabling the collective management of provincial affairs. Did Sir Julius know that he was in for a rough few months, as cabinet ministers and student activists vigorously opposed the reforms? In the end the government won the day.

Premiers stood down or became Deputy Governors. Governors were appointed, some famous names amongst them, (Sir Michael Somare became Governor of East Sepik). The public service got ready for a shake up. There would be a move to shift qualified professionals to rural areas where they could be closer to the people. Some Provinces quickly implemented reformed structures and set about the business of government. Others were less sure. For all the talk about returns going more directly to the people could not this mean more control by central government, especially over emotive issues like mining rights and mineral resources?

Sir Julius Chan was reassuring. In his opening speech he said, "These reforms, Mr. Speaker, strike a necessary and healthy balance between central and local power. They spell out a bright and bold future for Papua New Guinea."

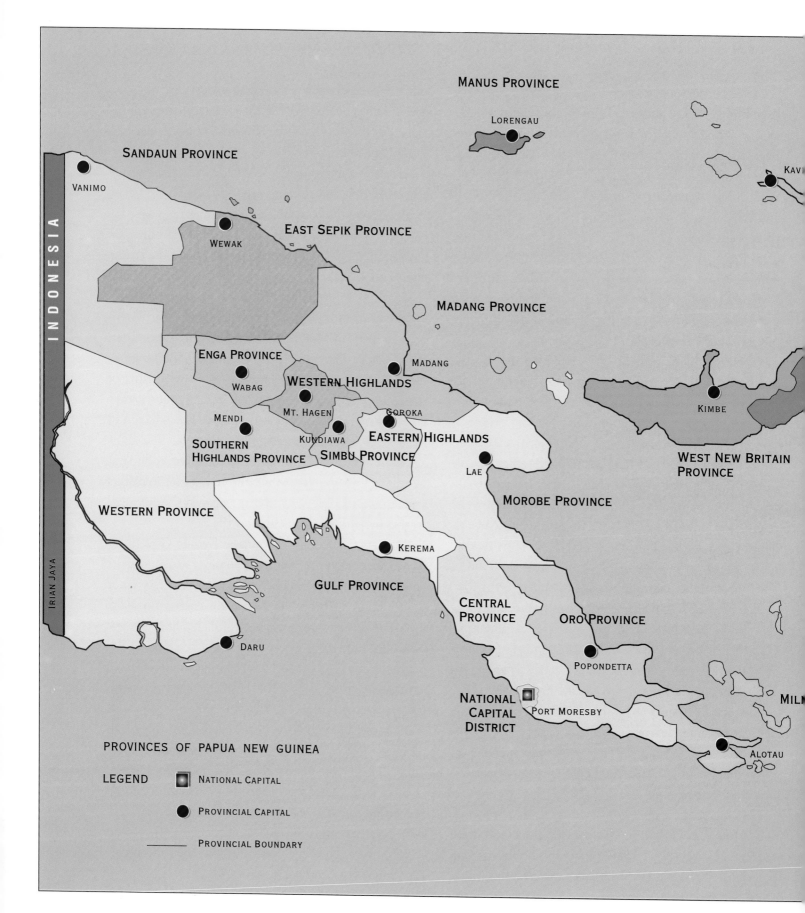

MANUS PROVINCE

LORENGAU

KAVI

SANDAUN PROVINCE

VANIMO

INDONESIA

EAST SEPIK PROVINCE

WEWAK

MADANG PROVINCE

MADANG

ENGA PROVINCE

WABAG

WESTERN HIGHLANDS

MT. HAGEN

GOROKA

MENDI

KUNDIAWA

EASTERN HIGHLANDS

SOUTHERN
HIGHLANDS PROVINCE

SIMBU PROVINCE

LAE

KIMBE

WEST NEW BRITAIN
PROVINCE

IRIAN JAYA

WESTERN PROVINCE

MOROBE PROVINCE

KEREMA

GULF PROVINCE

CENTRAL
PROVINCE

ORO PROVINCE

DARU

POPONDETTA

MIL

NATIONAL
CAPITAL
DISTRICT

PORT MORESBY

ALOTAU

PROVINCES OF PAPUA NEW GUINEA

LEGEND

NATIONAL CAPITAL

PROVINCIAL CAPITAL

PROVINCIAL BOUNDARY

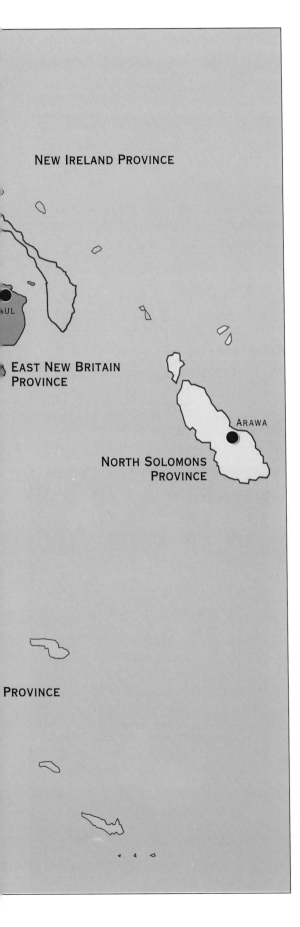

NEW IRELAND PROVINCE

UL

EAST NEW BRITAIN
PROVINCE

ARAWA

NORTH SOLOMONS
PROVINCE

PROVINCE

Look at a map which delineates the provinces of Papua New Guinea and you can imagine how it was drawn. Straight lines go north to south, east to west, the curved lines follow the chains of highest mountains. Yet, by early 1970 when decisions were being made to retain the provincial administrative unit as an element in the government of PNG, there was little dissatisfaction with these groupings. In general the clans and tribes and language groups that make up this various country had come to some accommodation which recognised mutual support and interest.

And so it was that the four regions are subdivided into nineteen provinces each of which celebrates an individual cultural identity.

By region, and moving roughly from west to east, the provinces are: Western, Gulf, Central, NCD (National Capital District, Port Moresby), Milne Bay, Oro, Southern Highlands, Enga, Western Highlands, Simbu, Eastern Highlands, Morobe, Madang, East Sepik, Sandaun, Manus, New Ireland, East New Britain, West New Britain and the North Solomons.

Wet, watery Western Province is Papua New Guinea's largest and least populated province. With the evocatively-named Fly and Strickland Rivers crossing it from top to bottom and famous for its swamps and its floods, it lives in the imagination like the last uncharted territory awaiting its discoverer.

In fact the area itself and the Fly River in particular was 'discovered' by western explorers at a relatively early stage in the history of Papua New Guinean and European contact. Named after the ship carrying the French navigator D'Urville, who had noted its potential navigability on his second journey to the area in 1842, the Fly River was followed nearly 1,000 kilometres up towards its headwaters by the Italian explorer Luigi d'Albertis in 1876.

The Fly, at 1,200 km, is Papua New Guinea's longest river.

Later explorations took place this century, the last great journey being the coast to coast crossing of the country in the 1927-28 expedition led by Ivan Champion and Charles Karius. They set out from Daru, near the mouth of the Fly in the Gulf of Papua, climbed 3,000 metre high mountains to enter the headwaters of the Sepik River, PNG's second longest, and travelled down it for 1,100 km to reach the coast near Wewak on the Coral Sea.

Many different tribes lived the area now described as Western Province, and the response to some of the early explorers and the many missionaries who followed was sometimes violent. Cannibalism and head-hunting were regular practices of people in this area. Naturally this was one of the first parts of their ritual culture to be opposed by every outsider, particularly by the missionaries, many of whom arrived under the auspices of the London Missionary Society. From the late-nineteenth century to this day missions have been active in the area and it is now heavily Christianised.

By all accounts, the culture that Christianity has now replaced was a deeply complex interweaving of beliefs about ancestral and other spirits, mediated by sorcerers and strongly differentiated by gender. Men and women had completely different life experiences. The centre of all power and activity was the men's house, full of artefacts required by them for the practice of their rituals. The artefacts of the Gogodala people of the lower Fly are particularly remarkable, featuring abstract clan symbols which are painted on canoes, dance masks, drums and statues and often using images of crocodiles and snakes.

Traces of the old life-style still remain in Western Province, if not in terms of religious belief, then at least in the styles of house and the kinds of food that are eaten. Because much of the province is subject to flooding, especially in the delta area, many villages consist of houses built on stilts. People catch fish, but the basic staple is sago.

Sago is the solidified, gel-like starchy extract obtained by first scraping then washing the inner fibres of the trunk of the sago palm. Fortunately there is a plentiful supply of these palms, because sago is eaten every day, in fact to such an extent that nutritionists see it as problematic. A diet consisting predominantly of sago will be deficient in protein. Western Province is not noted for its vegetable gardens, so unless care is taken, vitamin and mineral deficiencies can also occur.

Until recently, Western Province has been relatively untouched by industrial development but all that has now changed, as the massive and controversial gold and copper mine of Ok Tedi lies within its northern borders. Ok Tedi started producing gold in 1984 and copper in 1987. Processing the ore from which the copper concentrate is obtained, creates a vast amount of residue, called tailings, which has increased the amount of sediment that flows down the Fly River and has been accumulating in it and on the surrounding flood plain, together with pollution from elements like mercury which are used in the mining process.

Western Province, like its neighbour, Gulf, is undeveloped compared to the rest of the country. In the main town of this watery province, women have to carry water to their homes. Many hopes are pinned on the benefits that will accrue from the profits of the mine.

265

GULF PROVINCE

Gulf Province lies between central and western province next to National Capital District and has supplied many of the people who have become the leaders and organisers of the national life of Papua New Guinea. But Gulf Province itself is one of the least developed of the nineteen provinces. Much of the pattern of land use and many of the activities of its people speak of ancient economic necessity rather than innovation.

Gulf contradicts a huge, fanned-out coastal plain, covered in forests and well-endowed with swamps and waterways. As its name implies, it is the hinterland of a great, curving bay, the Gulf of Papua, with its 640 miles of coastline and its rich stock of prawns and other marine creatures. Inland, the province extends up to the crest of the Armit range of mountains. Some half of the land area of Gulf Province is mountainous and timbered, with a highest peak of 2775 m.

The large rivers which cross the plains of Gulf Province on their way to the sea include the Purari and the Kikori, which are PNG's third and fourth

largest. So far, the swampy, coastal plain has not been crossed by roads and economic development has been slow. Many of the coastal residents of Gulf Province derive a living from fishing, growing copra and making artefacts. Gulf is famous for its masks,

dancing boards, drums and figures representing important spirits.

The cultural life of Gulf Province was previously renowned for its uniqueness, with some of the people, although missionised, maintaining much of their traditional way of life well into this century. This consisted of separate lives for men and women, with the men, in particular, engaging constantly in ritual practices and ceremonials in specially constructed longhouses. But those that remained were destroyed by the people themselves in the years just before the second World War, and the old ways have not been resumed.

Nowadays the reality is more banal and the citizens of Gulf Province are anxious about getting work and government services. The oil pipe-line from the Kutubu oil field in Southern Highland Province passes through Gulf and oil has been discovered in Gulf Province itself. There is a feeling among the leaders of Gulf that the long years of underdevelopment are about to end.

Central Province tends to get left in the shadow of the national capital Port Moresby. It would be equally easy to say that Moresby draws people, water, vegetables, recreational facilities and a wealth of historical and cultural significance from Central Province. Central should not be thought of as a 'Cinderella' province.

Central lies on the south coast of PNG and extends inland to the Owen Stanley mountain range. The great majority of the population are drawn into Moresby to work in government or business or to sell fruit, vegetables, fish and betel nut in one of the many markets. Otherwise subsistence farming and fishing are the main activities. Central has a particularly strong athletics record and are prominent in rugby league, cricket and volleyball. There are no less than 32 local languages but there are several distinct groups with strong traditions.

The Motu, who live in the coastal areas were courageous seagoing people who took off once a year in their lagatois, big sailing canoes, to exchange pots and shells for sago and logs from the Erema people of eastern Gulf Province. This 'Hiri' trade is celebrated annually in Port Moresby with the Hiri Moale show. The Motu people also traded pots, axes and shell with the Mailu islanders in eastern Central and with people from Milne Bay. The Motu co-existed with the Koitabu people living in the hinterland with whom they exchanged fish and shell for vegetables. The Motu-Koitabu were more wary of the Koiari people who lived in the hills around the Sogeri plateau.

Even today the Koiari people are feared and tourists are warned to enter their lands with caution. A caution that might be worth attention were it not for the delights on offer in the Varirata National Park which occupies much of the Koiari's traditional hunting ground. The Koiari lived in tree houses. There is now some dispute about whether this was so that they could look out for enemies or whether the houses were used as a retreat in times of clan dispute. They hunted wallabies, cuscus, and other forest animals They also grew crops around the village using slash and burn agriculture, so most of the forest would have been cleared some time in the past and has regenerated.

The National Park has created a number of walks and picnic sites which make a delightful outing for Moresby families. The more sharp eyed might spot a bird of paradise. There are many varieties of trees, plants and butterflies. There are pitcher plants and fern baskets and many sorts of fungi. It is a naturalists dream. Some of the trails are quite jungle like considering the proximity to the big city. It is possible to stay overnight in Varirata - an attractive option for birdwatchers who want to catch a glimpse of some rare species.

There are other day-trips into Central Province. The Gerebu Plateau located near Doe village about 45 minutes drive from Moresby has a natural lake and a mini waterfall which never dries up even during the driest of dry seasons. There are caves which are rarely explored either by local people or outsiders because village elders have restricted visiting for fear of disturbing resident spirits. One of the caves has unusual pillars of rock which the local people call stone posts - they seem to change their shape every time eyes are set on them. The Gerebu plateau has clear, clean creeks and rivers rapid and deep enough for diving, rafting and canoeing.

Linking the north and south coasts, the Kokoda Trail was first used by miners in the 1890's but it was World War 2 that 'put it on the map'. After the bombing of Pearl Harbour in 1941 the Japanese moved on PNG sending the navy to Port Moresby and the army round the back via Popondetta. What they hadn't realised was that the trail was a switchback footpath across some of the most rugged country in the world, plunging up and down, the gullies infested by leeches. There was no chance of maintaining a supply line. The courage and suffering of those who fought there has never been forgotten. The Kokoda Trail is one of the most popular bush walks in all of PNG.

There are few greater contrasts in Papua New Guinea than that which meets arrivals at her capital city Port Moresby. On one side there are the stilt houses of the original inhabitants, the Motu people of Koki and Hanuabada, on the other side the multi storey concrete and glass blocks of the business district. Several miles away the dramatic new architecture of the Parliament building, the National Museum and the new Government Centre rise up at Waigani. The National Capital District, like many cities, is really a collection of villages and suburbs spread out in a ten mile radius around the deep harbour at Moresby which first attracted a British sea captain in 1873 to make it his base.

NCD now has 230,000 inhabitants. It is Melanesia's largest city and PNG's most populated area by far. Governor Bill Skate describes it as a unique province, for people from every other of PNG's 19 provinces lives here. They are drawn by government duties, by commercial opportunities and sometimes, with unfortunate consequences, by the bright city lights and dreams of pavements of gold.

A person's place of origin affects their chances of work and their social life. The Melanesian 'wantok' (literally 'one talk') system of clan responsibility still operates. A single salary may still be dispersed among many family members. Unemployed youths seek distant family and live with them until they outstay their welcome and find themselves out on the street. They have little alternative but to turn to criminal activities to survive. It has given Port Moresby a bad name. The 'rascal' problem is overplayed but there is no doubt that it exists. Governor Skate intends to solve it by putting the youths to voluntary work. "A physical programme, like roads or bridge building, is something that is highly visible and they can feel proud of. We're getting the Defence Force to loan us engineers for a civil action programme which will engage the unemployed youth in beautifying the city."

Beautifying the city was high on the agenda of outgoing Mayor David Unagi. "I want people to

know that Moresby is a place where people can live peacefully," he said "We have problems, our infrastructure, particularly the roads, need improving. We have to do something about the water supply. This is a capital city. It is growing fast and we have to do something about these things." David Unagi persuaded National Government to engage in a K60 million road improvement scheme and a K125 million airport redevelopment scheme. Construction has already begun. "It should make Jackson's the best airport in the South Pacific," says Minister Unagi, "a fitting gateway to PNG tourists and business people."

Everyone who visits NCD comments on the water problem. Geographers say it lies in a rain shadow. Local residents who suffer an unusually harsh climate of rain, storms, dry spells and high winds, just know that all too often they have no water in their taps. It has become a major issue. Only 60-70 % of Moresby residents have piped water. The system was put in 40 years ago for a population of 70,000. There is no way that it can cope with a population which will reach half a million by 2015. The supply comes from the Sogeri valley in Central Province but it comes through a single 800 mile trunk pipe. The debate revolves around how best to deliver adequate water to every district.

There are wide discrepancies in living conditions amongst Moresby residents. Not all have electricity. Many use kerosene for fuel. Some still use firewood collected from the denuded hills around the city. One quarter of Moresby residents live in squatter settlements. Moresby also has PNG's tallest building and most luxurious housing. It has nearly 500 kms of sealed roads, far more than any other province, with 693 licensed PMV's for passenger transport and a further 233 licensed to Central Province which lies at 10 mile. The miles are calculated as the distance from Town which is on the original harbour front. Moresby is the biggest coastal shipping port and the second biggest import centre after Lae.

The location of the Government in Moresby created a boom in office and housing construction. The government payroll gives NCD the steadiest econo-

my in PNG. It can look to the future with a big oil refinery at Motukea Island in Fairfax harbour, a new ship-building yard and a container wharf. It is perhaps fitting that Moresby still looks to the sea. For the sea was as important in the past as it will be in the future.

The original inhabitants of this area settled about 250 years ago. Building their houses on stilts over the sea, they traded fish for plants with the Koitabu people living in the hinterland. They were two separate language groups. The Motuans spoke an Austronesian language like many Pacific islanders. The Koitabu spoke a language used by mountain people. Over the years the two have combined to form Hiri Motu which, with Tok Pisin, is now the major language of communication. The two groups celebrate their origins once a year with the Hiri Moale festival. In September 1995 it will be extra-special for it will be combined with the celebrations of 20 years of Independence.

The Motu Koitabu people survived their harsh conditions, monsoon rains from December to April and tinder dry conditions during the rest of the year, by sailing on the South East monsoons hundreds of kilometres to Kerema in Gulf Province, returning two months later on the North Westerlys carrying sago and betel nut. This epic voyage will be remembered in NCD in 1995 by the building of four lagatois, great two-masted sailing canoes, and re-enacting the farewell and welcoming ceremonies. The Hiri was much more than a trading trip. It was a test of manhood and an opportunity for Lagatois captains to become 'big men' wealthy and prestigious.

Today villages vie for the privilege of building a ceremonial lagatoi. But just how much of the ancient ritual is still incorporated is left unsaid. In

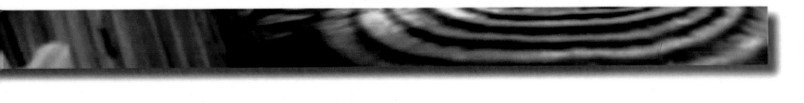

the past a bau-bau (bamboo pipe) would be passed to each crew member as they joined. While the boat was being built the captain and the owner would drink only coconut milk or soup, while striving to obtain ritual purity. Magicians started their work as the first logs were set, casting spells over every part of the construction to ensure that the lagatois would sail straight and to ward off evil spirits who might attempt to sink it. Food taboos on the boat were strict. There were potions and chants for every calamity.

While the Motuan men were away on their dangerous expedition the women made tattoos on all female children. It began when the little girls were 5 to 6 years of age. Each year new tattoos were added and each year, when the lagatois appeared on the horizon, the girls would be taken out into the sun to show off their tattoo. Some tattoos were very special. The first born daughter of a lagatoi captain had a 'tear drop' tattoo below each eye. Tattooing would only be finished on marriage. Very few Motu Koita girls elect to have more than a token tattoo on their bodies today. But at the Hiri Moale festivities they will appear with tattoos drawn on the bodies with felt tipped pens. Decoration without pain.

In addition to sago, which was brought back in great clay pots, the lagatoi brought betel nut. Outsiders often find betel chewing pretty disgusting, especially when they see the red cud spat out on the ground. Moresby pavements are stained red with betel juice. Traditionally betel nut was a very genteel habit, only indulged in by men on returning lagatoi. To exchange betel was a great honour and to sit and chew together was regarded as a spiritual experience.

At the Hiri Moale festival in 1995 these old traditions will be remembered once again. Lagatois will sail once more in the bay. There will be canoe races including a race between 2 Gogodala war canoes and a Keapara war canoe. There will be singing and dancing and choirs and sky-diving and official presentations. It is a day when the National Capital District can forget its present problems and proudly to share traditions with all the many Papua New Guineans who have now made the city their home.

No, Milne Bay does not want a road connection to the rest of PNG. The Owen Stanley mountains have inhibited travellers for thousands of years and there is no reason why they should be breached now.

Milne Bay Province spills out of the eastern end of PNG scattering tiny atolls, coral reefs and volcanic islands into the Pacific. Previously regarded as a 'Cinderella province', Milne Bay is now in boom-time, wealthy from the rewards of mining concessions and ready to develop its own infrastructure, people and economy.

Flying from the government offices in Alotau, Provincial Capital of Milne Bay is a bright flag. It is coloured red for tradition, blue for the ocean. It has a white stripe for sandy beaches and a vertical green stripe for green vegetation where progressive developments are taking place. A yellow star symbolises Venus which often appears in the east of Milne Bay at dawn. Myth says it is the star which missionaries and sailors used when they brought Christianity to the province.

"The missionaries brought change. They had agencies which developed us spiritually and even economically until the government came in. You cannot talk of the history of Milne Bay without including them", insists Elijah Digwaleu, Secretary to the Cabinet. The first Marist mission on Woodlark Island was established in 1847 and was rapidly followed by Anglicans, Wesleyans and Catholics, all of whom set up schools and health centres. They set the pattern of language use and education in the entire province. More recently they have been joined by a number of Seventh Day Adventist missions in Alotau and Samarai.

"The Churches brought us a lot but they also killed a lot of our culture. Milne Bay people were strong believers in witchcraft. It made them afraid. It was a mode of control. It created good behaviour. If you walk past a boat and see a little piece of string then you know there is a spell attached. You don't touch the boat. Remove the string, and anyone can take it", muses Elijah Digwaleu. Yet for all his fears Milne Bay is one of the more peaceful provinces of PNG. It does not have a law and order problem. It is rich in traditional practices and intent on governing itself wisely.

Eighty percent of the population of Milne Bay lives on an island. The islands fall into groups more often than not named after explorers: D'Entrecasteaux, Goodenough, Fergusson, Normanby, Trobriand, Woodlark and the Louisiade Archipelago. The province has 2,120 kilometres of coastline. Centuries

before the Europeans 'discovered' Milne Bay people traded between the islands, most famously in the Kula ring, a ritual exchange of necklaces and armlets which bound islanders together through a series of strenuous sea voyages in outrigger canoes. Even today, all inter island trade is conducted under the aegis of Kula expeditions.

The importance of Kula was brought to the rest of the world by Polish anthropologist Bronislaw Malinowski who wrote about it in "The Argonauts of the Western Pacific" in the 1920's. He also wrote about the islands of love - the Trobriand Islands - and left an impression of free-loving, short skirted young women, which rather mistakenly lives on today. His "Coral Gardens and Their Magic" describes Trobrianders as great gardeners. To be known as 'tokwaibagula', a good gardener, and having a big pile of yams at harvest time is a mark of prestige. Yams are not just food, they are part of an elaborate scheme of social relationships which set out patterns of power and prestige culminating in the Paramount Chief - who has the tallest and most elaborately decorated yam house of all.

Each group of islands has its own characteristics. Trobriand is flat, has a hierarchy of chiefs and matrilineal inheritance. Goodenough is one of the most mountainous islands in the Southern hemisphere. Woodlark is famous for ebony forests and for being the site of the biggest gold rush in the country. Fergusson has numerous extinct volcanoes, hot springs and geysers. Normanby is hilly. The peoples of Milne Bay have somehow survived the influence of missionaries, notorious blackbirders (indentured labour for the Queensland sugar plantations), gold miners, planters and soldiers. On big occasions the people still dress in traditional costumes and beat drums to revive their ancient cultures.

This is the background to the current Provincial Government's aims and plans for Milne Bay. "Here in Milne Bay we have a five year plan, the first of its kind", says Jones Liosi, Premier of Milne Bay in 1995. "My plan is to serve the last first - bottom up planning." So the first priority is to open up rural areas to growth. "It is absurd", says Liosi, "that our potato growers who have successfully planted and grown long English style potatoes on Normanby for generations have to hump them down the hill-sides on their backs for hours before loading them into boats for distribution. They should have a road or at the very least a bush trail." Normanby is a fertile island. Hybrid cocoa farmers can produce a good yield. But they too are hampered by negligible infrastructure.

Transport is simply inadequate at the moment, says Jones Liosi. Boats and canoes are the main form of transport. Milne Bay has a scant 400 kilometres of road and 330 registered vehicles for a population of 157,294 persons (1990 census). But it does have 23 airstrips including a runway at Alotau capable of taking international flights.

The second most important strand in the plan is 'social services'. The Provincial government of Milne Bay is critically aware of the poor record for health in almost all districts. Malaria and tuberculosis are major problems. But it was the appalling record of maternal and infant deaths in the Trobriand Islands that prompted one of the most exciting developments in social services.

Ten years ago visitors to Losuia, the Government station on the main Trobriand island of Kiriwina, were shocked to see children dying from malnutrition. In a joint effort Milne Bay Province and UNICEF called in an aid worker to assess the problem and implement a solution. They were fortunate in finding Jo Anang, a Ghanaian aid worker and nutritionist. "From my experiences in Ghana, I knew it's not just a matter of going into a village and talking to people but of going into the village and talking to the person who is the most appropriate, the person who understands how people feel and who can be with the mothers everyday." In a two pronged approach, Jo Anang went both to the Paramount Chief and to the women themselves to find out who should be involved in a training project.

Much to his credit, Paramount Chief Pulayasi Daniel has broken a centuries old taboo and involved himself in women's affairs. Father of eleven children and husband to four wives, Chief Pulayasi was nevertheless aware that many of his malefolk laughed when he took an interest in the village births project. He is quite clear, "Basically it's to do with people. When you deal with people, you worry about them, and part of the population is women and children", he said. "For women alone to look after children is not enough. Men too must change their attitudes and look after their children." Because of his active leadership the people of the Trobriands have become more aware of the importance of maternal child health care.

Traditionally none but close kin, a mother or a sister could assist with a birth, certainly no woman from another clan. The breakthrough came when the village chiefs selected one or two women, usually women with children, to attend basic training sessions at a centre near the clinic in Losuia. Selected women went through a three week residential course, leaving their children behind. "They are happy here, only problem is if their husband's don't like it" explained Nurse Susan. Most of the VBA's are illiterate so a card system was designed to refer mothers to the clinic and to the care of the VBA. The scheme started in 1992 and now has 97 trained VBA's. Success is evident in the dramatic decrease in maternal and infant deaths and an overall improvement in nutrition. The scheme is now being administered by Kenneth Kalubaku and a team from different villages. They have just extended the programme to train a group of women from the mainland.

Ultimately the success of the five year plan and all its various social programmes will depend on the success of economic development and the continued flow of funds from Milne Bay's major resources such as forest, mining and oil palm.

While Milne Bay would not come high up the list of PNG log exports, logging is none the less an importance resource for the province. The provincial government would like to see more processed logs bringing more money into the province. They are now encouraging boat-building - capitalising on the early work of the Kwato ministry which combined practical skills with missionary work. There are now several boat-yards around Alotau where master-craftsmen like Pastin Jack build everything from dinghies to 39 foot fishing boats using local hardwoods. Once Milne Bay boats were famous, now there is a chance that they will once again be seen all around the coastline of PNG.

The boats and even the incipient fishing industry seem meagre compared to the impact of the Misima gold mine. During its construction over 1,400 people were employed on the project at any one time. Currently there are over 300 Misimans and 150 expatriates operating the mine and it brings important revenue into the provincial government through the inter-

est of MRDC the state owned mining company which holds a 20% share.

The only comparable export earner is oil palm. Fly into Gurney airport for the capital Alotau and you immediately notice the oil palm plantations below you. The first palm oil left Alotau in 1991. At present the company employs 1,100 people of whom six are expatriates. It is not oil palms, but coconut palms which will attract tourists to Milne Bay.

The provincial government is keen to encourage tourism but not the 'wrong sort' of tourism. He knows that Milne Bay has all the elements of a tourist paradise but he is anxious. "I don't want people to be spectators in their own grounds. I want them to participate" declares Jones Liosi. Maybe he would be reassured by this account of Trobriand cricket. It was originally introduced by the Church as a distraction from more sexual pursuits.

"When the menfolk want to bowl a maiden over, they play cricket", writes Michael Mackintyre. "Trobriand cricketers dress as they would for war - painted faces, feathers, bodies glistening with coconut oil to ensure courage and ankle-bands to promote speed of reaction. Before the game bats are painted with war colours of black and white and, by magic, endowed with potent hitting powers. Once the game is under way, spells are used by bowlers to swerve and swing the ball and mystify the batsmen. Like ritual warfare, cricket gives the men the chance to flaunt their mas-

culinity before an audience of admiring girls who favour a fetching outfit rather like a diminutive skirt with no knickers".

If the tourists want to share in the fun they can take home some exquisite carvings many of which favour erotic themes. The legend of the Trobriands lives on.

278

In 1951 the Mt. Lamington volcano blew up and killed 2,942 people in the province of Oro. It was the largest natural disaster in the recorded history of Papua New Guinea. The eruption destroyed the District Headquarters at Higaturu and all the town buildings on the northern side of the mountain. Subsequently the capital was shifted to Popondetta, where it remains to this day.

But the volcanic activity which caused such a tragic loss of life at that time is also the reason for one of Oro Province's main natural resources - its soil. Volcanic soils, renowned for their fertility, cover the whole area and Oro Province at any season is a sea of green, with grasslands, cultivated fields, plantations and virgin forests as far as the eye can see.

Oro Province occupies a large section of the coastal plain sweeping down to the Solomon Sea on the northern side of the Owen Stanley range but with 10 volcanoes and other mountains going up to over 4,000 metres, it includes a variety of terrain. The people of Oro farm, fish and make distinctive artefacts, and because of the potential of the land for agriculture there have been a number of resettlement projects, with persons from outside the area being assisted by the government to set up there.

Oro is the home of the world's largest butterfly. Called the Queen Alexandra Birdwing, it has wingspan of up to 30 centimetres. In fact it is so large that it is said that it was first collected by bringing it down with a shot-gun! The Queen Alexandra Birdwing is unique to Papua New Guinea and found only in Oro Province where there is concern about its survival as its habitat undergoes change. A conservation project has been set up with World Bank money to investigate the situation of the Queen Alexandra Birdwing, starting with a survey to determine the population size. Oro will then take whatever action is needed to ensure its survival.

During the Second World War Oro Province, then part of the separate territory of New Guinea, was invaded by Japanese troops who proceeded to advance towards Port Moresby along the Kokoda Trail. They succeeded in capturing much of the trail before being stopped by Australian troops at Imita Ridge in Central Province and driven back to Oro. American and Australian troops combined to force the Japanese out of Oro in January 1943, seven months after the first invasion. There was an extremely high loss of life, especially among the Japanese. At Popondetta Airport a crashed aircraft has been elevated on a plinth as a memorial to this time and in the surrounding jungle there are many other such remains.

Today the people of Oro live in quieter times and their main concerns are for improvements in their standard of living. The necessity for a cash component in their livelihood is partially met by growing cash crops such as coffee - the robusta variety on the coast, and the arabica variety on higher land - and palm oil, a component of magarine. The fruit of the palm is crushed in a factory at Higaturu before being exported from Orobe wharf in Oro Bay. Cocoa and copra are also grown for export.

Politically, while senior government officers are proud to be able to state that they are the only province in the country that has never been suspended, they also see clearly that, in Oro Province as in every other, there is considerable scope for improvement in the quality and extent of public services, and in the relationship with the national government.

"We suffer from this big-man mentality", declared Arthur Jawodimbari, Provincial Secretary. "Too much time and energy is wasted playing politics."

Premier Douglas Garawa, the Deputy Governor Designate and an elected member himself, agrees. "In 1993 there were three provincial governments in one year alone. I myself have survived five votes of no-confidence in three years. We are beset by petty-minded politicians who are in politics for their personal advantage only, and we do not think we get the co-operation we deserve from central government."

At the same time, the very fact that some politicians and senior civil servants can see what the problems are and feel free to discuss them must be a good sign for the future.

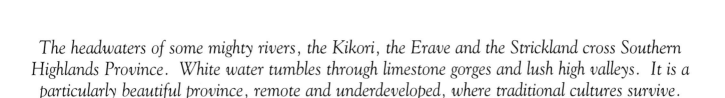

The headwaters of some mighty rivers, the Kikori, the Erave and the Strickland cross Southern Highlands Province. White water tumbles through limestone gorges and lush high valleys. It is a particularly beautiful province, remote and underdeveloped, where traditional cultures survive.

The climate in the south west of the province, at lower altitudes like Lake Kutubu, is humid and semi-tropical. But at higher altitudes, the provincial capital Mendi lies at 1,400 metres above sea level. Temperatures are lower and some areas are prone to sudden severe frosts which are calamitous for food and cash crops. Food gardens and cash crops were destroyed in 1994 by frost and by natural disasters, flood, landslide and drought.

Most of the natural vegetation is rainforest, with alpine woods and grasslands above 3,000 metres. Swamps occur at all levels. More than 60% of the province is still covered in forest. People's subsistence activities (cutting for gardens) inevitably change the natural appearance of this vegetation. More recently, economic and social alterations of infrastructure, especially from mineral resource developments, will change it more radically.

The Southern Highlands had a population of 317,437 in the 1990 census. That indicates a tremendous increase in 10 years, which concerns the provincial government. There is already pressure for land. There are also many young unproductive people who demand more goods and services. Until very recently people were engaged solely in a subsistence economy, the introduction of a modern cash economy has had a tremendous impact on their lives.

The development of mineral resources at Kutubu, Kare and to some extent Porgera drew skilled and unskilled to the mines and left only a skeleton productive labour force back in the villages. While the benefits in terms of employment opportunities, business spin-offs and infrastructure have to be acknowledged, so do the bad effects: creeping inflation, prostitution, drunkenness, robbery and pollution. In the future the Southern Highlands government is going to

insist on long term strategic plans to counteract these negative effects of mineral resource explorations and developments. In the short term it has declared a total liquor ban and established a high-powered Peace and Good Order Committee.

The Provincial government has pushed through a five year development plan which it hopes will accommodate both economic development and social expansion. Services should be distributed equally to the people of the Southern Highlands. The maintenance of traditional family values to create a sense of belonging and responsibility among all family members must be encouraged. Village level health schemes and Child Survival Programmes have been welcomed. Many of these goals are being achieved despite downturns in resource allocations and government cash flow problems.

When Europeans first came to the Southern Highlands in the 1930's, they called it a Papuan wonderland. When they found the lovely Lavani Valley in the 1950's, they talked of lost Shangri-la. There is something very attractive about

the area. Since the 1970's there have been roads and bridges built by the Australian Army Engineering team. It also has the Highlands highway. There are several airstrips which connect the area with the rest of PNG.

The people live in scattered hamlets, grow sweet potatoes for their staple food, have ceremonial exchanges of pigs, cassowaries and other valuables. They use intensive farming methods to grow food including beans, sugar-cane, pit-pit, bananas and greens. They treasure the coconut flavoured karuka (Highlands pandanus) nuts. Houses are built on the ground with walls of wood slabs or mud to keep out the cold.

Visitors to the area may well stay in one of eco-tourism's most successful ventures, the Ambua Lodge at Tari. From there they are invited into the settlements of the Huli people who inhabit the Tari valley. There are 38,000 Huli. They have many striking characteristics but certainly the most photographed are the Huli wigmen. Huli men's wigs are great head-pieces of human hair decorated with feathers and flowers. The wigs are grown and made to mark the transition from boyhood to manhood. Traditionally Huli men were warriors, they lived apart from women. Indeed they distrusted and feared women who were considered a source of sickness and debility. Huli men still dress up, put on paint and oils and paraded themselves. Tourism has encouraged them. The Huli men leave a bright imprint in every visitors mind.

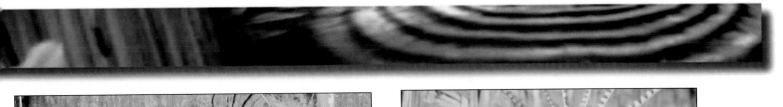

Enga, like other parts of the Highlands, was unknown to the rest of the world until it was reached by explorers in the years before World War II. An Australian patrol led by Taylor and Black in 1938 arrived first. They found a society of agriculturalists with pig exchange as the main economic arrangement.

Enga was created by administrators in 1973 from portions of what had been Southern Highlands and Western Highland Provinces. Much of the land is mountainous and a third of it over 2,000 metres above sea level. The high elevation of the province makes for a cold climate. The habitable south and central areas are quite densely populated, with low wooden house s scattered in the high valleys.

The people are subsistence farmers with coffee as the main earner of cash. The food grown now includes English potatoes and cabbages as well as sweet potato, taro, bananas, yams and other tropical

vegetables. Enga Province has mineral wealth also and Porgera, in the north west of the province, is the site of one of the world's larger gold mines.

Although there are nine separate dialects, this is few by PNG standards and these are dialects of the same language group.

Enga, like other parts of the Highlands, was unknown to the rest of the world until it was reached by explorers in the years before World War II. An Australian patrol led by Taylor and Black in 1938 arrived first. They found a society of agriculturalists with pig exchange as the main economic arrangement.

Both the formidable geography and the fierce reputation of the Engan people has tended to deter outsiders. Consequently Enga is possibly the least modernised or missionised of any province, with many tra-

ditions unchanged. Life is conducted according to customs that have prevailed for many years. Singsings, the name for gatherings and celebrations where singing and dancing occur, are still common. Pigs are still the best form of wealth and a good number of pigs is necessary to indicate status. Money itself is not well understood. Marriages involve brideprice. 'Payback' is common and tribal fighting is considered to be a legitimate way of settling disputes.

'Payback' is compensation for an offence, either social or physical. It occurs in all other parts of PNG. Knowledge of payback is embedded deep in the consciousness of most people. They understand its logic, even if they are Christians for whom the forgive of sins is fundamental. Payback is usually in the form of money or pigs. A clan will exact payback on behalf of one of its members. Failure to give payback is itself a serious crime and, if compensation is not forthcoming, violence might ensue, such as the burning down of a house or damage to other property of the clan of the person who caused the offence. Murder is sometimes committed in the name of payback. An innocent and uninvolved clan member can be the victim. In fact payback is one of the main reasons for murder. Adultery is considered one of the most serious crimes and often attracts payback. Car accidents are a relatively new and lucrative occasion for payback.

Disputes about payback can escalate into actual warfare, which is conducted with axes and bows and arrows and results in injuries and, occasionally, deaths. Tribal warfare is not uncommon but nor is it an everyday event. Disputes will normally be resolved with a payment of payback, whether or not the case has also been dealt with by the courts.

Compensation is, of course, also a fundamental concept in western law and compensation to landowners forms the basis of the arrangements by which mining rights are assigned to mining companies. Enga Province has had experience of both the benefits and the problems associated with mining for some time now. Mt. Kare, now closed, was the province's first mine. Porgera began producing in 1990. It processes 10,000 tonnes of ore a day. It has brought a great deal of money to Enga Province, much of it now vested in the Porgera Development Authority. Millions of kina have now been paid, something like a thousand times more than Pogera district was used to receiving as a support grant from the national government. The essential contradiction of pouring money into a non-cash economy has resulted in total disruption of the traditional lifestyle and much wastage. However, people in Porgera are coming to terms with their situation and beginning to invest in local businesses.

Western-style development and, in particular, the introduction of those western ideas which emphasise individual rights, may bring certain benefits to Engan society. The 'big man' system which dominates so much of PNG's politics is particularly strong here. Concepts like equality, democracy, freedom of speech and individual human rights are not as compelling as whatever custom dictates. Whatever the 'big man' says should happen, happens. Women, for example, have no autonomy of action and a wife is the property of her husband. A change in this way of thinking will probably be a long time in coming in Enga.

Mount Hagen, capital of Western Highlands Province, has the air of a frontier town, with its flat-roofed modern buildings, some two or three stories high, and its wide, dusty roads thronged with incomers from the surrounding villages.

Mt. Hagen provides the 350,000 people of the Western Highlands with administrative services, a court, a hospital, shops and a famous market. Situated in the Wahgi Valley, a region well-known for its agricultural produce, it has both historical and geographical significance as a staging post in the development of the Highlands region.

Only 60 years ago, the Wahgi valley and much of what is now known as the Western Highlands was a closed book to the rest of the world. It was first visited, definitively, by Europeans in the years just before the Second World War. Michael Leahy and his brother Danny, both gold prospectors, and James Taylor, an Australian District Officer, led a large expedition across the Chimbu mountains. Their aim was to set foot in the valley which they had previously only sighted from a reconnaissance flight in a small aircraft.

On that occasion Michael Leahy had written in his diary: "We flew over the new valley and laid to rest for all time the theory that New Guinea is a mass of uninhabitable mountains. What we saw was a great flat valley, more than 20 miles wide and not telling how many miles long, between two mountain ranges with a very crooked river meandering. Below us was evidence of a fertile soil and a teeming population, a continuous patchwork of gardens, laid off in neat squares like checkerboards with oblong grass houses in groups of four or five, dotted thickly over the landscape...."

If the white men were amazed by the valley and the people who lived there, it was nothing to compared with the amazement experienced by the people themselves, who had never seen white people before. A common response to the sight of these large pale creatures was one of fear and dread. They were not thought to be men, but the spirits of ancestors, possibly returning with evil intent.

Somehow this first contact between the races was achieved without many casualties. Gradually other

Europeans penetrated the mountain. At first it was more gold prospectors, then missionaries, followed after the war by the Kiaps, Australian patrol officers who strove to keep the peace between the new European settlers and local people and to stop tribal warfare. A significant event in the early 60's was the completion of the Highlands Highway which came all the way up to Mt. Hagen from the coast at Lae. This formed the basis of Western Province's present reputation as the transport and communications centre of the Highlands region.

Independence in 1975 was the cue for the departure of many settlers and the beginning of yet another phase in the crowded history of this area in the late 20th century. Building on what it has always been best at, Western Highlands now leads the country in the number of agricultural jobs. Coffee and tea are grown on plantations as well as smallholdings. The neat, checkerboard gardens which impressed Michael Leahy now produce a range of introduced cool-weather vegetables like spinach, broccoli, cauliflowers, broad beans and cucumbers as well as the traditional sweet potatoes, bananas, sugar cane, and greens. Pandanus palms and bamboo groves dot the landscape. Most of the vegetable growing is carried out by women and the beautiful gardens are their creations.

The people of Western Highlands Province were quick to respond to the new opportunities offered by the transport links which gave them such a central position. Even before Independence Western Highlanders were organising themselves into companies to protect their interests and keep control of their own wealth. One such group of companies, Wamp Nga is famous for its success over the past 25 years. 'Wamp Nga' means 'belonging to everyone' in the local Melpa language. Owned by the local government, it started as a motor business, Wamp Nga Motors, and is now a Highland conglomerate with interests as diverse as hotels, real estate and computer retailing. Wamp Nga also owns the Shell agency for the whole Highlands region. In an era of increasing privatisation it stands out as a shining example of successful local public ownership, evidence for all who need it that businesses in PNG can thrive on purely local initiative and energy.

Women too can be successful in business in the Western Highlands. Maggy Wilson runs a hotel just outside Mt. Hagen which is a model of style and comfort. Called 'Haus Poroman' (House of Friends), it is laid out much as a traditional village, with a collection of separate small thatched houses gathered around a large main building. With walls made of woven pandanus palm and bamboo, it is an intelligent response to the needs that tourists have for authentic experience and it is proof that local life-styles and modern comfort are perfectly compatible aims.

The Mt. Hagen Show, which takes place annually in August is an amazing, world famous event which puts on display a riotous assembly of dancers, drummers and musicians from all over the province and beyond. Like the other Highland shows, it is an opportunity to revel in the cultural diversity which still survives in a province which is otherwise taking every opportunity it can to develop along modern lines.

Simbu is a small mountainous province locked in the middle of the Papua New Guinean Highlands. At its northern boundary it has the country's highest peak, Mt. Wilhelm, at nearly 15,00 feet (4,509 metres). It is the most rugged of all PNG's provinces. Almost 50% of the land is mountainous, with deep narrow valleys and fast flowing rivers. The name Simbu is sometimes corrupted to Chimbu. Legend says that it was named thus because when steel axes and knives were given to the tribespeople they said they were "simbu" - very pleased.

Simbu is one of the more densely populated provinces in the country. The Simbus are renowned for being energetic and enterprising people, competitive in all economic and social activities. Not surprisingly, Rugby league has a big following. There is a local saying, "When the rugby ball was first kicked off from Sydney, it bounced off Loyd Rodson Oval in Moresby and landed here in Kundiawa, the capital of Simbu." During the season truck loads of supporters follow wherever the local team, the Warriors, plays.

Kundiawa grand finals attract up to 5,000 spectators.

Population pressure has forced one fifth of the people born in Simbu to migrate to other provinces. This is despite the population growth rate being one of the lowest in PNG. Those who live in Simbu are expert gardeners, who leave no accessible square metre of earth unturned. They have developed ways of draining and enriching soil that helps them grow food on the same steep hillside year after year at high altitudes. The Simbu landscape is like a patchwork of gardening effort. Sweet potatoes are the staple food, except along the southern border where sago takes over.

Archaeologists believe that people lived in Nombe near Chuave 24,000 years ago. They have also found pig's teeth in Chuave dated at 10,000 years. Pigs are still the main meat and are eaten at all ceremonial feasts. Pig killing was traditionally a great ceremony and is now re-enacted along with food exchanges, marriage and compensation ceremonies to encourage young people to value old traditions and to hold onto them. It is hoped that these events and the annual Simbu Women's Show will be sufficiently attractive to draw more tourists into the Province. At present only 3% of the population are engaged in any form of cash economy. Tourist revenue would be most welcome.

There is plenty in Simbu to attract tourists. Both Simbu men and women are skilful at making artefacts, carvings and bilums. The crafts are sold along busy pathways or even taken into town and hawked from office to office.

For the daring and adventurous visitor there is mountain climbing. Mt. Wilhelm has both a visitors cabin near the peak and a lodge. One guide book mentions the most delicious strawberries ever tasted, at the start of the walk. However it is a very high mountain and should be treated with respect. It can get very cold, it often gets fog-bound and sometimes it even snows. Climbers can suffer from altitude sickness, sunburn and hypothermia all in one day. There are at least six other mountains with good walking trails, rich in flora and fauna. There are caves, rock shelters, rock paintings, burial sites, salt making sites and an ancient stone axe quarry. What's more it has, reportedly, some of the most exciting white water rafting in PNG. The river Whagi goes through deep chasms, under small rope bridges over long stretches of rapids and past waterfalls.

The northern half of Simbu is pretty well served with a dense road network reaching into just about every village in the area. The southern half has no form of road network at all. The only way into some parts of Karimu is by plane. People there rely on the small airstrip for all their store goods, medical supplies and transport to the outside world. Road transport around Simbu is by any form of moving vehicle, from the back of an open pick-up truck to the occasional government vehicle. It is not uncommon to see people coming into town on big dump trucks. Simbu sits astride the Highlands highway, PNG's central artery, between Goroka and Mt. Hagen.

The upgrading of the Highlands Highway from Lae to Madang through Goroka and Hagen in 1968 was a watershed in the history of the Highland Provinces and of Eastern Highlands in particular.

Before that, the Eastern Highlands had witnessed barely three decades of European contact, from the first missionaries and gold prospectors, through the era of the Kiaps to the post-second World War influx of Australian settlers. All had their agendas and their achievements and their galleries of heroes and villains.

After the road, however, a new dynamic was put in place and the economic reality of the province was exposed to sight. Coinciding with the end of the colonial period and the departure of many of the settlers, the movement of human beings and produce along the road showed just who the people were, who lived in

these previously isolated, separate valleys, and what crops they produced. The variety of the different Highland tribal groups was matched by the range of agricultural produce, with cash crops like coffee and potatoes journeying up and down alongside local vegetables like fern, kau kau (sweet potato) and pit pit, together with livestock which included cattle and sheep as well as the traditional pigs and chickens.

The Eastern Highlands today is a fascinating patchwork of different patterns of land use. Agriculture remains the main activity of the 300,000 Highlanders who occupy the 11,200 square kilometre province. They grow coffee, citrus and potatoes on a commercial scale, together with many other vegetables for the local market. Honey is exported to Germany. Trout are raised in fish farms. Cattle, goats and sheep graze on the grasslands that cover many of the broad valleys between the high mountain ranges.

As in many rural societies where traditional methods are the main means of cultivation, it is the women who do most of the day-to-day agricultural work. They are the true farmers, maintaining the gardens, weeding, hoeing and watering the crops, then har-

vesting them and selling them at market. They are also responsible for some of the most vivid craft work, making bilums (knotted string fibre bags) for both their own use and to sell. Highland women carry huge loads in these bilums, which are suspended from head-bands. Anything from firewood to babies may be found within.

The cultural transformation of Highland society in the post-contact period is a result not only of roads and the introduction of a limited cash economy, but of other major forces such as missionisation, the education of children in the state school system and, increasingly, exposure to urban life-styles. The latter has had two marked effects: the adoption of Western dress, often purchased from dealers in second-hand stores, and the consumption of alcohol. For most of the colonial period the sale of alcohol was banned to all but foreign nationals. Since Independence, provinces have decided for themselves about prohibition. Eastern Highlands Province permits the sale and consumption of alcohol.

Goroka, the capital of Eastern Highlands Province, is an attractive small town set on a plain at the head of one of the broad sweeping valleys which are typical of the Eastern Highlands. It is the location of a number of offices and institutions, including the Goroka Teachers College (a faculty of the University of PNG), the Medical Research Institute, the Melanesian Institute and the head-quarters of the Raun Raun Theatre, a theatre company that specialises in community plays. The environs of Goroka are made beautiful by the presence of many trees, mostly introduced by the first European residents, and there is a famous hotel, 'The Bird of Paradise', which is a true social centre.

Morobe Province consists of the land around the Huon Gulf. Including the bulge of the Huon Peninsula. It is Papua New Guinea's most populous and most diverse region in terms of both culture and geography. PNG's second city, Lae, is its capital, and has its own local administration. Morobe Province, which has had to fund much of its development itself in recent years as funds from the national government have declined, is an example of relatively successful local provincial government, and is striving to retain its autonomy in the face of the recent administrative changes

The diversity which informs all accounts of Morobe is truly amazing. In one small area of 34,000 square kilometres - Morobe is a medium-sized province by PNG standards - there are more than 100 language groups, with all that that implies for different customs, cultures and lifestyles. The people were fierce warriors, and the

cause of much of old New Guinea's reputation as dangerous and hostile. Early settlers stayed on the coast. Now, almost too late, the intrinsic fascination of this complex web of human cultures is obvious. Artefacts from the Huon Peninsula, as seen in museums or shops or in the villages where they are still made, are tantalizing glimpses of lifestyles that are bound to change.

Geographically, Morobe consists of some of PNG's most jumbled and fortress-like mountains as well as one of its biggest and broadest valleys. It contains both coastal swamps and lakes. Its tallest mountains, at over 4,000 metres or more than 13,000 feet, are not in the Highlands as such, but in the mountain ranges that rise straight out of the sea on the Huon Peninsula. Climatically Morobe includes both some of the wettest and some of the driest areas of PNG. Lae, one of the wetter places, has four times as much rain as the area of its airport, which is only about 50 km away.

While some of the land is too rugged for any sort of cultivation, and a lot of it is covered in rain-forest, the province as a whole lends itself to a variety of agricultural activities, from cattle-ranching in the grassy Markham valley to copra, cocoa and tea plantations. Cardamom and chillies are also grown.

Rain forest covers much of Morobe. The Wau Ecology Institute in the heart of a forested area is a fund of expert knowledge on all aspects of forest ecology, with recent research to their credit on the medicinal plants of the forest. Together with the University of Technology at Lae, and the Forest Research Institute, also at Lae, it helps to establish the province as a centre of intelligence about the land and its natural reserves.

Forest-based industries in Morobe centre on Bulolo, not far from Wau. Gold was discovered in creeks and rivers of both these places in the 20's and 30's, and some small-scale mining goes on to this day. But now the main exploitative industry is forestry. Bulolo in particular is a timber town. A vast quantity of timber has been and continues to be extracted from the forests in this area, most of it still in the form of logs although it is the declared policy of the Government to phase out the export of logs in place of sawn timber, and to achieve this by the year 2000. Bulolo, by the way, was the site of one of PNG's earliest timber industries. After the gold was exhausted people turned to the trees. The bare, eroded hillsides in the area show the effects of this.

But Morobe does not have to rely on the exploitation of its natural resources as a source of wealth. More than some other provinces, it has the skills of its people to offer. Morobe has commercial, manufacturing and industrial activities. It has nineteen wharves and a coastal shipping industry. It has recently acquired a vast fish canning factory, said to be the largest in the Pacific. Three hundred people work here, mainly women. The mackerel they put in tins in this Malaysian-owned factory comes from the other side of the world. This is Morobe's role in what has become a global fishing and marketing enterprise.

However the quality of life for the inhabitants of Morobe Province is not determined only by the income-generating possibilities that exist there. The action or inaction of government officials and the kind of public services that they provide, or fail to provide, is equally important. This is a question that exercises the Administrator of Morobe Province, Ainea Sengaro. On his office wall is a whiteboard listing the agreed expenditure on such things as bridge maintenance, road building, and work on wharves, airstrips and the water supply, with a record of money spent.

"Socially, economically and politically Morobe is a province which is doing better than most but

which is still far from satisfactory in many ways," said Sengaro. "There is really no reason why we should not be able to achieve what we want for the people of Morobe. There is a financial crisis but we raise most of our income right here in the province. The only way I can explain the shortfall between what we want to do and what we achieve is by putting at least some of the blame on the kind of politics we have in this country. I believe that too much energy is used up in political position-taking of one sort or another, and the straightforward skills of administrators are not being given a chance."

In this way at least, if not in others, Morobe is very like its neighbours, and indeed like every province in PNG. All are hampered by the same obscure economic malaise, and all blame the political process, although, in a democracy, that is very like taking the blame oneself.

Sengero has a robust response to the question of what he is going to do about the situation in Morobe while he is its Administrator. "I am going for increased efficiency, with much more frequent reporting procedures, and rigorous checking of actual achievements," he said. "And I shall try to avoid the worst effects of the political process."

130,000 people live in city of Lae, a provincial and regional capital with the spacious feeling of a town that has been in existence for some time, without losing its connection to the land. Large tropical trees, their trunks covered in ferns, make occasional shady avenues and the open spaces between buildings are rich in vegetation. In the rainy season - July, August and September - heavy showers fall, providing the main reason for the abundant growth.

Nowhere is this growth more apparent than in Lae's Botanical Gardens, Papua New Guinea's largest botanical gardens and once reputed to be the best in the South Pacific, a magnificent area of land close to the centre of town which was first laid out by Andree Miller, the Australian botanist. The gardens have become somewhat run-down, but are still the location for serious botanical work. Every now and then the botanists at Lae discover a new species, most recently an orchid with nut-brown flowers which looks like carved wood. Vanda helvola was previously thought to be the same as the Burmese orchid of that name, but actually turns out to be different. PNG is of course famous for its orchids and Morobe Province has adopted one of the Dendrobium species as its emblem. The Morobe Shower is an orchid with a white blossom marked with mauve.

Once traders in PNG began to do more than exchange local produce, Lae was bound to prosper and become the sort of place that would end up having botanical gardens. Located near to the mouth of the Markham River, which winds down to the sea through

the vast, wide Markham Valley, it began its 20th century existence as part of the German colony of New Guinea. In 1900 German traders set up a branch of the New Guinea Company there. They were soon followed by missionaries, but in 1919, after the German defeat in World War I, the territory was ceded to Britain and effectively delegated to Australia. The main activities in the early part of the century were whaling, fishing for pearl shell, trading, and missionizing. There was a persistent flow of gold prospectors. Lae, with its wharf and its access to the established trading posts in the islands, was a focal point. If Rabaul in East New Britain was the administrative centre for the islands, Lae performed the same function for mainland New Guinea. Banks, schools, shops and churches all developed. The discovery of gold inland at Wau and Bulolo in the 1930's was a spur to further changes.

During the war Lae was occupied by the Japanese and there was intense fighting and many casualties in the immediate area before they were defeated by the Australian and American forces. The military cemetery can be found at the top of the road next to the Botanical Gardens. At the end of the war in 1945 Lae was littered with the debris of military occupation, but at the same time another era of opportunity was beginning with the arrival of Australian settlers and administrators and the opening up of the Highlands. Lae began to prosper again. It was the main port for Highlands traffic and still is. In 1973 PNG's second university was sited here. Known as the Unitec, it specialises in subjects such as mining and business studies and it contains PNG's only Centre for Intermediate Technology.

Today Lae is having something of a struggle to maintain its commercial and administrative functions and its reputation as PNG's second city, in the face of declining financial support from central government and from the same kind of urban problem that affects Port Moresby. Some degree of 'raskol' violence always brings its accompanying paranoia. This takes its toll on every activity, not least on the enjoyment of Andree Miller's once-beautiful Botanical Gardens.

Madang is a province of contrasts. It has many of Papua New Guineas highest mountains, greatest rivers, most beautiful sandy beaches, most island volcanoes and biggest mix of languages (175). In the middle of the main coastal strip lies Madang town, probably one of the most beautiful towns in the whole country if not the whole South Pacific region.

Madang province is divided in two by the 210 kilometre long Ramu valley which separates the coastal Adelbert and Finisterre mountain ranges from the central Schrader and Bismark ranges. It lies on a fault zone and has many earthquakes. The total land mass is 28,339 square kilometres which includes four major islands. But with the inclusion of the sea area (which is important when considering fishing rights) it occupies 94,000 square kilometres.

The Province is divided into six districts, the smallest of which is the island district of Karkar, the largest the Middle Ramu. Karkar has an active volcanic crater which erupted in 1974 and again in 1979 killing two volcanologists who were monitoring volcanic activity on site. It is also the most densely populated district with 73 persons per square kilometre. In contrast the Middle Ramu has a population density of 6 persons per square kilometre.

The people of Madang fall into four distinct groups, islanders, coastal people, river people and mountain people. Scientists found evidence of human settlement some 15,000 years ago near Simbai. For hundreds of years the Yabob and Bibil people traded between the coastal areas and the highlands. Great sailing canoes brought pots from Karkar island to Western Morobe. Shells, salt and wooden bowls were traded for stone axes, feathers and women from the Asaro, Simbu and Jimi valleys in the Highlands.

Today the fertile coastal strip produces coconuts and copra. The Ramu valley is productive cattle country and produces almost all of PNG's sugar requirement. The islanders depend on seafood, root crops, bananas and tropical fruits. Taro is a staple food but sweet potatoes are more important in the mountains.

The total population of Madang is 252,411. There are two large hospitals, thirty one Health centres and 173 Aidposts. 38.5 % of those aged 7-16 attend school. 45.9 % can read at least one language of which 29.5 % is English, 40.3% Tok Pisin and 40.9% local. 40% of those 10 years and older work for money contributing to the cash economy by selling crops (vegetables, betelnut, bananas, cocoa, coconuts, fruit, coffee), fish, pigs or services.

Madang has a well-developed infrastructure to cope with future development.

The Provincial capital, Madang, is centrally located in a naturally deep sheltered harbour which is linked to roads and air-services. It is an international seaport through which copra, cocoa, cardamon, chilli, woodchip and sawn timber is exported. Small, locally owned coastal vessels provide regular shipping services along the coast and to the islands. Access to the interior by the Ramu river is provided by barges or motorised dinghies and dug-out canoes.

Madang is justly proud of its beautiful harbour and its facilities.

The Province has 31 airstrips varying in size from the international runway at Madang to grass strips in rural areas. Currently the Madang runway takes regular F28 Air Niugini services direct from Port Moresby, Cairns and Jayapura. There is a plan to extend the runway to take much bigger planes. The 12995 Provincial Premier, Matthew Gubag, has a gleam in his eye when he envisages 747's landing from Hong Kong, bringing tourists and businessmen to the province.

Madang has 1762 km of roads of which 74 km are sealed. Roads run along the coast and connect with the Highlands Highway in Morobe. There is a plan to extend north into Sepik. The provinces which make up Momase region, (Morobe, Madang and Sepik) are keen to promote tourism on a region-wide basis. The road system will be crucial to that plan.

"Tourism", said Premier Gubag, "is the gold of Madang". Madang town is a major attraction. It is a town of parks and waterways, luxuriant trees and grassy pathways. It is remarkably free from the urban disturbances. Even late at night, people can be seen walking freely and unafraid. There are hotels, department stores, markets and artefact shops. A Museum and Cultural Centre looks to links with the sea - displaying models of traditional sea-going boats including the lalaoika, a one-masted canoe, and the balangut, a two-mast canoe that has made this area famous. The waters of the harbour are still crystal clear. Children can swim in safety. Harbour tours are easily arranged as are visits to one of the many tiny

tropical islands where people still live a traditional life as farmers and fishermen. For the more adventurous,

Madang is centre of an area of coral reefs - a divers paradise.

Undeniably the Province has great potential for tourism. Whether it is for sun, sea and sand or game fishing, adventure walks in the jungle and visiting hot springs and sulphur caves. Madang has it all from sea to mountain top. It is ready and welcoming.

However, Madang Province is one of the less developed Provinces in Papua New Guinea. But Premier Gubag is ready to change that. "My government is inviting investors to put up projects. We have land available, especially government land, let people come and set up their industries here. We have wonderful fishing grounds and extensive forests. Let anyone come who is interested in processing, cutting up timber, canning fish".

At present the Province is heavily dependent on the rural industries of agriculture, fisheries and forestry. Subsistence agriculture still plays an important part in the lives of 85% of the people of Madang Province. The main cash crops are copra, cocoa and coffee. Very recently spice crops have been established but they are insignificant compared to copra. Premier Gubag understands the copra farmers as he has farmed copra himself. There are 55 large plantations of copra in Madang, accounting for 18 thousand hectares, but almost as much acreage, 16 thousand hectares, is held by smallholders. The province produces 20 -25 thousand tonnes annually.

All the coastal regions look to the sea and the possibility of a great harvest of fish. The Momase Smallholder Coastal Fisheries Development project has been extended to Madang from Morobe Province. Currently it is funded by the German government who had historic links with the area. It is hoped to extend still further to East Sepik and Sandaun Provinces. The East Ship Fishing Company of Philippines has been fishing in Madang waters since 1990 harvesting about 300 tonnes of tuna a month. Plans are on the table for not one but two canning factories, which the government are confi-

dent would attract more interest in the resources of the sea.

Canning is to fishing what saw-mills is to logging. Madang wants to attract investors to establish saw-mills "on the spot where they are harvesting the logs", says Matthew Gubag. "Even further, we want to see them processing, cutting up timber and making furniture right on the spot". Madang has one of the largest forest resources in the country amounting to 700,000 hectares of which 200,000 is under logging lease and another 195,328 is on proposal for issuing Timber Permits. About another 250,000 hectares are potential logging area. There are many Wokabaut Sawmills distributed throughout the Province but none are on a scale which could maximise the potential of Madang's natural forest.

Madang's first contact with the Europeans was in 1871 when the Russian biologist, Nicolai Miklouho-Maclay explored the Rai coast. He introduced pineapples, mangoes, beans, pumpkins and other foods. Later the Germans came and built tobacco, cotton and coffee plantations. In 1886 Johannes Flierl started the first Lutheran mission in Madang. 40.3 % of the population are Lutheran today.

In 1942 Japanese soldiers captured Madang town. For nearly two years villagers had to suffer Allied bombing, food shortages and disease epidemics until allied soldiers recaptured the town in April 1944. Now both Japanese and Europeans are welcomed in Madang, as visitors not as invaders. Madang's future could rest as much with its neighbours in Asia as to its links with Australasia. It is to the outside world that it is looking for investment. It is to the outside world that it holds out a warm welcome to anyone who will help bring badly needed development.

The great Sepik river flows through the imagination leaving traces in the collective memory and artefacts in museums around the world. Like the Congo in Africa and the Amazon in South America it dominates the hearts and culture of PNG and the provinces through which it flows.

East Sepik Province is the second largest province in PNG It has a land area of 42,800 square kilometres and a population of over a quarter of a million people - 90% of whom are rural dwellers. It is largely undeveloped. It is isolated from the rest of the country. There are no road connections south to Madang and the roads north to West Sepik are earth-formed and subject to flooding. It is highly dependent on air transport. But it is the most visited of all PNG's provinces. At present 60% of all visitors to PNG go to East Sepik – to the river.

The Sepik River is 1,126 km long and navigable for almost the entire distance. It starts in the northern mountains and winds gradually down to the sea. It frequently turns back on itself and has often changed its course leaving dead-ends, lagoons, oxbow lakes or huge swampy expanses which turn into lakes in the wet season or dry up to make grassland when the river is low. There is hardly a stone or rock within 50km of its banks. If a stone is washed down villages treat it as sacred and place it in front of the village haus tambaram (spirit house). At the end of the wet season water tears great chunks of mud and vegetation out of the river-banks and these floating islands drift downstream often with small trees and animals aboard. When it meets the sea the river stains it brown for 50 or more kilometres from the shore. Islanders claim to have drawn fresh water straight from the sea.

From the Sepik's mouth the province's 190 km coastline ranges over the Murik lakes delta to a narrow shelf west of Wewak. There are very few coral reefs but there are beautiful beaches with proper swaying palm trees and plenty of white sand. Wewak, the provincial capital is an attractive town with neat and tidy housing, lush tropical vegetation and gentle hills.

The newly appointed Governor Sir Michael Somare and the provincial government of East

Sepik want to develop Wewak as a tourist hub. But while they think mass tourism might be alright for Madang they believe it would destroy the Sepik. There is a delicate balance between bringing in much needed development and destroying the livelihood and culture of the indigenous people. One solution under consideration is to preserve the Upper Sepik and encourage small numbers of elite tourists to use Wewak as a base from which to explore the Middle Sepik. However to achieve this more limited objective, they would need to extend the Wewak runway, seal more roads (sealing the road from Wewak to Pagwi would cut the journey time in half) and upgrade hotel accommodation. Sir Michael Somare would like to attract more tourists from South East Asia using northerly air routes.

There has been a constant stream of visitors from Japan to Wewak to pay homage to their war dead from World War 2. The Japanese held the Sepik region for most of the war but the struggle was bitter and long. It was May 1945 before Wewak fell and the remaining Japanese troops withdrew into the hills. It was not until

September 1945 that General Adachi finally surrendered with the surviving 13,000 out of 100,000 troops. At Mission Hill there is a Japanese War Memorial to mark a mass grave, though the troops buried here were exhumed and returned to Japan. It is a quiet, reflective place with a fine view out across the headland and islands just off the coast.

Most visitors to East Sepik to go to PNG's cultural treasure house - the villages of the Middle Sepik. The provincial government intends to develop a village guest house network. They also need to safeguard health (by ensuring safe water and sanitation) and security (by more reliance on two-way radios). They are aware that they must oppose logging where it comes into conflict with tourism. The river must be kept free of the dreaded water hyacinth and some attempt will have to be made to regulate the expansion of river cruises.

River cruises have been the backbone of Sepik tourism and in general they are very well run. But large boats can swamp canoes whose occupants in turn ask exorbitant compensation. Visitors can be rude, obnoxious and

disruptive. Bad feelings and jealousies have occurred in less favoured villages. And there is a question whether performing traditional ceremonies for tourists weakens their spiritual significance and power.

Somehow the art of the Sepik has survived. Traditional carvers stayed in business because insects and borers attacked the wooden masks, hooks, stools and door-posts and they had to be replaced. Now it is tourism which keeps carving skills alive. 90% of the men are skilled wood-carvers. And deep below the surface old myths survive. The crocodile which features in many 'airport' or tourist carvings also appears in the Iatmul people's stories about their origins. In the beginning there was the salt water crocodile. It helped the land to rise above the water. Boys are scarified on initiation to produce patterns of crocodile skin on their backs and arms. Iatmul men keep the skulls of saltwater crocodiles in their cult houses.

Haus tambarans (spirit houses) are common to both river and hill tribes. Architectural styles vary but the high forward leading prow of the Maprik area is the most well-known. Some are huge, standing on great carved piles. They can be 40 to 50 metres long stretching 25 metres into the air. It is a men's house where men meet and store their sacred masks and musical instruments. Once the missionaries burnt them down and destroyed the idols but since one of them was successfully charged with arson the practice has been discontinued.

When the current provincial government took over they found services in a parlous state. District offices are falling apart. Health services are quite inadequate with a high infant mortality and maternal morbidity. Sir Michael Somare recognises that there has been an almost total reliance on the Churches, particularly the Catholic Church, to provide health and education services. He wants the government to collaborate with these agencies to help the people to health and prosperity.

East Sepik has a rural economy of subsistence agriculture and cash crops of coffee, cocoa, copra and rubber. The new provincial government is determined to improve the system of agriculture to encourage cash earning and wage employment for rural households. They have encouraged farmers to diversify, supplying seeds for the production of spices: chillies, pepper, nutmeg and vanilla. Already 17,000 farmers have engaged in the project and 15 tonnes of chillies have been produced.

East Sepik was the first government to realise the need to register all customary lands. It passed a Provincial Act that enabled the government to assist customary owners to register their land. It is a system which allows for group ownership and should inspire confidence in investors. The people of East Sepik are self-reliant they support themselves from their own gardens and grow cash crops to supplement their income. All coffee and cocoa is small-holder produced. They are being helped by a number of feeder programmes to introduce new varieties of hybrid cocoa or with livestock. The provincial government imported some big pigs to begin a breeding programme for pork and bacon production. It was similar thinking which persuaded the extension services to provide feed, pens, solar panels and freezers to encourage small-holder crocodile breeding. The East Sepik river system is a natural habitat for crocodiles. More than 50% of crocodile skins harvested from the wild come from Sepik. But farmers have been less successful raising them in captivity.

The future for the people of East Sepik will depend on it's governors' ability to bring investment, tourists and services to the backwaters of the great river.

In the far north-west of PNG, where the 'sun goes down' is one of the most unchanged provinces in the country. Sandaun, or West Sepik as it was once known, is a large undeveloped province on PNG's border with Irian Jaya. It has only two towns, Aitape and the capital Vanimo. In some areas there are no people at all or just scattered settlements.

"Because it is neglected there is a lot of jungle. People live in the style of our forefathers, our great grandparents. I see little of what is talked about in National Parliament benefiting our people," said Deputy Governor Peien Aloitch. "I see school children in remote areas without any clothes, or with torn clothes. I think we should pay more attention to them". Certainly Sandaun has one of the lowest levels of literacy and educational attainment of any province. Sandaun people have the lowest life expectancy and the highest death rate for children. It has very limited infrastructure, few roads, no telecommunications network except along the border. But it does have 57 airstrips, a year-round safe anchorage at Vanimo and a very low crime rate. It also has the largest single area of commercial timber in PNG.

Forest and timber dominate the Sandaun economy. The port at Vanimo may see four or five large freighters a week loading logs and cut timber. The logs are stacked high on the wharves. Huge hardwood kwila trees en route for Malaysia and Singapore. In 1992 110,600 cubic metres of logs valued at over 11 million kina were exported from Sandaun. Two thirds of them came from the Vanimo Timber Project. "We know how many logs are being harvested and exported overseas. We know how much forest there is. How can we know how many fish there are in the sea?" queried Peien Aloitch once a fisherman himself. "Better to develop logging and leave fishing to the local people."

Along the coastal strip local people live in well-found wooden houses in large villages. There is a good road from Vanimo to the

border. All but a kilometre and a half is sealed. The last section is awaiting landowner agreements. The border is no longer a problem in the sense that there are no skirmishes or refugees as in the '70's and '80's but it does exercise a powerful pull on Sandaun. Shops and restaurants carry Indonesian foodstuffs. A boat leaves Vanimo every Thursday with shoppers taking advantage of cheaper, more available goods in Jayapura. Anyone living within 14 kms of the border carries a Border Crossing Pass which entitles them to pass unhindered. Those from further afield have visas and customs like any other frontier. The border is a typical colonial slight of hand. A ruler-straight line drawn across a totally unknown area with no regard for the people living on it or near it. On both sides there are families who have intermarried and there are

shared cultural customs. There are even shared gardens. There is also the presence of the Australian engineering battalion and a company of the PNG Defence Force – just in case.

The Province is divided into six districts three of which lie on the border and get special funding. Of the others, only Telefomin has a cash economy and that is largely from growing vegetables for the Ok Tedi mine in neighbouring Western Province. The Min people in Telefomin benefit from Ok Tedi to the tune of K1 million a year. It is spent on bridges, water, schools and airstrips. Telefomin is looking forward to the development of the Frieda River copper mine for they can expect a similar deal. It hopes to upgrade its Technical High School to train workers for the mine which will be the first in the Province.

Sandaun has benefited from the National Government's 'Look North' policy. Trade with Malaysia and Singapore, Taiwan and Korea has increased. Pein Aloitch wants to sell Vanimo as the tourist gateway to Asia. There are traditional arts and crafts and numerous war relics to share with foreign visitors. One recent discovery has done more to enhance Sandaun's international reputation than any other. Ironically, it is a shy forest dwelling creature - a unique species of tree kangaroo. In the local Olo language it is called 'tenkile'. It is found nowhere else in the world.

"Our isolation has given us strength and energy to survive", said Simeon Malai, Secretary of Manus Province. It could well be that Manus' geographical isolation, it is the smallest and least visited of all PNG provinces, has reinforced certain characteristics. Manus people are self-reliant, gifted. They care passionately about their island, about each other and their families. There is a tremendous pride in Manus culture and heritage.

Manus has the smallest land area (2100 square kms) and population (32,713) of any province. It is the most northerly province of PNG. A scattering of 208 islands along the equator give it an 800 km border. The largest island, Manus, is part of the Admiralty group. Most of it is rugged mountain covered in forest.

Traditionally its people are fishermen and farmers, who export copra, cocoa and timber. However one of the big successes for Manus, and its top export, is well-educated young people who get jobs outside the province and send money home. In 1994 Manus received K9 million in remittances. This achievement lies deep in the history of Manus.

Manus islanders were always great mariners sailing large outrigger canoes, some up to 10 metres long with three sails, to trade extensively around the islands. A Spanish sailor was the first European to find them and some Spanish touches remain - the airport is on an island called Los Negros. Germans attempted to

colonise Manus in the early 20th century but the fierce independence of the people and the infertility of the soil inhibited colonisation. It was World War 2 which made the biggest impact. First the Japanese and then the Americans caused much damage to villages and built huge bases. The Americans used Seeadler Harbour, a fine protected anchorage, to harbour its fleet in preparation for an assault on the Philippines. At times there were more than 600 vessels docked there. A year after the war they left but not before scrapping everything.

It was this wartime exposure to outside influences that initiated the development of education in Manus, though it began in a curious way. It led to cargo cults one of which, dubbed the New Way, has an impact today. Cargo cults had appeared sporadically in PNG. It was a way of explaining the extraordinary technology of Europeans - it must have come by supernatural means. Paliau Moloat led the movement in Manus. Although it shared many of the attributes of cargo cults, it is now recognised as one of the first post-war independence movements. It brought together diverse, often warring tribes in unified resistance to the Australian administration. It was a radical Church movement which resulted in throwing over old cults and rituals and rebuilding European style villages, schools and government. Paliau was imprisoned for his activities in 1949 but later released and eventually awarded a knighthood.

The Paliau movement gave Manus a head start on the rest of PNG. By the early 1950's a minimum of 4 years schooling was compulsory for every child on Manus. Some classrooms had 400 pupils but dedicated teachers won hearts and minds. Manus has the highest literacy rate in PNG and the highest proportion of pupils who have completed Grade 6. 42% of the schools are run by Churches. Government and Church work together on Manus. "We are a 100% Christian community" said government official Paliau Lukas. For those unable to attend secondary school there is a "School of the Air". In PNG it is unique to Manus. These high standards of education have led not only to good jobs off the island but to Manusians taking more than their share of positions of power and influence in PNG.

Perhaps it was also due to high educational attainment that Manus tried time and again to develop a plan for the future of the province. Expert opinion was bought and found wanting. It was only when political scientist Steven Pokawin took over the leadership that a plan was devised which appears to work. Casting aside the top-down approach, they asked for an expert demographer from the University of PNG and, with WHO funding, began a random sample survey of 30% of the population. It was based on interviews, district by district, village by village about what people perceived their basic minimum needs to be. The breadwinner, man or woman, was asked to set needs in an order of priority. The answers came back, for the majority of districts shelter came first. So that was put into the new plan.

The whole approach is characteristic of Manusian traditional emphasis on independence and self reliance. "Since Independence people had become dependent on hand-outs. In 1975 probably 95% of the cash in the economy came from the National Government. It was a disaster to initiative and to dreams. If God created you to be a doctor, then look to it. Go see what you can do to help yourself achieve a medical degree. But recognise your needs. Recognise what is realistic and then solve the problem your self", declaims author of the plan, James Pokris. "Once the people have identified their problems then it is the political responsibility of Church and government to make the projects happen."

In the last ten years Manus has some notable achievements. The shelter programme was begun by offering designs and setting villagers to building the houses themselves. By 1991 every village in Manus had at least 4 permanent dwellings. In 1995 they have at least 16 per village built out from light timber frames with corrugated iron roofs and solar panels. This is where the remittance money goes. It also goes on outboard motors.

Manus is a province of islands. 75% of the people are dependent on sea transport and there is a network of coastal vessels linking outlying islands. In 1975 there were 10 outboard motors on Manus and 5 speedboats. Now there are 5,000 speedboats and 10,000 outboard motors. It means that each family on Manus has on average 2 outboards and a speedboat - all bought with remittances.

Manus is rich in fish and marine resources, especially trochus and pearl shells. All live fish export has been banned within a 3 mile zone leaving it to subsistence fisherfolk. The 3 to 12 mile limit is for local and ex-pat ventures only and the 12 to 200 mile zone falls within the National

Government remit. Manus is most anxious to preserve stocks, by understanding where the breeding grounds are and protecting them from exploitation. No-one is allowed to cut mangrove swamp, the breeding ground for many crustaceans. The estuaries are left undisturbed. Every schoolchild in Manus is taught the importance of preserving these places to conserve the future.

Unfortunately the lesson was learnt too late to save the West coast of Manus. Palius Lukas explains, "Manus does not have the huge forest resources of other provinces but it did agree to harvest 84,00 cubic metres a year for fifteen years. Since 1987 logging has brought in a revenue of 15k million and that has been redistributed to the people. But it has cost them dear. The West coast is scarred. 4,000 people have been torn from sustainable subsistence to dependency on rice and tinned fish. Where rivers flowed and you could harvest fish and crustaceans or keep pigs, now there is nothing but dry gullies. In 6 years all has been lost. There have even been outbreaks of lawlessness in this peaceful island." It is a sad story.

In true Manus style the response is to ban logging, despite the fact that it is the only project currently earning money, and to plan a major spiritual revival which will make people conscious of the importance of family life (and the value of

small scale enterprise). Churches and government have to pull together to care for fatherless children and unwed mothers. Youth groups and community centres are encouraged. Morning devotions are part of every Manus day. Spiritual renewal is second to shelter on the Manus plan. Next came medical care, family life, peace and harmony, population and family planning, water, food, communication, money, education and land.

Of all these communications is well on the way to being exceptional, not just in PNG, but in the whole South Pacific. Part of the plan was to build a rural telephone network initially with 2-way radio and then with VHF and SSB links. Already every community of 100 persons has a solar powered radio available, usually in a school or community centre. The next stage will be links by satellite to the internet - going global. Modern communications could well be the key to unlocking the door to tourism.

Past attempts to encourage tourists failed because, James Pokris says, "Tourism was geared towards creating another Waikiki Beach in Manus. It should be linked with shelter. Well planned, it should provide stimulant for village people to have better housing. Let tourists use village houses where monetary benefits may be shared to the villages and not just the hotels and main shops in Lorengau". Now they are looking at attractions like white water rafting and sea kayaking. They plan the first world championships in sea-kayaking in 1997. The championship is not just a sporting event but an opportunity to share Manus' concern its water-ways, both coast and river. The paddlers will be attracted to a pristine environment and taught how to care for it. It will probably involve just about every aspect of island life. It would certainly put Manus on the tourist map. And if sea-kayaking sounds too strenuous there are marvellous caves, beaches, dive sites, and the village where famous American anthropologist, Margaret Mead, lived which has a memorial to her work and to the Pere people she lived amongst.

Manus may be small and unvisited but it is big in ideas and determined to go its own way. "The rest of the country hides behind conventions", says Secretary Simeon Malai. "Manus has moved in a different direction. It challenges all agencies to be imaginative and creative. This is the way to go".

NEW IRELAND PROVINCE

There is a long thin island lying between one and five degrees south of the equator in a north westerly direction. It claims to be one of the most peaceful and law abiding places in the whole of the South Pacific. It is New Ireland, or Niu Ailan (the new island) in pidgin.

New Ireland is no more than 10 kilometres wide at its widest and 350 kms long. A spine of mountains falls straight to the sea in the west but leaves a narrow fertile coastal strip on the east. There is a population of 87,000 most of whom live in the south of the island. There are twenty different languages. While close neighbours might understand each other, language becomes incomprehensible further away down the island.

Many traditions are similar: matrilineal descent, big man leadership, weapons and tools but there are marked differences in house and canoe design, in burial rites, marriage ceremonies and ritual. It has high literacy rates, at least 61% can read. Three fifths attend Church-run schools. There are some famous sons including the present Prime Minister Sir Julius Chan.

New Ireland has the only National Fisheries College in PNG. It was founded in 1977 with the assistance of the Japanese Government. It offers a two year course in tropical fisheries. It has just commissioned a new boat built in Australia. Students take day-trips to gain practical experience of long-lining and trawling. The college takes both boy and girl students from all over PNG though the principal confesses they have had to teach the Highlanders to swim first.

The provincial capital, Kavieng, boasts a good size airfield with a modern airport building. It is soon to be expanded to take international flights and increased traffic for the Lihir goldmine and the Sasemi fresh fish markets of Japan and the USA. Following the Rabaul volcanic disaster Kavieng is bidding for new routes by air and by sea. After waiting for nearly 40 years it is to get a new multi-purpose wharf. The new wharf will also service Lihir, a tiny island off the east coast. The gold is buried in an ancient, collapsed, volcanic caldera.

The Lihir gold mine is without a doubt the biggest thing to happen to New Ireland in its history. Lihir will be the biggest gold mine in the Southern hemisphere. Initially it will employ 7,000 people which is equal to the total of islanders on Lihir. It will have a dramatic impact on their lifestyle and that of all New Irelanders.

At present the economy is kept afloat by Poliamba Pty Ltd. Poliamba produces oil palm and cocoa. It was created by the Commonwealth Development Corporation in response to an appeal by community leaders who were concerned at how few employment opportunities there were locally. In colonial times the Germans had planted copra in large plantations along the length of New Ireland. The trees were past their best, the plantations had become derelict and the price of copra had fallen. The CDC suggested rehabilitating the old plantations and a K54 million investment package was put together.

Poliamba is a social programme as much as a business investment. About 500 people are employed directly and another 750 work on contract planting, weeding and harvesting fruit. Contract work allows people time to garden, fish, help with community projects or just malolo. Workers live at home and remain valued members of village society. Poliamba built its own mill, its own tanks capable of storing 4,000 tonnes of oil and its own wharf. The oil is shipped out to Malaysia for refining before being turned into magarine, cooking oil or even ice cream. It is a huge investment but it has not forgotten the small producer. Small landowners are encouraged to plant and deliver direct to the mill.

Key to many local developments is the sealing of the highway. Baron Buliminsky had the highway built down the island seventy years ago. Poliamba sealed a seventy kilometre section to their factory and now New Irelanders are looking forward to the completion

317

of the remaining 130 kilometres as part of the Lihir deal. It is anticipated that local business will triple with the highway and it will open up the island for tourism.

Bilas Peles, the islands of Tranquillity appeal to adventurers and eco-tourists. The New Ireland government is looking for projects which will promote culture and environment and bring maximum benefits to the people. The biggest surprise is the success of cycling. Both coasts offer outstanding cycling with good flat roads, little traffic, plenty of water (fresh and salt) and friendly people. Not so surprising but equally good is the diving. There are wrecks and reefs and over thirty islands which are natural breeding grounds for fish. While between the islands there are schools of barracuda, turtles, rays, dolphins and sharks.

Sharks occur in many of the cultural traditions of New Ireland. 'Shark calling' refers to the remarkable ability of certain men to call a shark to their canoe by voice or by a rattle until it can be snared in a noose. Canoes and fishing scenes are the subject of many colourful baroque carvings. Malangan carvings were totemic figures made to honour the dead and used in funerary rituals and soul boats. Malangan art is in museums in Europe and the USA. But the art or carving nearly died out before the son of a famous carver resurrected it. Now New Irelanders can enjoy their own cultural heritage.

September 1995, sees East New Britain with its own anniversary to celebrate. It is just a year after the volcanic eruptions that virtually destroyed the capital, Rabaul, and turned the surrounding area into a field of ash. It is remembered as being a frightening but also an exciting time.

Sunday 18th September was a night of continuous earthquakes. At five in the morning there was an exceptionally large quake and billowing clouds began issuing from Mount Tavorvor, one of the several cones that surround the bay of Rabaul. There was a noise like continuous thunder. Ash began raining down and the sky darkened rather than getting light. The inhabitants began running from their houses.

"People didn't know what to do", said Theresa Peter, a local resident. "Children were running one way, parents another. The evacuation vehicles were not in position. People got in whatever car they could Some cars were commandeered. Fifteen thousand people lived in Rabaul itself, so you can imagine the confusion."

Despite the confusion, and the fact that a second volcano, Vulcan, began erupting, there was little loss of life. The people of Rabaul helped each other to safety. A few days later the eruptions themselves stopped, although a rain of mud and ash continued to fall for months.

The result was a scene of tremendous devastation. Most of the buildings in Rabaul had collapsed under the weight of ash, which spread over a huge area to the south-east of the city, with the new 800ft high cone of Mt. Vulcan right in the middle. The roads and the airport were obliterated. The telephone system had been one of the first victims of the disaster. There was no water, and no electricity.

"Before the eruptions, Rabaul was the main town in the islands region", said Governor Francis Koimanrea. "It was a beautiful town with avenues of flowering trees, popular with tourists. Politically stable, it had a good administration and was a hub of commercial activity. Many people had come to live there from outside the area, attracted by the work opportunities and the pleasant surroundings".

A year later, the huge task of cleaning up Rabaul is not complete.

The functions of the capital have been split between Kotopo, a township further round the bay, and Vunadidir, up in the hills, where government officials have set up camp in buildings that were previously a college for administrators. Land has been purchased by the government and is being made available in small lots for resettlement, though many of the people who had come to live in Rabaul from other provinces have returned to their original homes. Rabaul itself is still a mess of collapsed buildings and heaps of ash.

"We had a lot of assistance from government, from the other provinces and from international donors", said Francis Koimanrea. "The Gazelle Restoration Authority, which was set up earlier this year, has also been assisted in its funding by outside agencies. We are very grateful for this. However it is not until one has witnessed the utter devastation caused by events such as this that one can appreciate the scale of the work needed to recreate all that makes up a busy, modern provincial capital and much remains to be done".

As a province, East New Britain relies on both subsistence and plantation agriculture together with forestry, fishing, coastal shipping and commercial activities to provide its economic base. Copra and coconut products are important, as is cocoa. The province is fertile, with well-established plantations and gardens and considerable forest reserves. A relatively long period of contact with a variety of outsiders has resulted in a stable society with functioning social systems such as schools and health services - and a tolerance of tourists. The Gazelle Peninsula is proud of its network of sealed roads. It is because of all this that it is clear that, while the loss of Rabaul has been an unmitigated disaster, East New Britain will overcome this and move on, the events of 1994 taking their place among the others that have marked Rabaul's colourful past.

"Economic development has been one main feature of our Province. We are ranked one of the big four in the country", said Provincial Secretary Sebulon Kulu.

"We are contributing K88 million towards the National purse." West New Britain is PNG's volcano, oil palm and timber centre. There are 13 volcanoes in the Province of which 3 are active, one dormant and the rest extinct. It is these rich volcanic soils which are the source of WNB's wealth of timber and palm oil.

The Western half of New Britain island was sparsely developed during the colonial period except for scattered coconut plantations. Compared to the eastern end of the island it seems relatively untouched even today. But it is a delightfully friendly place with a great tradition of dancing and music. It became a separate administrative district in 1966 after 80 years of German and Australian rule from Rabaul. Between 1950 and 1960 the government brought big areas of fertile unused land for resettlement schemes and agriculture development. Two major nucleus estate-smallholder oilpalm projects were developed.

According to the 1990 census WNB has a population of 130,625 people, 314 rural villages, 433 rural communities, 20 resettlement schemes and 39 plantations and estates. Many people came to WNB as plantation labourers or settlers. One fourth of the population was born outside the island. This is the highest rate for any province. Unfortunately it

has caused trouble with the villagers and plans have been announced to repatriate illegal settlers. WNB also has a high birth rate which is creating a land shortage and tribal conflict in some areas.

Many hundreds of years ago the people of WNB were engaged in trade and exchange networks involving shells, pots, canoes and carvings between New Britain and Morobe and Madang on the mainland. Today Nakanai, spoken on the north east coast and mountains, is the first language of one fifth of the local people. Tok pisin is the main second language. Shell money was used for bride price in many areas but is fast being replaced by kina and toea. Many groups have developed their own cultural artefacts. The Nakanai have a variety of bark cloth masks including hoods representing pigs or fish.

Among the Kilenge people of Cape Gloucester, carved wooden bowls and pots from the vitiaz strait trade are also traditional bride price items. The Kilenge make giant pointed masks called bukomo with bright, simple facial features. They also carve and paint canoe prows with simple designs representing bush animals or plants related to family groups.

Witu islanders make large conical masks of bark cloth, with large triangles pointed around the eyes. The Arowe people traditionally carved life sized human figures. Kandrian people make unique shields of three paralleled pieces of wood lashed together. The Kaulong and Senseng people are the only Melanesians to blow guns to kill animals, birds and fruit bats in the rain forest. Darts are blown through 4 metre long tubes of bamboo, a sudden breath of air can shoot as far as 50 metres.

In exchange for allowing loggers into its vast timber resource WNB has plenty of roads and bridges and a Kimbe-Bialla Highway. The provincial government has been encouraging small-holder development of some cash crops: coffee, spices, coconut, cocoa and poultry and pig units. There is also the hope that tourists will be attracted by the people, the extraordinary active volcanic landscapes with geysers and hot-springs. Or they might come for the diving which is deemed stunningly beautiful by divers who rave about clear water, volcanic caves draped in stag horn coral and reef drop-offs. There is a lot on offer in the quiet half of New Britain island.

There are two things that people remember about the North Solomons. Firstly they recall that the people who live here are reputed to have the blackest skin on earth and, secondly, that the world's largest copper mine is here.

The people are so black that the name by which they call other Papua New Guineans is 'redskins'. This indicates that they have been genetically isolated for a long time or that they are part of a larger group that has not survived.

For many years, headlines have reminded outsiders of the bitter conflict over the copper mine, which ended in the closure of the mine, the loss of many lives and the destruction of entire villages. A dispute over land and mineral rights had grown over the years into an armed secessionist movement. Today, a fragile peace agreement is still holding.

Talking about this province, people tend to use the name of the island which contains the mine,

Bougainville. North Solomons has two adjoining main islands, Bougainville and Buka, and 166 smaller islands scattered over 450,000 square kms of sea. Bougainville is almost all of volcanic origin. A series of mountain ranges form a central spine of high peaked mountains, underground caverns and lakes. Bougainville has many natural harbours. Buka, by contrast, is mostly coral that has been raised up from the sea. The Bougainville Copper Ltd. mine is in the Crown Prince range of mountains. Coconut and cocoa plantations cover most of the coastal land. North Solomons is in PNG's most active earthquake area.

From the opening proper of the mine in 1972 (though it was started in 1969), to its closure in 1989, Bougainville enjoyed a productive economy and one of the most effective government and education systems in PNG. The arguments and history of the conflict make up a long and complicated story, much written about elsewhere, but the lessons of Bougainville are reflected in the current efforts to reform Provincial government throughout PNG and in the laws regarding land rights and compensation.

The chief task is of rehabilitation. The population of North Solomons is estimated at 130,000. Those living in the small islands and in the Buka area arranged a peace in 1991. They wanted their lives to return to some sort of normalcy. Government services in the form of teachers, public servants and non-public servants were asked to return. Interim authorities were set up and with the assistance of the Council of Chiefs, schools and health centres re-opened. As soon as areas were declared safe by the Security Forces, essential services were set up. Small-scale rural economic activities were restored. By the end of 1993 full productions of cocoa and copra were being exported from Nissan and Buka. Now the effort is being extended to Bougainville itself.

It is a massive task. Whole villages been displaced. In 1994 there were approximately 50,000 people, almost a third of the population, living in care centres. The whole infrastructure was disrupted. There is a huge repair and rebuilding job to be done. Roads need maintenance as do wharves and airstrips. International aid is at hand as long as the peace holds.

It may not be too long before North Solomons is open to the casual traveller once again. There they will find a people whose clan membership is traced down the maternal line. The crafts and customs are complex. Best known are intricately patterned baskets woven by the Siwia and Telei people of south west Buka. They may hear a bamboo flute band or a group of drummers. They will certainly hear stories of the great mine and the trouble it brought to this island in the South Pacific.

OVERVIEW

No one knows exactly when man first set foot in PNG, but evidence of his early presence has been found at a number of locations. In New Ireland, stone tools indicate human habitation more than 30,000 years old. On the Huon Peninsula, axes excavated from volcanic ash attest a civilisation that reaches back a further 10,000 years.

At Kuk, just outside Mount Hagen, a recently discovered drainage and mounding system, for both wet and dry cultivation, bears witness to the sophisticated agricultural communities that must have been spread all across the highlands thousands of years before their European counterparts took to cultivating the land. Archeological investigations indicate that a constant flow of hardy, adaptable peoples have streamed into Papua New Guinea from various parts of Asia and that the complex process of displacement and assimilation have led to exceptional diversity in all areas of art and culture.

In the Eastern Highlands there is cave art, stone artifacts and large-scale terracing of hill slopes for agricultural gardening, dating back tens of thousands of years. In Enga and the Southern Highlands, stone mortars and pestles have been unearthed, probably used for crushing and powdering nuts. Coastal civilisations at Balof Cave and on New Ireland are more recent. Lapita pottery has been found on Mussau Island, New Ireland and Manus Province. However, the most obvious difference between the growth of civilisation in Papua New Guinea and that in many other parts of the world is that the former never developed into city-states. Paradoxically, the sophistication of agricultural techinques may have prohibited the growth of such intense masses of population since virtually none of the crops could be stored or transported over great distances. The result was highly developed but small and local agricultural units, optimising the cultivation of their own specific environments.

Many of these early agricultural practices may have been disappeared when the sweet potato was first introduced into the country. The 'kaukau' or sweet potato soon became a crucial part of the staple diet in the highland valley communities where it was readily adaptable to the temperate climate. By the time the Europeans first penetrated into the Highlands in the 1930s, the thriving population of that region was close to a million. Like the ancient cultures of Central and South America, the Papua New Guineans did not have the wheel. Nor did they have looms. But excavations reveal that they had a rich material culture. Chinese glass beads and the remains of bronze drums on Lou Island are testament to international trade links over 2,000 years old. Obsidian tools carved in Talasea in West New Britain in 1500 BC have been found nearly 4,000

kilometres away in Fiji. There were complex trading networks around the coast and between the coastal and highland regions. Often the goods travelled circuitous routes to their destinations since the tribes would only trade with their immediate neighbours. Valuable commodities such as salt, obsidian, shells, oil, pigments, pottery and stone were traded around the country.

Undisturbed by European intrusion for tens of thousands of years, the people of these islands built up their own civilisations and cultures.

Undisturbed by European intrusion for tens of thousands of years, the people of these islands built up their own civilisations and cultures. Then early in the sixteenth century, Portuguese and Spanish navigators first met the islanders and gave them a new name. In 1526 Jorge de Menezes called the land Ilhas Dos Papuas, the last word being a Portuguese corruption of the Malay term for curly hair. Seventeen years later, in 1545, Ynigo Ortiz de Rexes renamed the country Nueve Guinea, because it reminded him of Guinea in Africa. Caught between an arbitrary label and a rather demeaning slang word, the name Papua New Guinea has nevertheless stuck. For a long time, Europeans mistakenly thought that the inhabitants of PNG were related to the negro peoples of Africa.

The Spaniards and the Portuguese were followed by the Dutch, who consolidated their hold on the East Indies in the 17th century. Although they were clearly not averse to finding gold in the area, their main efforts were concentrated on the lucrative Spice Island trade in mace, nutmeg and cloves. There was no obvious wealth in Papua New Guinea and interaction with the inhabitants was limited to stopping for food, firewood and water. During the next centuries, the mainland and islands of Papua New Guinea were visited by British, French and Dutch mariners, many of whom left their names or the names of European places behind them. It was not until 1828 that the Dutch claimed sovereignty over the west part of the island of New Guinea. Coastal communties started to become accustomed to contact with whalers, pearlers, sandalwood cutters and traders of various kinds. As the fledging colony of Australia developed, there was an increasing need for cheap indentured labour to work in the sugar plantations of North Queensland and an unscrupulous 'blackbirding' industry arose.

Ships would visit islands in the Milne Bay, New Britain, New Ireland, Bougainville and the Solomons to forcibly 'recruit' young men to work as labourers in Australia, Fiji and Samoa. This sometimes led to violent clashes with local clans, but 'kanaka' labour was instrumental in getting large-scale commercial agriculture successfully established in those countries.

English cartographers were soon mapping the edges of their international domain. In 1847, Captain Owen Stanley surveyed the Papuan coast, immodestly naming the country's central cordillera after himself. Thirty years later, in the southern part of the country, the Englishman John Moresby located a break in the fringing reef and went on through it to find a large natural habour and a village, Hanuabada. This harbour and the town that replaced the village is now known as Port Moresby.

The future capital, however, grew very slowly. Its European population remainedfairly static except for a brief invasion by gold prospectors in 1878. Reports of gold on Laloki River outside the town spurred more than a hundred hopefuls to travel from Cooktown in North Queensland. Within six months they were all back in Australia again. By 1897, Port Moresby had a resident white population of only 33.

In 1848, the Dutch formally incorporated the eastern end of mainland New Guinea into their empire. That part of the country is now Irian Jaya and is part of Indonesia. When Germany annexed northeastern New Guinea and the Bismarck Archipelago as Kaiser Wilhelmsland in 1884, the growing and exportation of copra was a major commercial activity on Gazelle Peninsula. Several previous attempts by British navigators to annex Papua New Guinea had all ended abortively, including one by Captain Moresby himself in 1873. However, only three days after the German announcement, Commodore John Erskine officially raised the Union Jack over British New Guinea. Four years later, in 1888, it became a British colony. The actual demarcation lines between German and

British New Guinea were drawn up over a table in Europe by bisecting the country with a ruler, then dividing up the eastern half. Papua New Guinea became the proud 'possession' of Britain, Germany and Holland.

'Taim bilong masta' is Pidgin for the colonial period, the 87 years from 1888 to 1975.

In the early 1880s, Sir Peter Scratchley, Special Commissioner to the Crown, was sent out to manage the affairs of this latest addition to British Imperial interests. He established his residence on a hillside near the village of Hanuabada, overlooking the beach of Konedobu, now the official residence of the Governor General. With only a small annual purse, the British colonial administrators could not do much more than visit the coastal communities and try to impose the law. Scratchley died of malaria in 1885 and Papua New Guinea did not have official colonial status until 1888, but during his short tenure he set a government policy that became the prototype for ensuing generations of British and Australian administrators. Scratchley was an enlightened man and recommended to his superiors in London that the Papua New Guinea government should employ and serve the native people as well as the empire.

The German administration in the northern part of the country was administered on a very different basis. Managed by businessmen, the German Territory was in effect a private company, originally floated in Berlin in 1884 and aimed at creating a profit-based plantation economy. Legal and domestic administration played a secondary role and was essentially designed to maintain an accessible labour force. The Germans energetically set about 'purchasing' prime fertile tracts along the coast and establishing a chain of trading stations while they experimented with various kinds of tropical crops. Their efforts resulted in the copra plantations along the northern mainland coast from the Sepik to the Markham, on the Admiralty Islands, New Britain, New Ireland and Bougainville. This venture was a commercial success and it underwrote the export economy of the territory for the next thirty years, but with a heavy price to pay on both sides. Many of the German colonialists died of malaria and other diseases and the Papua New Guineans suffered under an oppressive regime, the local people being indentured and beaten when they did not comply to the 'Pax Germanica'.

The First World War had relatively little impact on Papua New Guinea despite the fact that the British and the German colonies of New Guinea lay side by side. In 1914, an Australian naval expeditionary force of 2,000 men was sent to Rabaul, the capital of German New Guinea, where the small contingent of German soldiers were asked to surrender. In the skirmish that followed, one German, six Australians and thirty New Guinean enlisted soldiers lost their lives. From that point on, not another shot was fired for the remainder of the war. When Germany surrendered in 1918, Australia took over the task of administering both halves of the country. Even after the newly formed League of Nations appointed Australia as guardian of the Mandated Territory of New Guinea, it governed both halves independently.

The years between the two great wars were full of excitement and activity in PNG. The search for gold had led administration patrols deep into the country and previously unknown peoples were encountered and filmed. Further searches for minerals and oil began in earnest, following up on earlier indications that the country had vast reserves. Minerals were discovered in large quantities whereas the oil boom had to wait another fifty years.

When war broke out again in Europe in 1939, it looked as if Papua New Guinea would be as little affected as it was a quarter of a century earlier. But the Japanese had other plans. On December 7, 1941 the Japanese Air Force attacked Pearl Harbour and Papua New Guinea suddenly found itself the only barrier between the

invaders and the Australian mainland. This was the beginning of the New Guinea Campaign, generally acknowledged as one of the bloodiest battle arenas in the entire South Pacific War. In 1943, Admiral Yamamoto, the Commander-in-Chief of the Japanese Combined Fleet and the architect of the raid on Pearl Harbour, was shot down over Buin on the island of Bougainville.

The Japanese launched an air attack on Rabaul on January 23, 1942. After bombarding the town, they landed 20,000 soldiers and made Rabaul the South Pacific headquarters of the Imperial Japanese Army. The Australians, and the Americans who were later sent to reinforce the 'diggers', were only too aware of what might happen if the Japanese invaded the Australian mainland and they fought ferociously in the forests of PNG to prevent them. The Japanese tried to capture the capital, Port Moresby, but were severely defeated at the famous air battle of the Coral Sea. As a final effort, the Japanese threw all they could into a last campaign, the Kokoda Trail, but to no avail. The allies had

won, but thousands of Papua New Guineans and Australians had lost their lives. The Japanese numbers of killed and wounded were equally high.

The Papua New Guineans served the war effort both as soldiers and as carriers. More than 3,000 men were engaged on the Kokoda campaign alone, toiling up the track with supplies and back down again carrying the wounded on stretchers. Many a soldier owed his life to these 'angels', as they were called, ordinary villagers who risked their lives to help the military. September 1995 is thus not only the twentieth anniversary of the independence of Papua New Guinea, but the fiftieth anniversary of the end of the war.

World War Two had a profound effect on the nation. For many, it was the first time they had ever left their towns and villages and they discovered an entirely new world. More importantly, the war radically altered people's attitude towards the Europeans. Their mask of superiority had fallen. They were vulnerable.

The Australian government fully acknowledged the 'debt of gratitude' they owed Papua New Guinea and soon after the war had ended they assisted generously in developing the infrastructure of PNG society, building roads, schools and health centres. During the 5 years between the end of the war and 1950, the Australians poured 16 million pounds into the PNG economy, more than 40 times the amount spent by the administration in the 5 years leading up to 1939. A Director of Education was appointed and English adopted as the official lingua franca in the belief that it would foster

national unity in a country that had over 700 individual languages. The new order also meant increased spending in the public sector. New emphasis was placed on public works and utilities. Aside from education, the health service and roads, aid was used to set up sophisticated communications and electricity systems.

The two decades leading up to Independence were an exciting era for the two halves of Papua New Guinea. For the first time nationals began to take part in the development of their country. Australia was committed to granting PNG full independence. A national flag and crest were designed and Papua New Guinea officially adopted as the country's name. In 1973, the assets of two Australian airlines operating in PNG were amalgamated and the new national carrier, Air Niugini, was established.

Papua New Guinea was granted home rule in October 1973 and full independence in September two years later. The first Governor-General, Sir John Guise, made it clear that the colonial flag was being lowered, not torn down, a view endorsed by Prime Minister, Michael Somare, when he said: "We have been more fortunate that many other countries. We have been lucky because we have reached full nationhood without the fighting and bloodshed experienced by so many other former colonies." But the Prime Minister also made it clear that PNG owed its independence not to the Australians or the United Nations but to the people who had worked hard for peace and unity. Sixty-nine years of Australian administration had come to an end.

This book is a commemoration of that event and a celebration of the 20 years of Independence since then.

Papua New Guinea proudly celebrated its twentieth Anniversary of Indpendence on September 16th. 1995. The Prime Minister, The Rt. Hon. Sir Julius Chan, GCMG, KBE, MP gave the following speech at the opening ceremony.

This is a special day; a special day for all Papua New Guineans. It is a day for pride in having come this far, and for all we have achieved in the 20 years since gaining our Independence.

We are in the company of special friends today, and many distinguished guests - His Majesty, the King of Tonga, five Presidents, nine Prime Ministers and

three Secretaries-General - of the Commonwealth, ASEAN and the ACP - and the Queensland Premier, a Church representative from the South Pacific and many of our friends from the pre-independence era.

This alone is a recognition that there are many people who wish to share our celebrations with us.

Today is also a day for reflection - to measure the goals we set ourselves 20 years back into our history, and to see whether achievements matched aspirations.

I cannot help remembering this day 20 years ago – in fact, I am flooded with memories. On the 16th day of September 1975, we lowered the Australian flag with great dignity and with sadness - and then

raised the new Papua New Guinea standard in its place. It has flown proudly ever since.

Foremost in my memories are, of course, those I stood side by side with, on that day. Without them Papua New Guinea could not have achieved its Independence. Sir Michael Somare, our first Prime Minister, Sir John Guise, our first Governor-General - and our generation of fellow politicians.

How united we were then.... We all had the one goal, and we were pushing for it with equal vigour. We

were then just plain Michael, John, Albert, Pita, Ebia and Julius. We didn't seem to separate into opposing camps.

I also cannot forget all the other Members of Parliament, led by Mathias Toliman and Tei Abal, who ensured the stability of our new State even though they had strenuously opposed the onset of Independence. They helped from the most loyal and most responsible Opposition our Parliament has ever seen.

We must also remember all the public servants who, although they had been brought up in and had been totally loyal to the Australian Administration of the Territory of Papua New Guinea, became on that day most loyal and hard working officers of the Public Service of the Independent State of Papua New Guinea.

But our independence was not won by politicians and public servants alone. It takes the

collective will of a people to win independence for a State, and it was the people of Papua New Guinea who chose their leaders and accepted their leadership along a different path.

We owe a great debt of gratitude to all our founding leaders, and to the people and public servants of our new nation. Just as we owed then, we still do today, an immeasurable debt of gratitude to the people of Australia, and as a nation and as a people, we are truly appreciative of Australian generosity.

I remember the country that was born this day 20 years ago, and we were a country in a hurry. We still

are. There was much to be done and there still is. We knew that we had to come together as one people.

Many of .us still remember the cry of „AHEBOU" and „BUNG WANTAIM". Maybe the essential goal is not yet achieved, but no- one should believe that it won't be. We are nearer to it than we were 20 years ago,

We are closer to becoming true Papua New Guineans than ever before - we are beginning to see ourselves as a people.

Not just an amalgamation of separate groups - not just as Engans, Tolais, Toaripis, Dobuans, Bougainvilleans, Sepiks and Morobeans and as members of all the other diverse groups in our land - but as proud citizens of the one country.

But the process of building a nation does not happen overnight and to this day, clan, tribal and regional sentiments at times threaten our bonds as true Papua New Guineans.

As a nation we must address this issue, and the correct place - the only place - to do it is in the heart of each and every one of us. Until this challenge is taken on, we can never fulfil our potential for greatness.

Change never comes without some pain and achievements can't occur unless there is some honest sweat. By any measure at all, Papua New Guinea has indeed experienced pain and shed much honest sweat.

More pain, more sweat will be needed if we are to fulfil our own hopes.

We cannot just manage our affairs, we must make sure we manage them well. Why live in a dirty run-down house, a broken wil-wil and producing sloppy work? What is to be gained from rejecting criticism when that criticism could be deserved?

These attitudes are not rare and we cannot be proud of them.

We have experienced several shocks in recent years. Some of these have been external imports and many have been unwanted but home-made.

By no means are we in an unsalvageable position. We are in the process of forcing ourselves out of a mess, but it would be grossly foolish to say that all is well with one society, our economy and particularly with some of our attitudes.

It is in the latter area where we possibly face our greatest danger. We tell ourselves we are a resource rich country but we fool each other if we continue to think that these resources represent riches if they still lie in the ground.

341

There is no doubt that Papua New Guinea has been doubly blessed, in its people and in its natural resources. Yes, we are potentially rich but we will only realise that potential when make sustainable use of what God has so generously given us.

We tell ourselves that we have many proud traditions and customs forming a unique and proud Papua New Guinean culture. This is true, but we would be naive to continue retaining those which don't sit comfortably with our legitimate desire to be part of a modern and increasingly complex international economy. Sometimes the two can't sit well together.

We must accept that there is still room for more change and adjustment.

We have come a long way since 1975. Although it has sometimes been a case of three steps forward and one step back - or sideways - we are ahead. We have always managed to take corrective action, although sometimes perilously close to the last moment,

In 20 years we have built a nation and brought it to the point where it not only has a growing confidence in its own ability to set and correct its own course - to be Papua New Guineans - but also in its maturing relationships with the other nations in its region and indeed, in the world.

Today we are committed members of a number of international bodies - regionally in the Melanesian Spearhead Group and the South Pacific Forum - but also in the Commonwealth... in APEC, ASEAN and the United Nations.

We have selectively and strategically established 21 embassies and consulates in 16 countries, to develop international relationships and to uphold and promote our interest,.

Among all the nations of this world, there would hardly be another that has had to journey so far on so many fronts in the past 20 years. We have done well. We have achieved much and our country shows the potential to achieve so much more.

Yes, we have had our ups and downs on this journey, but every nation does, including those who have thousands of years of experience behind them, as the media shows us every day.

The greatest barrier to realising our potential sometimes seems to be ourselves - some of us must stop condemning every move for change that is made, blocking every turn away from the past and demanding too much without being willing to offer enough back in return.

We have made mistakes. There is no doubt about that, but we are learning from them. What we Papua New Guineans need to remember is that leaders too are human, and leaders can and do make mistakes. They are not celestial beings, but lie somewhere between being saints and sinners. Sometimes they are a mixture of both.

It is too easy to be over-critical - and many people are, both within Papua New Guinea and overseas. We should never lose sight of the fact that our journey has taken some of our people from an isolated tribal existence into the modern world in less than a lifetime.

343

In that context what we have achieved is quite remarkable. I pay tribute to the fathers of our nation, among them my peers, the three former Prime Ministers of Papua New Guinea, Sir Michael Somare, Rabbie Namaliu and Paias Wingti.

One of the most telling measures of the success of our journey is the skills of our people. In a generation we have gone from essentially a zero-skills base in terms of the modern world to today where we have doctors ... lawyers ... engineers ... pilots ... agriculturists ... geologists ... and many other skilled people.

Today they are coming to the fore. And in the next 20 years, their numbers will increase dramatically and drive this country ahead.

In this, they will be assisted by the millions of our people who are the essential backbone of Papua New Guinea - those who live away from our cities and towns, where they have lived for many thousands of years.

In the huts and villages on the coast, in our valleys and in our highlands. They are the wellspring of our national life. They are our strength. They always have been and they always will be.

I cannot forget the poor, the hungry, the sick and the disadvantaged. It is shameful that they exist in such numbers at this stage of our development. They must get a higher place on our ladder of priorities.

To achieve this - to provide an even spread of services - dramatic structural changes have taken place over recent months, and the systems applied for delivery of services to the rural areas have been improved. The effects of these changes have already taken hold, but it is still early days.

Change is nothing be frightened of. It is a sign of life, and we need it if we are to grow as a nation. But the keyword is consultation and the password, adaptability.

Key among any changes made are the ones that will help solve law and order problem. It has been a problem that has dogged our young nation and done considerable damage - to our county's peaceful men, women and children and to our reputation on the international stage.

The vast majority of Papua New Guinea people are friendly, decent and peace-loving, but a small minority of violent, criminal lawbreakers are draining our lifeblood away.

The causes of crime and violence are many and complex. While increased police activity - and my Government moved on this earlier this year - will go some way to dealing with it, the real answer to the problems will be found only when we, as a nation, tackle their root cause.

Here we are talking about education and employment opportunities. We are talking about young people who have left their villages and who no longer have traditional support and discipline. While essential values remain constant in our towns and villages, it has been the method of control that has changed.

Sometimes there is no control at all.

We will always have law and order problems until we can fully involve our young people in a modern society. We must give them the opportunity to mould meaningful lives, to have the dignity of work, to earn a decent living. When that happens, our crime levels will fall.

This is a challenge for all of us - not just for the Government, but also for all the people of this country and for the private sector. It is a challenge we must meet head-on.

We have to look at the education system and how it can better meet the needs of a growing population, and provide a workforce for our country's future growth.

We need to continue with the positive new direction of our health services, where there is now a National Plan in place to take our country to the year 2000 and beyond.

The life of this country lies in the immunisation of our children, and the overall health of mothers and their babies.

To our newer generations - and you are the hope and lifeblood of our nation - I urge you never to accept or offer second-best. Second-best in the services you receive from the State, or second-best in what you yourselves offer to your nation - no matter what you do.

Do not fall into the trap of simply blaming your leaders, bosses or

your co-workers for everything that may be wrong. Look into yourself. Blaming others is most often just fooling ourselves and our nation.

We need to take that critical look inside ourselves and admit that large sections of our society have become experts at the game of supply and demand - or demand and supply. They demand and

the Government is expected to immediately and automatically supply.

They have gotten it all wrong. The State is you - the people.

Papua New Guinea has been a society of self-sufficiency in the past, where everyone survived by their own efforts and those of their families. We have to recapture that attitude. Unless and until we do, then we will never achieve progress for ourselves and our society.

Papua New Guinea has to be a partnership between the State and the people.

My fellow Papua New Guineans, let us enter our second 20 years with a commitment to do better ... to work harder ... and to give more of ourselves than ever before.

I say this to all our people , but especially our leaders, politicians and public servants. I say it to all Papua New Guineans.

We are the nation that has survived the Bougainville crisis. We are coming out of it with more compassion, strength, determination and unity than ever before. We are the nation that has survived floods and famines, earthquakes and volcanoes.

Natural disasters and those that are man-made - we have survived them all and we are stronger for them. We are more resilient and better equipped for the future. In twenty short years - and they have gone pretty fast - this nation has known more than its fair share of suffering.

Through it all we have grown.

Part of the reason we have dealt so well with adversity is the inherent strength of our many ancient cultures - the desire to tend to each other's needs, the willingness to share. However, it is also the strength of our „newer cultures" that has seen us through -

our churches, our workers, our academics, our business sector, our multi-cultural society.

Yes, we have much to be proud of and a strong foundation on which to continue building our nation. But - remember that this country can only be as good as we ourselves make it. So why don't we all strive to make it great?

That is my commitment, and the commitment of my Government to make Papua New Guinea great.

Today we renew that commitment. We refocus ourselves on what it is to be Papua New Guinean. We focus again on all the things that make Papua New Guinea so special.

I praise the hard work done by the National Events Council - its Chairman Joe Tauvasa and all the council members. They have done great work to organise the celebrations throughout our land, they have done great work to bind our people together as celebrants for this special day.

I say thank you also to all the representatives from nations near and far, for your time and effort in

sharing with us this most memorable day in our nation's life, and also to all my fellow Papua New Guineans.

To you I say, be proud to be Papua New Guinean. One People. One Nation. One Country. And as I ask God to bless Papua New Guinea, I also remind all of us that on this planet, God's work is really our own. We are the ones who have to translate God's wishes into reality.

And in working for that reality let us share our vision for Papua New Guinea.

Let us see the Bird of Paradise fly towards the stars. Let us know that Papua New Guinea can keep on rising, and let us continue to work for a future in which all Papua New Guineans will...

Know ourselves as a nation of many, different, worthy cultures..

Unite on the basis of respect for all other people...

Never forget that people come first, including the interests of children and future generations...

Develop our load and other resources for growth, improved quality of life and capacity-building for self-reliance.... and

Uphold the law, including the National Goals in our Constitution.

Let the Kundu or the Gaba sound out the news of our commitment to Papua New Guinea's future.

Ahebou. Bung Wantaim. Unite and Good night.

Cabinet

Septem

**Rt. Hon. Sir Julius Chan
(GCMG, KBE, MP)**
Prime Minister & Minister for
Foreign Affairs & Trade

**Hon. Arnold Marsipal,
(OBE, MP)**
Minister for Justice &
Minister for State Assis-
ting the Prime Minister

**Hon. Sir Albert Kipalan
(KBE, LLB, MP)**
Minister for Lands &
Acting Minister for
Health

Hon. Kilroy Genia (MP)
Minister for Public
Service

Hon. Moi Avei (MP)
Minister for National
Planning

**Hon. Joseph Onguglo
(MP)**
Minister for Education

Hon. Parry Zeipi (MP)
Minister for Home
Affairs

**Hon. Michael Nali
(MP)**
Minister for Civil
Aviation, Culture &
Tourism

**Hon. Paul Mambei
(MP)**
Minister for
Environment

**Hon. Robert Nagle
(MP)**
Minister for Housing

**Hon. John Giheno
(MP)**
Minister for Mining &
Petroleum

**Hon. Samson Napo
(MP)**
Minister for Industrial
Relations

Ministers
er 1995

Hon. Peter Yama (MP)
Minister for Transport
& Works

Hon. David Mai (MP)
Minister for Agriculture
& Livestock

Hon. Chris Haiveta (MP)
Deputy Prime Minister &
Minister for Finance

**Hon. David Unagi
(MP)**
Minister for Provincial
& Local-level
Governments

**Hon. Andrew Baing
(MP)**
Minister for Forests

**Hon. Titus Philemon
(MP)**
Minister for Fisheries

**Hon. Paul Tohian
(MP)**
Minister for Admini-
strative Services.

**Hon. Castan Maibawa
(MP)**
Minister for Police

**Hon. Joseph Egilio
(MP)**
Minister for
Communications

**Hon. Nakikus Konga
(MP)**
Minister for Commerce
& Industry

**Hon. Mathias Ijape
(LLB, MP)**
Minister for Defence

**Hon. Paul Wanjik
(MP)**
Minister for
Correctional Services

GOVERNMENT DEPARTMENTS
TELEPHONE & FAX NUMBERS

Prime Minister
Morauta House,
PO Box 6605
Waigani, NCD
Papua New Guinea
Tel: + (675) 327 6625
       + (675) 327 6616
Fax: + (675) 327 7328

Agriculture & Livestock
PO Box 417
Konedobu, NCD
Papua New Guinea
Tel: + (675) 321 3002
Fax: + (675) 327 2495

Central Bank of PNG
Douglas Street
PO Box 121
Port Moresby, NCD
Tel: + (675) 321 2999
Fax: + (675) 321 1617

Civil Aviation & Tourism
7 Mile, Jacksons Airport
PO Box 684
Boroko, NCD
Papua New Guinea
Tel: + (675) 325 1764
Fax: + (675) 325 5399

Commerce & Industry
Central Government Office
PO Box 375
Waigani, NCD
Papua New Guinea
Tel: + (675) 327 1102
Fax: + (675) 325 2403

Correctional Institutional Services
Headquarters Credit House
PO Box 6889
Boroko, NCD
Papua New Guinea
Tel: + (675) 327 7524
Fax: + (675) 325 7298

Education
PSA Haus Independence Drive
PO Box 446
Waigani, NCD
Papua New Guinea
Tel: + (675) 327 2335
Fax: + (675) 327 4648

Environment & Conservation
National Parliament
Waigani, NCD
Papua New Guinea
Tel: + (675) 327 1687
Fax: + (675) 327 1873

Defence Force PNG
PNGDF Hq, Murray Barracks
Free Mail Bag
Boroko, NCD
Papua New Guinea
Tel: + (675) 324 2270
Fax: + (675) 325 6117

Finance & Planning
Vulupindi Haus
PO Box 710
Waigani, NCD
Papua New Guinea
Tel: + (675) 328 8000
Fax: + (675) 328 8141

Fisheries & Marine Resources
PO Box 165
Konedobu, NCD
Papua New Guinea
Tel: + (675) 327 7350
Fax: + (675) 327 7351

Forestry
Frangipani St. Hohola
Po Box 5055
Boroko, NCD
Papua New Guinea
Tel: + (675) 327 7800
Fax: + (675) 325 4455

Foreign Affairs & Trade
Waigani, NCD
Papua New Guinea
Tel: + (675) 300 1121
Fax: + (675) 325 4467

Health
Headquarters - Hohola
PO Box 3991
Boroko, NCD
Papua New Guinea
Tel: + (675) 324 8601
Fax: + (675) 325 0826
       + (675) 325 9870

Higher Education
Okari Street
PO Box 5117
Boroko, NCD
Papua New Guinea
Tel: 325 0479
Fax: 325 8406

Home Affairs & Youth
Sports Complex
PO Box 7354
Boroko, NCD
Papua New Guinea
Tel: + (675) 325 4170
Fax: + (675) 325 4190

Industrial Relations
Labour and Employment
Cuthbertson St., Credit House
PO Box 5644 Boroko NCD
Papua New Guinea
Tel: + (675) 321 1114
      + (675) 321 3855
Fax: + (675) 327 7480

Investment Promotion Authority
Investment House
PO Box 5053
Boroko, NCD
Papua New Guinea
Tel: + (675) 321 7311
Fax: + (675) 320 2237

Justice & Attorney
Central Government Bldg
PO Wardstrip
Waigani, NCD
Papua New Guinea
Tel: + (675) 327 1502
Fax: + (675) 325 9265

Judiciary, National Court
Court House, Waigani
PO Box 7018
Boroko, NCD
Papua New Guinea
Tel: + (675) 325 7099
Fax: + (675) 325 7732

Mining & Petroleum
Private Mail Bag
Port Moresby, Post Office
Papua New Guinea
Tel: + (675) 321 4011
Fax: + (675) 321 7958

National Computers Centre
Central Government Bldg
PO Box 336
Waigani, NCD
Papua New Guinea
Tel: + (675) 323 1841
Fax: + (675) 325 0391

National Housing Commission
Koura Way, Tokarara
PO Box 1550
Boroko, Ncd
Papua New Guinea
Tel: + (675) 324 7200
Fax: + (675) 325 9918

**Ombudsman Commission
   of PNG**
Garden City Buildingg,
Angau Drive
PO Box 852
Boroko, NCD
Papua New Guinea
Tel: + (675) 325 9955
Fax: + (675) 325 9220

Public Service Ministry
Central Government Offices
PO Wardstrip
Waigani, NCD
Papua New Guinea
Tel: + (675) 327 1901
Fax: + (675) 325 0520

Royal PNG Constabulary
Police Headquarters
PO Box 857
Konedobu, NCD
Papua New Guinea
Tel: + (675) 322 6100
Fax: + (675) 322 6113

Trade Union Congress
PO Box 4279 Boroko NCD
Papua New Guinea
Tel: + (675) 325 7642
Fax: + (675) 325 7890

National Parliament
Magani Crescent ,Waigani
PO Parliament House
Waigani, NCD
Papua New Guinea
Tel: + (675) 327 7411
Fax: + (675) 327 7410

**Minister of State Assisting the
   Prime Minister**
Morauta House
PO Box Wardstrip
Waigani, NCD
Papua New Guinea
Tel: + (675) 327 6761

**Village Services & Provincial
   Affairs**
Headquarters - Waigani 2nd Floor
PO Box 1287
Boroko, NCD
Papua New Guinea
Tel: + (675) 327 7544
Fax: + (675) 327 7546

Works Supply & Transport
Headquarters - Waigani Drive
PO Box 1108
Boroko, NCD
Papua New Guinea
Tel: + (675) 324 1139
Fax: + (675) 324 1400

Lands and Physical Planning
Morauta Haus
Wardstrip - Waigani
PO Box 5665
Boroko, N.C.D.
Tel: + (675) 327 6423
      + (675)327 6472
Fax: + (675) 327 6733

**National Boadcasting
Commission**
Hubert Murray Hwy - 5 Mile PO
Box 1359 Boroko NCD Papua
New Guinea
Tel: + (675) 325 5233
Fax: + (675) 325 6296

SUBSCRIBERS

ADDRESS TELEPHONE & FAX NUMBERS

Air Niugini
PO Box 7186
Boroko, NCD
Papua New Guinea
Tel: + (675) 327 3415
Fax: + (675) 327 3416
        + (675)327 3380

Airways Hotel & Apartments
Jackson Pde. Saraga St.
PO Box 1942
Boroko, NCD
Papua New Guinea
Tel: + (675) 324 5200
Fax: + (675) 325 0759

Angco Coffee Limited
1 Airport Road
PO Box 136
Goroka
Eastern Highlands Province
Papua New Guinea
Tel: + (675) 72 1677
Fax: + (675) 72 2154

Avis Rent-A-Car
Nationwide Rent-A-Car Pty Ltd
PO Box 1533
Port Moresby, NCD
Boroko, NCD
Papua New Guinea
Tel: + (675) 325 8299
Fax: + (675) 325 3767

Bible Society Of PNG Inc.
Hubert Murray Hwy - Koki
PO Box 335
Port Moresby, NCD
Papua New Guinea
Tel: + (675)321 7893
Fax: + (675) 321 4544

Boc Gas
Cig Papua New Guinea Pty Ltd
Mangora Street - Lae
PO Box 93 Lae
Morobe Province
Papua New Guinea
Tel: + (675) 42 2377
Fax: + (675) 42 3649

Boroko Motors
Head Office
Waigani Drive
PO Box 1259
Boroko, NCD
Papua New Guinea
Tel: + (675) 325 5255
Fax: + (675) 325 5321

Bng Trading Company Ltd
Burns Philip Building
Champion Pde - Pt. Moresby
PO Box 75 Port Moresby, NCD
Papua New Guinea
Tel: + (675) 320 0600
        + (675) 321 2933
Fax: + (675) 320 0458
        + (675) 321 2939

Chamber Of Commerce & Industry
PO Box 1621
Port Moresby,
Boroko, NCD
Papua New Guinea
Tel: + (675) 321 3057
Fax: + (675) 321 3077

Chamber Of Manufacturers
PO Box 598
Port Moresby, NCD
Papua New Guinea
Tel: + (675) 325 9512
Fax: + (675) 323 1839

Chevron Niugini Pty Ltd
Credit House - Cuthbertson St.
PO Box 822
Port Moresby, NCD
Papua New Guinea
Tel: + (675) 321 1088
Fax: + (675) 322 5566
        + (675) 322 5588

City Pharmacy
Head Office & Wholesale
Waigani Drive
PO Box 1663
Port Moresby, NCD
Papua New Guinea
Tel: + (675) 325 9044
Fax: + (675) 325 9042

Coastal Shipping Company Pty Ltd
Voco Point
PO Box 1721 Lae
Morobe Province
Papua New Guinea
Tel: + (675) 42 3180
Fax: + (675) 42 1686

Coffee Industry Corporation
Head Office - Goroka
PO Box 137 Goroka
Eastern Highlands Province
Papua New Guinea
Tel: + (675) 72 1266
Fax: + (675) 72 1827

Collins & Leahy Pty Ltd
PO Box 557 Goroka
Eastern Highlands Province
Papua New Guinea
Tel: + (675) 72 1555
Fax: + (675) 72 1718

Colin Ritchie & Associates
Exploration Services Pty Ltd
Babaga St. Tokarara
PO Box 436
Boroko, NCD
Papua New Guinea
Tel: + (675) 325 6707
Fax: + (675) 325 3623

Coral Sea Hotels
PO Box 1215
Boroko, NCD
Papua New Guinea
Tel: + (675) 325 3865
Fax: + (675) 325 2751

Computers & Communication
Tamara Rd. 6 Mile
PO Box 1023
Port Moresby, NCD
Papua New Guinea
Tel: + (675)325 7466
Fax: + (675) 325 8772

Daltron Electronics Pty Ltd
PO Box 1711
Boroko, NCD
Papua New Guinea
Tel: + (675) 325 6766
Fax: + (675) 325 6558

Ela Motors
PO Box 74,
Port Moresby NCD,
Papua New Guinea,
Tel: + (675) 322 9400
Fax: + (675)321 7268

Employers Federation Of PNG
Burns House - Champion Pde.
PO Box 490
Port Moresby, NCD
Papua New Guinea
Tel: + (675) 321 4772
Fax: + (675) 321 4070

Fairdeal Liquors (PNG)
Varahe St. - Gordons
PO Box 4207
Boroko, NCD
Papua New Guinea
Tel: + (675) 325 8925
        + (675) 325 8827
Fax: + (675) 325 0061

Forest Industries Association
1,GB House, Spring Garden Road
PO Box 4037
Boroko, NCD
Papua New Guinea
Tel: + (675) 325 9458
Fax: + (675) 325 9563

Gulf Papua Fisheries Pty Ltd
Munidubu St. Konedobu
PO Box 1277
Port Moresby, NCD
Papua New Guinea
Tel: + (675) 321 2247
       + (675) 321 2247
Fax: + (675)321 2462

Guard Dog Security
Ago St. Gordons
PO Box 648
Port Moresby, NCD
Papua New Guinea
Tel: + (675) 325 9653
Fax: + (675) 324 4858

Gulf Papua Fisheries Pty Ltd
Munidubu St. Konedobu
PO Box 1277
Port Moresby, NCD
Papua New Guinea
Tel: + (675) 321 2247
       + (675) 321 2247
Fax: + (675) 321 2462

Harbours Board
Head Office Stanley Esplanade
PO Box 671
Port Moresby, NCD
Papua New Guinea
Tel: + (675) 321 1400
Fax: + (675) 321 2440

Helandis Management Services
Ground Floor Rdf Haus
Jacksons Parade
PO Box 4848
Boroko, NCD
Papua New Guinea
Tel: + (675) 325 7648
Fax: + (675) 325 4580

Higaturu Oil Palms
Head Office
PO Box 28
Popondetta, Oro Province
Papua New Guinea
Tel: + (675) 329 7131
       + (675) 329 7161
       + (675) 329 7177
Fax: + (675) 329 7137

Hornibrook NGI Pty Ltd
Head Office
PO Box 1396
Boroko, NCD
Papua New Guinea
Tel: + (675) 325 3099
Fax: + (675) 325 0387

Howard Porter (PNG) Pty Ltd
Mataram Street
PO Box 672 Lae
Morobe Province
Papua New Guinea
Tel: + (675) 42 5622
Fax: + (675) 42 6039

Ilimo Poultry Products Pty Ltd
Sogeri Road - 14 1/2 Mile
PO Box 1885 Boroko, NCD
Papua New Guinea
Tel: + (675) 328 1100
       + (675) 328 1101
Fax: + (675) 328 1245

Industrial Centres
Development Corporation
Haus Tomakala
Level 4 - Suite 41
Po Box 1571
Boroko, NCD
Papua New Guinea
Tel: + (675) 323 1179
Fax: + (675) 323 1109

**Investment Corporation
Fund Of PNG**
Ang House - Hunter Street
PO Box 155
Port Moresby, NCD
Papua New Guinea
Tel: + (675) 321 2855
       + (675) 321 2435
Fax: + (675) 321 1240

International Education Agency
Bava Street - East Boroko
PO Box 6974
Boroko, NCD
Papua New Guinea
Tel: + (675) 325 3814
Fax: + (675) 325 8193

Islands Nationair
PO Box 488
Boroko, NCD
Papua New Guinea
Tel: + (675) 325 1835
Fax: + (675) 325 5059

Lae Biscuit Company Pty Ltd
Mula St. (Cnr. Morobe Ave.)
Po Box 1331 Lae Morobe Province
Papua New Guinea
Tel: + (675) 42 2499
Fax: + (675) 42 1524

Law Society PNG
Garden City Bldg, Angau Drive
PO Box 1994 Boroko, NCD
Papua New Guinea
Tel: + (675) 325 8483
Fax: + (675) 325 6609

Loloata Island Resort
PO Box 5290
Boroko, NCD
Papua New Guinea
Tel: + (675) 325 8590
       + (675) 325 1369
Fax: + (675) 325 8933

Mainland Holdings Pty Ltd
Head Office
PO Box 196 Lae
Morobe Province
Papua New Guinea
Tel: + (675) 42 1499
Fax: + (675) 42 6172

McIntosh Securities (Png) Pty Ltd
Level 4 - Defens Haus
PO Box 1156
Port Moresby, NCD
Papua New Guinea
Tel: + (675) 320 0321
Fax: + (675) 320 0323

MBA (Airlines) Pty Ltd
Jacksons Airport
PO Box 170
Boroko, NCD
Papua New Guinea
Tel: + (675) 325 2011
       + (675) 325 2102
Fax: + (675) 325 2219

**Mineral Resources Development
Corporation Pty Ltd**
8th Floor - Investment Haus
Douglas St.
PO Box 1076
Port Moresby, NCD
Papua New Guinea
Tel: + (675) 321 7133
Fax: + (675) 321 7603

Mobil Oil New Guinea Ltd
Head Office
5th Level - Credit House
Cuthbertson St.
PO Box 485
Port Moresby, NCD
Papua New Guinea
Tel: + (675) 321 2055
Fax: + (675) 321 2025

**National Provident Fund Board
Of Trustees**
Po Box 5791 Boroko, NCD
Papua New Guinea
Tel: + (675) 325 9910
       + (675) 325 9522
       + (675) 325 9652
Fax: + (675) 325 9738
       + (675) 325 5503

Net Shop, The
Morea Tobo Rd. - 6 Mile
PO Box 5860
Boroko, NCD
Papua New Guinea
Tel: 325 8222
Fax: 325 8994

Niugini Adventures Pty Ltd
Hunting & Fishing Sepcialists
PO Box 7373 Boroko, NCD
Papua New Guinea
Tel: + (675) 325 4394
Fax: + (675) 325 0524

**New Guinea Marine
Products Pty Ltd**
Munidubu Street - Konedobu
PO Box 1703
Port Moresby, NCD
Papua New Guinea
Tel: + (675) 321 1612
       + (675) 321 1777
Fax: + (675) 321 1474

Rugby Football League Inc.
PO Box 1095
Boroko, NCD
Papua New Guinea
Tel: + (675) 325 9733
Fax: + (675) 325 0646

PNG Banking Corporation
Head Office
PO Box 78 Port Moresby, NCD
Papua New Guinea
Tel: + (675) 322 9903
Fax: + (675) 321 1236

PNG Electricity Commission
Headquarters - Port Moresby
Wards Road
PO Box 1105 Boroko, NCD
Papua New Guinea
Tel: + (675) 324 3200
Fax: + (675) 325 0072

Price Waterhouse
Pacific Place - Musgrave St.
Port Moresby, NCD
Papua New Guinea
Tel: + (675) 321 2077
Fax: + (675) 322 2189

Ramu Sugar Limited
Gusap, PO Box 2183
Lae, Morobe Province
Papua New Guinea
Tel: + (675) 44 3291
Fax: + (675) 44 3295

Remington Pitney Bowes
Munidubu St.
PO Box 101 Port Moresby, NCD
Papua New Guinea
Tel: + (675) 321 1100
Fax: + (675) 321 3185

Securimax Security Group
PO Box 131 Mt. Hagen
Western Highlands Province
Papua New Guinea
Tel: + (675) 52 2817
Fax: + (675) 52 3888

Steamships Shipping & Transport
PO Box 634 Port Moresby, NCD
Papua New Guinea
Tel: + (675) 321 2055
Fax: + (675) 321 2025

Telikom
Headquarters
Telikom Rumana - Waigani
PO Box 1349 Boroko, NCD
Papua New Guinea
Tel: + (675) 323 1179
Fax: + (675) 325 9582

Trans Niugini Tours Pty Ltd
Po Box 371 Mt. Hagen
Western Highlands Province
Papua New Guinea
Tel: + (675) 52 1438
Fax: + (675) 52 2470
                E-Mail: 100250.3337 @
                Compuserve.Com

Treid Pacific (PNG) Pty Ltd
Portion 445 Kanage St. - 6 Mile
PO Box 6918 Boroko, NCD
Papua New Guinea
Tel: + (675) 325 4766
Fax: + (675) 325 4214

Tourism Promotion Authority
2nd Floor, Nic Haus
PO Box 1291
Port Moresby, NCD
Papua New Guinea
Tel: + (675) 320 0211
Fax: + (675) 320 0223

Vanimo Forest Products Pty Ltd
Po Box 41 Vanimo
East Sepik Province
Papua New Guinea
Tel: + (675) 87 1152
          + (675) 87 1245
          + (675) 87 1395
Fax: + (675) 87 1203

Westpac Bank PNG - Limited
5th Floor - Mogoru Motor Building
Champion Parade
Po Box 706
Port Moresby, Ncd
Papua New Guinea
Tel: (675) 322 0830
Fax: (675) 321 3367

Wills (PNG) Pty Ltd
Head Office - Modilon Road
Madang, Madang Province
Papua New Guinea
Tel: + (675) 82 3788
Fax: + (675) 82 3667

**Woo Textile Corporation
      Pty Ltd**
Head Office
Kennedy Rd. - Gordons
PO Box 5448 Boroko, NCD
Papua New Guinea
Tel: + (675) 325 2819
Fax: + (675) 325 8415

Churches and Missions

Anglican Church	325 5632
Apostolic Nunciature to PNG	325 6021
Assemblies of God	325 7659
Association of Baptist For World Evangelism	325 6571
Australian Four Square Mission	82 2575
Bahais of PNG	72 2016
Baptist Church	325 8432
Bible Society Of PNG Inc	321 7693
Catholic Church	325 9532
Christian Brothers - Vunakanau	92 1241
Christian Literature - Crusade Bookstore	325 3066
Christian Radio Mission	72 2670
Christian Union Mission	325 7836
Church of Christ	325 9059
Church of Jesus Christ of Latter Day Saints	325 2191
Church of Nazarene	325 6617
Churches Of Christ	82 3057
Evangelical Brotherhood Church Inc	326 1164
Evangelical Church of Manus Lugos	40 9017
Evangelical Church of Papua	321 7647
Fmi Sisters of Generalate House	92 7136
Filadelfia Kristen Kongregessen	52 1146
Four Square Gospel Church	77 1181
Franciscan Friars	93 5305
Goroka Four Square Church	72 1705
Green River Christian Centre	87 8917
Gutnius Lutheran Church	57 1033
Highlands Independent Baptist Church	57 4014
Highlands Nazarene Church	56 2335
Intern. Bible Students Association of PNG	325 3011
Islamic Society of PNG	325 9882
Jehovah's Witnesses	325 3011
Lae Lutheran Community Centre	42 5750
Leprosy Mission	359 1101
Life Outreach Ministries	326 0135
Lutheran Church	42 3711
Martin Luther Seminary	42 2699
Missionaries Of Charity	321 2201
Pacific Island Ministries	88 5925
Png Bible Church	326 1034
Port Moresby Congregation of Jehovah's Witnesses	325 6782
Presbyterian Reformed Church	325 8043
St. John of God Brothers	325 0025
St. Peters Channel Community	325 7613
Salvation Army	325 5507
Sisters of Notre Dame	56 2248
Society of The Divine Word	52 1812
United Church	321 1744
Westeyan Church	52 1359
World Outreach Mission	72 2590

ACKNOWLEDGEMENTS & CREDITS

The contributors wish to thank all those politicians, public servants, businessmen and others who took the time to answer our questions and supply us with information.

We should also like to acknowledge the following source books which proved invaluable in providing background.

'A Fact Book on Modern Papua New Guinea' by Jackson Rannells (OUP 1991)

'Papua New Guinea - People, Politics & History since 1975' by Sean Dorney, (Random House, 1990).

'Papua New Guinea: The Challenge of Independence' by Mark Turner (Penguin 1990)

'Papua New Guinea, a travel survival kit' by Tony Wheeler and Jon Murray (Lonely Planet Publications 1993)

'The Times of PNG' - fact sheets on the Provinces of PNG 1995

destination
Papua New Guinea

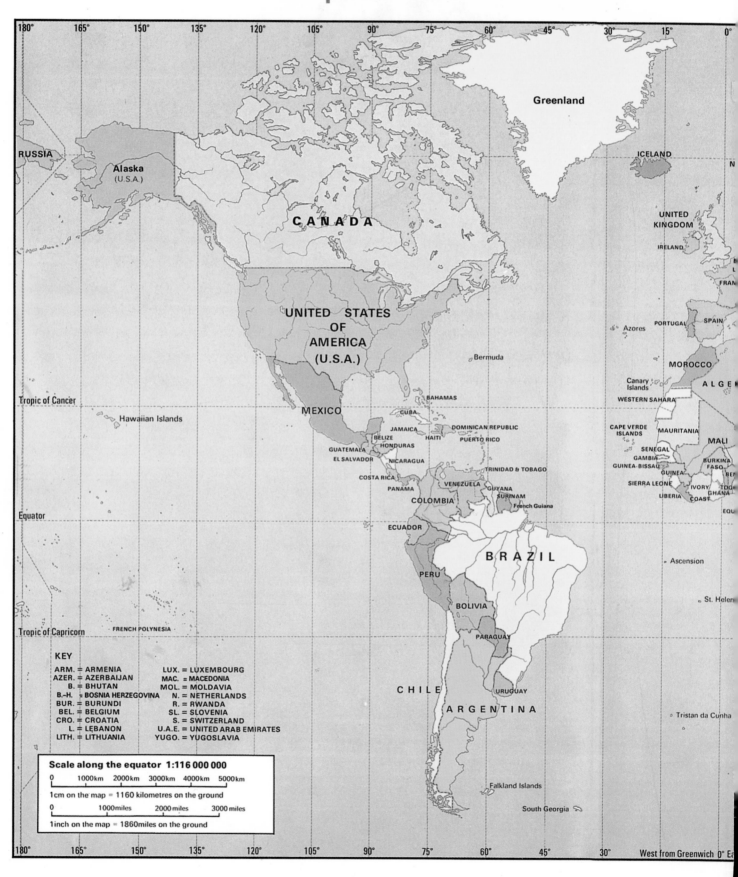

RUSSIA

Greenland

ICELAND

Alaska
(U.S.A.)

CANADA

UNITED
KINGDOM

IRELAND

FRAN

UNITED STATES
OF
AMERICA
(U.S.A.)

Azores

PORTUGAL SPAIN

Bermuda

MOROCCO

Tropic of Cancer

Canary
Islands

ALGE

Hawaiian Islands

WESTERN SAHARA

BAHAMAS

MEXICO

CUBA

CAPE VERDE
ISLANDS

MAURITANIA

JAMAICA

DOMINICAN REPUBLIC

MALI

BELIZE

HAITI

PUERTO RICO

SENEGAL

GUATEMALA

HONDURAS

GAMBIA

BURKINA
FASO

EL SALVADOR

NICARAGUA

GUINEA-BISSAU

GUINEA

BEN

SIERRA LEONE

IVORY
COAST

TOGO
GHANA

TRINIDAD & TOBAGO

COSTA RICA

LIBERIA

COAST

PANAMA

VENEZUELA

GUYANA

EQU

COLOMBIA

SURINAM

French Guiana

Equator

ECUADOR

B R A Z I L

Ascension

PERU

St. Helen

BOLIVIA

Tropic of Capricorn

FRENCH POLYNESIA

PARAGUAY

KEY

ARM. = ARMENIA	LUX. = LUXEMBOURG
AZER. = AZERBAIJAN	MAC. = MACEDONIA
B. = BHUTAN	MOL. = MOLDAVIA
B.-H. = BOSNIA HERZEGOVINA	N. = NETHERLANDS
BUR. = BURUNDI	R. = RWANDA
BEL. = BELGIUM	SL. = SLOVENIA
CRO. = CROATIA	S. = SWITZERLAND
L. = LEBANON	U.A.E. = UNITED ARAB EMIRATES
LITH. = LITHUANIA	YUGO. = YUGOSLAVIA

C H I L E

URUGUAY

A R G E N T I N A

Tristan da Cunha

Scale along the equator 1:116 000 000

0   1000km   2000km   3000km   4000km   5000km

1cm on the map = 1160 kilometres on the ground

0   1000miles   2000 miles   3000 miles

1inch on the map = 1860miles on the ground

Falkland Islands

South Georgia

180° 165° 150° 135° 120° 105° 90° 75° 60° 45° 30° 15° 0°

West from Greenwich 0° E